AMERICAN KINGS

Also by Seth Wickersham

It's Better to Be Feared:
The New England Patriots Dynasty
and the Pursuit of Greatness

AMERICAN KINGS

A BIOGRAPHY OF THE QUARTERBACK

ESPN SENIOR WRITER AND
NEW YORK TIMES BESTSELLING AUTHOR OF
IT'S BETTER TO BE FEARED

SETH WICKERSHAM

HYPERION AVENUE
LOS ANGELES · NEW YORK

First Edition, September 2025
10 9 8 7 6 5 4 3 2
FAC-004510-25238
Printed in the United States of America

This book is set in Chronicle and Clarendon
Designed by Amy C. King

Library of Congress Control Number: 2025932086
ISBN 978-1-368-09918-9
Reinforced binding

The authorized representative in the EU for product
safety and compliance is Disney Trading
B.V., Asterweg 15S, 1031 HL, Amsterdam, The Netherlands
email: DCP.DL-EU.bookscontact@disney.com

www.HyperionAvenueBooks.com

SUSTAINABLE FORESTRY INITIATIVE
Certified Sourcing
www.forests.org
SFI-01681

Logo Applies to Text Stock Only

For all who try

Fame requires every kind of excess. I mean true fame, a devouring neon, not the somber renown of waning statesmen or chinless kings.

—DON DeLILLO

If you ain't confident, you don't belong here.

—JOE NAMATH

PREFACE

I was a quarterback once.

Like thousands of American boys, I was drawn to the feeling of the ball in my hands, the power and possibilities at my command. I was tall, but not particularly tall. I lifted weights, but was not particularly strong. Throwing a football didn't come naturally. But I had an edge: I was obsessed.

I remember the first time I met a quarterback: Craig Morton of the Broncos, at Stapleton Airport in Denver, forty or so miles from where we lived in Boulder. Early eighties. I was maybe five years old. My dad spotted him at the luggage carousel. Morton wore a trench coat, I remember. Dad introduced himself and then me. Morton bent over to shake my hand, an impossible disparity of scale. He wasn't a superstar, but he was good. He'd once led the league in yards per attempt, the kind of weird quarterback stat, an attempt to quantify magic, that I later knew by heart. It felt like I was meeting a president, only cooler.

When I was six, we moved to Anchorage, Alaska, tucked up against the Chugach Mountains. Maybe it was the vastness of the landscape. Maybe it was the dark emptiness during long winters.

Maybe I was tied up in a fragile vision of myself and what I assumed the world found attractive. But I remember wanting, maybe even needing, to feel like I was exceptional at something. Watching quarterbacks made me want to be one. Did America offer a cooler job title? By age thirteen, I'd go out alone in the yard and throw a ball high against the sky and catch it and throw it again, chasing its arc, imagining and wondering. At the video store I found a tape from a few years earlier called *John Elway: The Fundamentals of Offensive Football.* Elway—he now was my guy. He had replaced Morton in Denver. He wore number 7, as Morton did years before, a cool quarterback number. He ran one way and threw the other, an exceptional feat made to look easy. The host on the tape said, "You'll sit down the first time and watch this tape all the way through, then head for your field and try it out," and I thought he was talking to me like he knew me. Then Elway arrived on-screen and addressed the viewer with the royal *we. Us.* Quarterbacks. In it together. He took us to the stadium and advised us to greet boos with casual indifference. He took us into the playbook and reminded us we had to be the team's best student. In the huddle we had to be leaders. At the line of scrimmage, we had to read defenses for intent and weakness. He taught us cadence. *Down. Set. Red twenty-eight, Red twenty-eight. Hut.* There were five checkpoints in receiving the snap, he said. The start of a play was madness, but not for us, he said. It *couldn't* be for us. We learned how to hold the ball; Elway said he put his ring and pinky fingers on the laces, his middle and index fingers off. So I did the same. He told us to hold the ball high at our throwing shoulder; drop it and you risked slowing your release. Keep your knees bent but stand tall. Step to the target, toes pointed at a forty-five-degree angle. Shoulders and hips perpendicular to the line of scrimmage so you can throw left or right with equal ease. Three-step drops, five-step drops, seven-step drops. Seven was the "exciting" one, he said, because it was the prelude to a deep throw. And at the end of the tape the host made it all seem attainable: "Maybe someday, who knows, when they're talking great quarterbacks on a Monday morning, they'll be talking your name."

Some boys become quarterbacks because they are born skilled. Some are pushed by parents and coaches. Others work hard at it because they crave a challenge and status, and because they simply love throwing the football. That was me. There was a purity to it. All quarterbacks talk about it, how the windup of throwing a ball takes less than a second, that cobra-like lash, yet you can feel a lifetime in it, frame by frame. . . .

As a sophomore at Robert Service High School, I was the junior-varsity starter. It felt like a miracle and a validation and a trajectory, the beginning of something. People looked at me differently, in the huddle and in the hallway. I was a quarterback.

Two moments from that season stay with me.

On a sunny afternoon against Dimond High, we had crossed midfield, and I called a pass: a play-action fake, half roll, with one option deep and two short. The head coach, a teacher and former high school quarterback named Brian Hosken, let me call plays. He wanted me to "think football"—down, distance, field position—wanted me to be a coach out there. I dropped back, and a pass-rusher shook free and wrapped me up. I spun away. I don't know how. Harried but opportunistic, an Elway impersonation, I fled left, eyes downfield, where, by god, I saw Anthony O'Meally, my best receiver, in space. I planted my feet. Something strange happens when your arm is cocked but before you throw. Time slows. You experience a kind of lucid thought. Quarterbacks know. I launched it downfield, 35 yards that felt like 60, as a defender drilled my rib cage. I didn't see the ball in the air, and didn't see Anthony catch it . . . I only heard a sharp rise of cheers from the sideline and from the stands at the rush of a completed forward pass—what only a quarterback can provide. Even now, all these decades later, when I lie in bed unable to sleep, I think of that play, breath by breath, second by second, until it relaxes me. That game, I threw a touchdown pass, that beautiful American phrase. High school quarterbacks never forget their favorite throws.

A week or so later, we played in the cold rain, an early-afternoon game that felt dark. All quarterbacks hate throwing wet footballs. The idea of quarterbacking is based on the fanciful but aspirational notion of total control. A wet ball is pure chaos. Late in the game we had a chance to win. Which meant I did. A two-minute drill, that precious and liberating thing. Quarterbacks speak of these as the most joyous moments, when the micromanaging of coaching is stripped away and it's all on you. We moved the ball down the field, a few throws and a few runs, marching on schedule . . . then Coach Hosken called a pass. It was a drop-back play, requiring me to scan options and decide. I set up in the pocket and felt pressure. I moved left and saw a receiver buttoned up near the sideline. He appeared open. But he wasn't. As I reared back, Coach saw the looming disaster and ran along the sideline close, yelling and waving his arms, imploring me to throw out of bounds. I threw to the receiver. A pass that needed to be low and outside was high and inside. An opposing player intercepted it. Game over. Afterward, I sat in the bench in a daze, head in hands. I watched through my helmet as rain hit the turf, gathering in puddles. My center, Aaron Collins, sat next to me and put his hand on my head. I didn't want to stand back up or leave the field. I just wanted to disappear.

Between the end of my sophomore year and the beginning of football season the next August, fueled by both moments, I was determined to unseat a senior ahead of me as the varsity starter.

I brought footballs almost everywhere I went, in case there was an empty field. I read books and recorded NFL games on tape and studied statistics. I threw to my dad in a church parking lot, with the snow cleared off, him in work pants and a parka, trying not to fall on the ice. I threw to friends and teammates. I threw to my mom and sister. I practiced techniques in front of the mirror. When I was alone, I threw to spots on a fence, imagining hands and windows. I viewed everything, from people moving in crowds to cars passing on the road, within a certain context, of objects and motion and windows. An assistant coach on my team named Tom Morrison had me to his house, and we sat in his living room as he punched in game tapes—"my film," in football parlance. There was one throw that he kept replaying, a pass over the middle, a moment where everything clicked. My footwork, perfect. My eyes, turning at the designed instant. My release, high and clean. The ball, on the numbers and in stride, giving the receiver a chance to run. "Doesn't get any better than that," he said.

I had gone to UCLA's football camp in Southern California and watched the country's top high school quarterbacks up close. And a half hour north of Anchorage, I went to Drew Bledsoe's father Mac's camp for the second straight year. The summer before, Drew had been about to play his final season at Washington State and was on the cusp of being the first overall pick in the NFL Draft. Now he wore a New England Patriots number 11 jersey and carried around a football with gold NFL branding. Everything I wanted, everything all of us wanted, was standing before us. During one session Drew stood near me as I threw a post pattern off what's called "a plant": five steps and the moment your back foot hits ground, you fire. I practiced it hundreds of times. "There's a ball," Bledsoe said.

That summer, Service High's varsity squad competed in a football tournament. I was the varsity backup. I threw a touchdown pass. One of the starters told me that I was the school's best quarterback. I had a skillset. More importantly, I had *momentum*.

The night before the first practice of my junior year, I lay in bed visualizing every aspect of what would happen. How it would go. How the air would taste. Clicks and snaps of fastening my shoulder pads. Danger and freedom of pulling down my helmet. Warming up: keeping my release point high and hitting my target between the numbers ten straight times from ten yards away, an exercise that was less about accuracy than about focusing my mind and calming myself. I pictured the coaches calling my name to enter the huddle, and once there I saw every player look at me for direction, all the big boys on varsity, linemen taller, receivers faster. All business. I imagined breathing deep before calling a play, stuff I had studied all summer on paper. Fox Pro Right 47 Pitch Reverse, or Bear Power I 22 Quick, or Fox Bone 48 Pass, or Fire Right Red Split 44, Boot 9, Zoom Swirl Out 52, or Pass Right Red 83, 616, or Pro Right Red 28 Quick Pass. Walking to the line of scrimmage, sensing opportunity in the forest on the other side, spotting something to exploit. Hands under center. Hollering a cadence. *Down. Set. Black fifty-two, Black fifty-two* . . . somehow seeing clarity in collisions and aggression.

The next day, I got my first snaps with varsity. My third play was a pass, a quick slant to the left. I dropped back and for the first time felt the speed of the game. My wiring broke down. I rushed thoughts and process. The mechanics I had committed to muscle memory collapsed. I threw left. The ball came out low. It hit a line-backer in the chest; he dropped it. That was it for the day. It wasn't what I wanted, but I had gotten a taste. The next practice wouldn't feel so overwhelming, I told myself. After all the offseason work-outs, all the times the coaches had seen me throw, I figured I'd get a little rope, get another shot tomorrow . . . and then the record scratched.

The next morning, our coaches divided up the varsity and junior-varsity squads. Varsity went right, jayvee left. They read off names. Guys I expected, a bunch of my friends, went to varsity. Then I heard it: "Wickersham. Over there." Jayvee.

I stumbled slowly toward the left. Someone shouted at me to not pout, and I tried, but I felt like the wind had been knocked out of me. I cried harder that night than I cried over my parents' divorce, harder than when the bank took our house. Something had been ripped away, an idea of what I was becoming or hoped to become. The coach thought what I needed most was playing time, and I wasn't going to get it on varsity. He eventually offered to move me to varsity if I wanted to switch to receiver. I took it. Out of pride, shock, as a means of saving face, I don't know. I had wanted to stand out but now just wanted to blend in. The following summer at foot-ball camp I jogged past the quarterbacks. I never forgave myself.

———

They do something that will never be fully comprehensible. They become mythical figures, in our minds and their own. They know what it's like to wait in the dark of a stadium tunnel, surrounded by cheerleaders and 80,000 people ready to explode at the call of their name, a wall of noise that fills their rib cages. They know the power of QB1 and the cosmic humiliation of QB2. They know what it means to say Tiger 12 Tom and Jerry Right Gun Trips Right Bunch F Shuttle. They know what it's like to hold the ball with two hands in the pocket, raise it high, just far enough to create a magical and exclusive torque, and to sling it forward, hips before shoulders, the ball released at the highest point, the flick of an index finger delivering the near-sexual rush of a tight spiral. They have practiced their autographs since childhood. They've earned letter jackets. They've picked jerseys, numbers 1–19. They absorb unbearable punishment and are spared it. They outdrink their linemen. Some sleep with world-famous women and some with women they've just met in bars. Most marry, some stray. They create attention to attract attention. They know what it's like to face outside forces trying to undo them, and to stare down the demons of fame and jealousy and money and doubt and hubris. Five of them at any given time on the planet are undeniably great. Three of those men earn gold jackets. They die alone, die with families, die with Christ, die quarterbacks.

Quarterbacking is not just a job but a way of being. A lifestyle. A kind of cool. A type of American that once didn't exist. The first forward pass was legalized three months after the Pure Food and Drug Act, the moment when the Gilded Age finally died and the Progressive Age began. Invention and innovation were orders of the day. Quarterback, QB, or just *Q*—it's the only position in American sports that's a literal and figurative noun, *and* a literal, figurative, and transitive verb. The very idea of the quarterback was and remains bound up with who we are and how we see ourselves on a national scale. Johnny Unitas was bedrock establishment. Joe Namath was rebellion. Joe Montana was pure cool. Quarterbacks know what it's like to want power and pressure at the highest level, to reach and to fall, to be covered in glory and shadowed by shame.

The most complex moments in sports are the few seconds before the ball is snapped in a football game and the few seconds after it. Quarterbacks command those moments and live with the consequences. Boxers are tougher, hockey players more coordinated, point guards faster and quicker, but quarterbacks have the hardest, most captivating job in sports. There's an *otherness* that separates those who can do it, a presence and a force field. Something that can't be fully shared, truly sustained, or easily explained.

What must it be like to be a quarterback? To be The Quarterback? How much thrill must be in it? How much wisdom? How much juice and joy? How much loneliness and hurt? How much folly and cruelty? How do you know a quarterback when you see one? Are its skills learned or innate? In the end, is what quarterback offers worth it, and does what it takes ever feel justified?

I was a teenager the first time I wondered those things. The following summer at football camp, a quarterback coach from the year before spotted me with the wide receivers, walked over, and asked, "What happened to you?" But it wasn't the right question, wasn't the one I'd carry with me all these years later.

The real question is *What might have happened?*

I

ORIGINS

John Elway sometimes watches his younger self—the Elway that I loved—on YouTube. More than reliving old memories, he likes to see how that guy stacks up to the current guys, the newest models. He's pleased with the answer. We're in a bar south of Denver on a May afternoon—as it happens, forty years to the day after Elway demanded and was granted a trade from the Baltimore Colts to the Denver Broncos in 1983. Quick to smile and slim at sixty-two, down thirty-five pounds from a few years ago when he was leading a manic life as the Broncos general manager, he's just flown in from "a good run" at the craps tables in Las Vegas. He sits with his back to the bar. The lunch crowd points and whispers. It's hard to imagine a professional athlete meaning as much to a city as Elway has meant to Denver over the years. We talk about beginnings. He tells me about earning his first letterman jacket: Granada

Hills Highlanders, 1977. A year earlier his father, Jack, had gotten a job as head coach at Cal State Northridge in the valley north of Los Angeles. Elway can still see the black leather sleeves and the kelly green wool. His name stitched in white. "Like a trophy," he says. He remembers the pins he put on the letter, remembers proudly walking the school halls. "Making all-league, trying to make all-city . . ." The jacket now hangs behind glass in a restaurant bearing his name, and the football field at Granada Hills bears his name, too. But there was a moment when one of the greatest quarterbacks of all time didn't think of himself as a quarterback at all.

Football was once the expression of a certain sort of omnivorous land grab, a bruising ground-level grind to take what we see as ours. But the spiral, a pass—the first known example of which probably came in 1885—and its particular and exhilarating and efficient carve through space, a pursuit and trajectory, metaphysical and mystical and metaphorical all at once, a demonstration of ambition and grace, untethered, bold, full of possibility, brought the game into the realm of discovery. Only in 2020 did scientists pin down the physics of a football in flight, why it turns over in the air rather than sinking to the ground. A spiral can be the offspring of a variety of arm angles, from over-the-top to three-quarters, sidearm, and even sometimes underhand, but no two are quite alike. Joe Namath's is different from Johnny Unitas's is different from Terry Bradshaw's is different from Joe Montana's is different from John Elway's is different from Tom Brady's is different from Patrick Mahomes's. That wrist snap and twist-swirl, that whip of the finger, it's a signature, like a strand of DNA, a statement of style and intent. If it didn't fly in that tight, silent spin, there would be no such thing as a quarterback. Not a magical one. Not of the kind Elway was. Not of the kind I wanted to be.

But it does, and because it does, the quarterback's power, pressures, and responsibility sometimes seem near limitless. The first time I saw Elway throw a football in person was November 24, 1991, Broncos at Seahawks. I was fifteen years old. The word I'd use to describe his ball's aesthetic now, but didn't think of then, is *determined*. He threw spirals that had muscular ideas and intentions, that knew what they wanted. The ball he threw, and the self-assured—if not outright arrogant—barely contained violence with which he threw it, conspired to make him execute things others wouldn't try, setting up deep in the pocket and calmly hitting impossible margins on the sidelines and invisible gaps between defenders down the middle of the field. Television never did it justice. You had to be there to see it, and once you saw it you couldn't shake it. Some of the best throws in Super Bowl history belong to Elway, even in the games he lost. In Super Bowl XXI, on a team devoid of stars and facing the New York Giants' Lawrence Taylor and one of the most stacked defenses in NFL history, coached by Bill Belichick, Elway ran left as the pocket collapsed and pulled up to throw deep. It was third and long, second quarter. If you watch it now and pause the video at the point of release, his body is leaning to the left, like a heeling sailboat, as the ball leaves his hand on a diagonal across the field, to the right. The receiver he hits is running a post route *away* from him. It looked casual; he never truly turned his arm loose, for fear of injury. Nothing about this throw makes sense. Elway lets fly on the hashmark at the Broncos' 14-yard line and Vance Johnson catches it on the run beyond the right hashmark at the Giants' 32-yard line. No physics explain it, just raw fearlessness and a gift applied to the max.

I watch it on repeat. You should, too.

In his best moments, Elway bent the logic of the football field the way Michael Jordan refused the laws of gravity and Wayne Gretzky manipulated objects, speeds, and angles. He played free, his own authority on what mattered and what was possible.

"You just feel like you can do anything," he says.

At fifteen, John Elway was a running back. Calvin Hill of the Cowboys was his favorite player. He wore number 35 because Hill did. He liked to run and to lower his shoulder on contact. Quarterback, as he knew it, was boring. All you did was hand off. And anyway, Elway's best sport was baseball. But in 1975, on the first day of ninth grade, on Military Hill in Pullman, Washington, his father told him who he was about to be. They were driving in the family's '73 Impala—Sheila the Chevy, the Elways called it—on the way to school, and John was talking about going out for running back, and Jack shook his head and quickly pulled the car over and put it into park.

Jack knew what he'd set his son up for, a particular kind of life and prophecy and duty as much as a position to play. A year later, when the family moved to Los Angeles and found Granada Hills, he chose a high school before he bought a house. The program had a progressive passing offense. It threw as a mandate and an imperative and a higher calling, as a way to set up the run rather than the other way around. That's where John was headed, where Jack was headed, where football, and maybe the country, was headed. Yes, John was the son of the new coach at Northridge. Yes, people saw him as a hotshot outsider coming to dominate. So yes, there was pressure. But the way to survive it, Jack was sure, was to throw. That's why they'd come. To throw. Jack saw something special in John. Not just the powerful arm—Elway calls it "my security thing"—but the engine inside him, an intense expectation of self and an idea of worth and identity, something burning. When John was just ten, father and son would play Ping-Pong matches until two in the morning, the boy always insisting on another chance to slay the old man and full of rage when he came up short. There were marks on the basement walls from where John threw paddles in anger. Jack wanted to nurture that fire, channel it, see where it could take his son. Raised in a small Washington logging town, the son of a plumber, Jack had made it to Washington State as a quarterback himself, but injuries cut his dream short. He proposed to his wife, Jan, after only a few dates and with only one condition: "I have to have a son."

Elway says he can't recall the exact conversation in the Impala. You're growing. It's time. You're not as fast as before, and you need to get stronger, but you've got this *thing*, a singular awareness and singular power. This is the moment. But he remembers the message like it was yesterday. Jack pulled over. Jack talked and John listened. "Fifteen minutes later, I got out of the car a quarterback," he says.

He was five-foot-ten, maybe 150 pounds at the time. And shy. Floppy blond hair and that arm said he fit the look, but little else did. Jack took him to see a friend, Washington State quarterbacks coach Mike Price, who peered past John's gangly frame, saw the potential, and offered one simple note: "Release the ball at the highest point of your motion." Elway says that conversation, and subsequent deliberate practice, unlocked his belief in his arm and self and set him on a path. Passing camps and workouts with friends running routes for him and word in the local papers that Granada had a phenom on its hands came quickly. National magazines followed. He was the chosen one, the first child star in this space, in the decade that took the concept to a higher level. But sitting with me in front of images of him on the walls of the Denver bar, posing for pictures and I-just-wanna-shake-your-hands with well-wishers, and collecting business cards from those who spot him through the crowd, the everyday of most of his adult life, what John Elway remembers best is the doubt. Jack hadn't told him to play a position, he'd told him to be part of a tradition, to step up to a mark, to stand out and to bear the weight of whatever came next. And they both knew it. There's a bust of John at the Hall of Fame in Canton—he's a made guy ten times over—but what *this* John Elway wants to tell me about *that* John Elway is the scale of expectations and the depth of fear.

"They thought I was *Joe Namath* coming in," he says.

———

Senior Night at Isidore Newman School in Uptown New Orleans. Class of '23. A warm October sunset. A tunnel of cheerleaders under the lights, with a line of football players waiting to have their names announced and to meet their parents at midfield, and little surprise over who will be called first.

He's in full uniform, wearing a kelly green jersey of his own, with a white number 16. He stands, slightly tilting back and forth, waiting. The field is bright and clean. He turns to his coach beside him.

"Do I run?" Arch Manning asks.

He is one of the top-rated high school quarterbacks in America. His talent and production and work ethic merit the status, but it's his name that makes the talent and production and work ethic feel inevitable. He's a Manning. His grandfather is Archie, a Southern icon. His Uncle Eli is a two-time Super Bowl champion, a New York icon. His Uncle Peyton is a two-time Super Bowl champion, a national icon. Arch knows no other kind of life. There's no hiding.

The crowd buzzes. A fervor awaits. The structures framing the stadium at Newman seem to mirror stages of his life. He'd started playing, almost as soon as he could walk, on the playgrounds behind the north end zone. Parallel to the sidelines are classrooms and buildings where he went to elementary school and then high school. As he approaches the south end zone, seventeen years old and at the beginning of something, he stands in the shadows of Manning Fieldhouse, named in honor of his father and uncles, all Newman alums. Tonight, as a senior, he commands the stage with little left to prove. In three months, he will be a freshman at the University of Texas. Anything other than a college career that ends with him being the first overall draft pick will seem like potential unfulfilled, an expectation both comically unfair and a reality of the life he has chosen.

Coach Nelson Stewart looks back at Arch. Stewart played with Peyton when they were young. He's known Arch since he was running on that kindergarten playground. He looks out to midfield now, to Arch's parents, Cooper and Ellen.

"Do a smooth jog," Stewart says.

"How fast?"

"Not fast."

Arch is nervous. Stewart can tell. Maybe Arch somehow knows it's the last night the world will feel this small. Maybe he wonders whether he'll ever feel this big again. Stewart tells him a quick story from his college years about almost falling on his face during player introductions. The kid laughs. The coach nods him on ahead.

The voice of the PA announcer calls out "Arch Manning" and continues with a rundown of honors, as the boy jogs, long-striding, to meet his mom and dad.

You can make the case that Arch Manning wasn't born on April 27, 2005, but on October 4, 1969. That night, Archie Manning's Ole Miss Rebels played Alabama. Archie was a handsome junior from Drew, Mississippi, a gifted, gritty kid carrying a deep hurt and living out a tireless urge to prove himself after his father's death by suicide. He liked quarterback. He studied those who played it, even as a kid. He reveled in the responsibility and the status it afforded him. It felt comfortable, manageable, an extension of self and ability. This was the first nationally televised night game in college football history. Archie threw for 436 yards and ran for 104 more, accounting for five touchdowns in a one-point loss, in what is now considered one of the greatest games of all time. He cried when the game ended. He was a legend, a folk hero, a song title, an All-American before he took an NFL snap, and even though he couldn't have known it at the time, he was the beginning of a family franchise that would show no signs of slowing down almost six decades later. Arch was part of a lineage before he was a glint in Cooper and Ellen's eyes. When Arch played fifth-grade flag football, Stewart and Cooper talked about moving him up to the middle school team but decided to keep him where he was, staving off the mania that awaited him. When he started high school, college coaches circled. He fit the part: tall, muscular, thick, handsome, driven and with a beautiful release point. The hype grew. Read the headlines—"The Next Manning" or "Better Than Peyton?" or "Overrated"—and you know it's been a long time since he felt like a little boy.

Arch can throw the deep out, he can settle teammates in the huddle, he can read a defense—summits for most, the price of entry for him. On Senior Night, as he stands at midfield, you can *almost* feel the weight of what lies ahead, the way it presses down on him, when he hopes someone might light the way for the short, tentative jog from the end zone to midfield, from what's now to what's next.

———

Mid-City Los Angeles, at about 4 p.m. on a March afternoon, Warren Moon is in no rush. A ceremony in his honor is underway at Hamilton High School, and the first speaker at the podium is well into her remarks. Moon wasn't given a shot to start as a Hamilton Yankee until his junior season because for a long time talented Black quarterbacks were rarely given the chance to play. But Moon led the team to a league championship in 1973 and went on to become one of Hamilton's luminaries. He's chatting, smiling for photos, hugging people he hasn't seen in years.

They're unveiling a mural of him today. It's painted to look like bright sidewalk chalk art. A Washington Huskies helmet in the upper left corner, a Pro Football Hall of Fame logo in the upper right. He's in his Houston Oilers uniform in the center of the frame, dropping back to pass, holding a ball high near the number 1 on his jersey. For Moon, sixty-five on this day, these moments are rarer now. There are few honors left to win. Hall of Fame in 2006, AP Offensive Player of the Year in 1990, NFL Man of the Year in 1989, nine Pro Bowls, five Canadian Football League championships, Rose Bowl MVP, and his number retired by the Tennessee Titans, the team the Oilers became.

A hundred or so people pack an outdoor corner of campus, between the locker rooms and Al Michaels Field, named after the famous sportscaster, also a Hamilton alum. Longtime, big-time NFL agent Leigh Steinberg—who's on the shortlist of people responsible for the quarterback's lofty cultural status—sits near me in the audience. Posters on the walls all around say WELCOME BACK. A thicket of green and white balloons hangs next to a concrete wall where the mural hides behind a black curtain.

The first speaker somehow messes up his name, an all-time great quarterback name—"Warren *Mune*"—as Moon walks slowly to his seat in the front row, stopped often and stopping often. His voice rises as he sees old friends and teammates—"You made it!"—and feels the warmth of being surrounded by people who know him, who knew him *when*. A rotating cast takes turns at the microphone, recounting his accolades, remembering his feats. "I know you're a Hall of Famer in the United States and Canada," one says. "But let's talk about the 1973 Hamilton Yankees football championship!" Then Norris Milton, Hamilton's current head coach, says, "It takes a lot for me to get shellshocked and starstruck, but now this is a surreal moment to see Warren Moon in person." A city councilman gives Moon a framed Los Angeles County commendation. Moon stands with the frame, holding it and holding his pose for an extra beat. Cameras click. He hasn't aged much since his playing days. He shaves his head and no longer has his signature mustache, but that's about it. His posture is perfect, game-ready.

"Don't sit down," the last speaker tells Moon. "It's your turn. Whoever was responsible for the script didn't do a very good job. Warren, you're up!"

"Warren Moon, everybody!" someone shouts.

"I've been introduced a lot of times over the last forty, forty-five years," Moon says, pausing until the audience giggles. "And that was the worst introduction I've ever received in my life."

He's been nervous about today's event. In 2017, he was named in a sexual harassment suit by a female former employee of his sports marketing firm. The parties settled in 2019. At the time of the lawsuit, Moon took what turned out to be a permanent leave of absence from his job as a radio analyst with the Seattle Seahawks, and he has largely stayed out of the public eye in the years since. Embarrassed and ashamed and angry at what he feels was a false accusation, he's tried to win back the trust of family and friends, he later tells me. Some sort of calm seems to wash over him behind the microphone now. Maybe they believe him. Believe *in* him. Or can forgive him. Or don't care. He speaks at first like someone who has a sort of stump speech, polished in repetition over the years, sticking to classic themes of gratitude, thanking people in his circle: Jack Epstein, the head coach who once gave him confidence when he needed it most. Rod Martin, a fellow Hamilton alum and Super Bowl hero linebacker with the Raiders. Old teammates. Steinberg, who "never gave up on me when I went up to Canada." His sisters, his niece and nephew, his brother-in-law. And then his mother, smiling from her wheelchair in the front row.

"She just turned ninety-five," he says. The crowd applauds.

Pat Moon was widowed, and Warren was left fatherless when he was just seven years old. Harold Moon, a laborer and an alcoholic, died of liver disease in 1963. Moon seems to change as he looks at his mother, both of them taking stock of the time that's passed, counting the cost. He's here remembering high school days when the team and the school looked to him to lead, but he was the man of the house long before he took a snap for Hamilton, cooking and mending clothes and looking out for his five sisters. His coaches and teammates didn't fully know it then, and many don't fully understand it now, but what he did on the field, the way he did it and the level he reached, was tied to how deep he could bury the hurt and pressure.

"I was handed the mantle of my household at a very young age," he tells those gathered. He took it seriously, he says. "A little too seriously."

He carried a briefcase in the hallways in high school. He had a vision of himself. Was set on becoming someone. He liked the idea that he could handle things, no matter the stakes, and he liked that people liked that about him. He was known by teachers and coaches and teammates and classmates, by his girlfriend Felicia, and by his aunts and uncles, as someone that "had a lot of maturity" for his age. Deep down, he knew that a lot of it was a front. He often pretended that life was better than it was. But he was also at the center of something. Ask him now what he misses most about the game, about his old job, and it's the hard stuff that he talks about first—at Hamilton and in Seattle, in Canada and Houston and Minneapolis. Two years after the ceremony, I'm sitting with Moon in the back of a restaurant south of Seattle. When he entered, a man at the bar yelled, "Hall of Fame!" Moon is nursing a cocktail and an appetizer, and he's telling me, with a kind of melancholic longing, about hurt and about the crushing headaches he got when he played, causing him to go home and collapse into bed after games, stress and pressure and fear and elation.

"It's taxing, man," he says. But then: "I used to sometimes *wish* I could get those migraines again."

He misses the pain?

Misses a job where effectiveness is measured by how much he hurt? Still craves a crushing, chain reaction of swelling, after three hours of spirals and shots to the ribs, all of which both defined his toughness and his limits?

"Yeah, I gave everything I had, mentally and physically. No matter how bad we won, no matter how bad we lost, I gave everything I had. And I loved that feeling."

———

South of Downtown LA, general managers and scouts gather at a track stadium at the center of the University of Southern California campus. On this March morning, 2024, it's USC's Pro Day, a chance for players to work out before NFL evaluators for the NFL Draft. Camera crews from three national television shows are here, along with representatives from all thirty-two clubs, for one reason. He loosens up in a building across an alley from the stadium, throwing a racquetball against a wall, kicking around a soccer ball. At 9:42 a.m., he comes out of a tunnel. Everyone turns. He nods at friends and family in the stands.

"What up, what up," Caleb Williams says.

Today is a formality, performative, a reality show, part of a machine that existed before Williams and will go on after him. Since 1966, when the National Football League merged with the American Football League, twenty-seven quarterbacks have been drafted first overall. In a few weeks, Williams is going to be number twenty-eight. He knows, the Chicago Bears—the team holding the first overall pick—know, the league knows, we know. He won the Heisman Trophy in 2022, his first full season as a starter. He brought eight offensive linemen to the ceremony in New York and wore a Gucci suit. That night, he slept with the trophy, the realization of not only years of work but of the belief that college football's grandest achievement was his destiny. He plopped back into bed after a predawn bathroom run and smacked his ear on the Heisman's extended hand.

Williams is not just an outstanding college quarterback; he's the first true professional amateur quarterback, earning millions in endorsements after a landmark 2021 Supreme Court ruling that college athletes could profit off their name, image, and likeness. He has a host of endorsements, of managers, a host of *stuff*. His team has produced a spreadsheet that estimates, if all goes well—if all goes as it's *supposed* to—he could be worth half a billion dollars in the coming years. His pursuit is of a role and a status and an arrival as much or more as it is of playing a game at the highest level.

Williams sifts through the gathered personnel, most of whom are awkwardly staring at him, or staring without staring, until he sees two men: Will Hewlett, his personal quarterback coach, and Tom Gormely, his physical therapist. He walks over.

"How do you feel?" Gormely asks.

"Good," Williams says.

Good is always relative for football players, even in the offseason. Williams spent much of the morning in a jacuzzi, soaking out pain in his arm and back. For most NFL prospects, the months between the end of college football season and the draft are a monotonous prelude, filled with long, humiliating, dehumanizing, and borderline-illegal auditions with flawed decision makers and methodologies. A multibillion-dollar industry has hinged on scouting which college quarterbacks will be great in the pros. NFL teams have more information than they can manage: footage of all of a quarterback's college games and even practices; video of all-star games, in-person observation, the NFL Combine, Pro Days, and private workouts; full medical information; drug-test results; background checks; psychological and intelligence tests; and interviews with former teammates, coaches, trainers, and others. No scouting processes have cracked the code, or even clarified it. Team owners are becoming more involved in evaluating quarterbacks, fully aware that their hired experts are experts only to a point. It's not much different than what happens a few miles away in Hollywood, where people in corner offices decide fates without a clue as to what makes a summer blockbuster.

Williams stretches, an array of drills that look basic but are specific to the job, loosening his hips and spine, mobilizing joints and tissues. The names are funny: HS Floss, QL Pretzel, IR Rocks, TS Pigeon, Cat Cow, Push Up + Calf Lunge, Psoas Reach, Worlds Greatest, Lunge and Rotate, Walking Hip ER. The TS Pigeon, for instance, calls for Williams to sit in a kind of yoga pose, left leg in front, right in back, hunched down as if preparing for a track race, and then slowly rotate his arm back and up. None of this is meant to be understood by mortals.

"Well, you can chill," Gormely tells Williams when he finishes.

Williams sits under a tent, changing into cleats, then lies down on the turf. He props his feet up on a folding chair, tapping his fingers on his chest. He meditates for about five minutes, nearly dozing off.

Hewlett stands nearby, checking a list of fifty color-coded items. Each one is a throw Williams will make today. Hewlett is one of the premier names in an industry that has exploded over the last twenty years, mirroring the cultural status of the profession: private quarterback coach. When Hewlett assembles what he calls "a script" of throws, he's compiling a narrative. When Williams drops back for the first of those throws, he's a character in a story.

Hewlett's job—for high school kids to NFL starters—is to deliver a specific American dream. He speaks to an idea, something that for most of the history of the quarterback didn't exist: that there's *a way to do this*. A way to *become* this, through technique, explanation, practice, and expertise, check or credit card accepted. A small part of Hewlett's role, for his most fortunate clients, is to manufacture the quarterback into a story that already exists. That means writing a script of throws—with little predictive value—for a Pro Day.

Hewlett's goal for today's spectacle is as strange and urgent as the event itself: He wants to prove that Williams cares about quarterbacking as much as being a quarterback. A script for a series of useless drills before representatives of thirty-two teams, thirty-one of whom won't employ him next year, is necessary because Williams needs to *show* that he takes them seriously. Excelling at artifice matters, multilayering absurdity.

"Gotta check all the boxes," Hewlett says.

But then Williams tells Hewlett that he's going to drop his "fucking nuts" before the scouts, making clear that he is not part of a process or machinery, much less part of a script. He will execute the menu of tasks—lining up under center, in shotgun, rolling out, throwing short and medium and long, to pass patterns with names like Whip, Swirl, Spray Out, Dagger, C.O. Option, Sail, Strike-Spray, Through Nod—but he will be a man alone out there, propelled if not sustained by a belief in and assertion of himself rather than system. It's a lonely and essential part of the equation. A handful of quarterbacks will *always* outstrip the story.

"Let's do it," Williams says.

He takes the stage. Some of the assembled minds stand together, others alone, as if angle and distance will provide clarity. There's a runway aspect to it all. Williams has a smooth arm, his passes accurate. After twenty or so minutes, he throws a deep post route, 65 yards in the air, to cap the workout. Script complete.

"Yeah, we're done," Hewlett says. "Helluva job, men."

Williams waves to the stands and waves to his future employers at the Bears, a quarterback that resembles an MBA test case. His significance is not just the expectation that he will be a great quarterback, but that he'll be the first of something new, a major-market superstar, fully formed as a player and as an entity—which he knows all too well might not matter if he lands in the wrong place.

Plantation Park, outside Jacksonville. A December morning in 2022. Colin Hurley stands on a football field while most kids his age are in class. He's fifteen years old and midway through his junior year at Trinity Christian Academy, where he has been the starting quarterback since eighth grade and has won two state championships. His heroes are Dan Marino and Cam Newton. He is being recruited by most major college football programs. His life has been engineered to make him a quarterback. He takes classes through a virtual high school, six days a week, consuming credits at an accelerated rate so that he can go to college early, and most of all, freeing up time for throwing and lifting and training and playing the part. Like Caleb Williams, Colin is a prodigy, both by choice and by system, a seductive and dangerous space. The days of waiting on the eventual viability of someone like Tom Brady, who spent the fall of his freshman year of high school as a backup on an 0–8 team and spent the spring playing baseball, seem long gone. There's often a dull panic in young quarterbacks that someone somewhere is doing something that they're not. Hurley trains with professional athletes, including NFL passers. He travels the country to various camps and flag-football competitions, venues to announce his presence as the next great one, among all the supposed next great ones. His is a fiercely limited existence in the hopes of an expansive life.

Colin is a boy, but he has the physical characteristics of a modern adult quarterback. He is tall and thick, with a profound ass that some college coaches grab. His release is quick but adaptable, and he's been clocked throwing a football sixty-one miles an hour, which his trainer says is one mile faster than the top recording for Patrick Mahomes. Most of all, Hurley carries himself like he expects all of what is out there for the taking, an unwavering belief that he and *this* are a matter of destiny, all the way to Canton.

It's quiet, except for the subtle sounds of the craft, which I love and miss dearly: the slap of leather on hands when the ball is snapped, breaths short and sharp, the rhythmic cleated toe-taps of a drop back, and finally, the rub of the ball leaving fingertips and hitting air. Nobody else is around, except one of Colin's buddies, a receiver named Miles Burris—and, as always, his dad, Charlie. Colin wears his hair long, sprouting like a weeping willow. He likes to shake it away from his eyes. He labors to stuff it under a helmet, much more than he labors when he throws. He completes a deep corner route, dropping the ball where Burris wants it—over his outside shoulder, a cradle more than a catch—but is still vaguely dissatisfied.

"One more," he says.

"Most important thing is to keep the ball away from the safeties here," Charlie says.

Next rep, same throw. "I think that one's better," Colin says.

"I try to stay hands-off," Charlie says to me, giving his son space. "I'm Dad."

Many quarterback stories can be broken down into two categories: too much Daddy, or not enough. Beyond that, most quarterback stories can be broken down into two subcategories: those who burn out trying to please their fathers, and those who have their own thoughts on the matter. Charlie Hurley doesn't look like a classic quarterback dad, which is to say that he doesn't look like a failed quarterback. He is short and jacked, like the tailback that he was, with faded tattoos along arms that remind you of the virtue of dumbbell curls. Among other police roles, he was a homicide investigator in Central Miami before he and his then-wife, Marion, decided to raise their two young sons in Jacksonville. Charlie has seen every kind of car accident, overdose, murder, mutilation. A loving hardass, he lives in a kind of existential panic. His job made him fear cars, guns, drugs, alcohol, and any of those things mixed with testosterone. His relationship with his son—both parasocial and as close as best friends—makes him fear his son being ordinary, all of this work being for nothing. Colin's one shot at greatness is also Charlie's one shot to help provide it. "I'm raising him to be a man in a cutthroat industry," Charlie says, "at the most cutthroat position."

One evening Charlie and Colin were watching *QB1: Beyond the Lights*, the Netflix series about high school quarterbacks. It was an episode with Spencer Rattler, a star out of Phoenix who was considered the nation's best high school quarterback in 2019, which, because of how these things go, means he was also considered the next college star, which means he seemed destined to be an NFL star, which means he seemed destined to transcend sports and land in our collective firmament. It didn't work out that way. It rarely does. During one scene, the intensity of Spencer's father, Mike, stunned both Hurleys. Colin pointed to the screen and looked at Charlie, shaking his head.

"We can do this," Colin said. "Just don't be like him."

Colin was fourteen years old when he said this to his dad, a child who acutely felt the momentum behind himself and his chosen line of work. He was thrilled and grateful and eager—and a little scared, even if, like many in this space, he refused to admit it outright. He saw danger out there, danger for *him*, if the apparatus were to collapse under its own weight. Most quarterbacks eventually realize that alongside the will required to attain physical and cultural supremacy is the capacity to self-destruct. Behind the eyes peering out from a face mask is an invisible battle to not break under strain from city to huddle to home, to not play roulette too much or too often, to not say fuck it and chase a thrill and wonder if they can tempt fate again. . . .

Charlie knows this, of course, and he controls for it by controlling his son's world. When the Hurleys moved to Jacksonville, Colin was already showing promise at throwing whatever ball happened to be in his right hand. Charlie found a trainer for Colin: Tom Gormely. He found a private quarterback coach: Will Hewlett. Those are the same guys that together or separately work with Caleb Williams, Super Bowl starter Brock Purdy of the 49ers, first-round draft pick Anthony Richardson of the Colts, and likely future Hall of Famer Matthew Stafford of the Rams, among others. The Hurleys entered the strange, year-round circuit of youth quarterbacking, of camps and competitions and flag tournaments and exposure, to college coaches and to agents and to online outlets obsessed with the premise and promise that genius can be spotted early. Throwing mechanics, arm care, strength and speed training, film study, brand building, marketing, media training, academics, offseason seven-on-seven tournaments and other quarterback showcases, nutrition, rehabilitation, recovery, financial literacy— Charlie has found ways to provide it all. It's worked, so far. Colin can't legally drive, and has yet to be fitted for braces, but he can quarterback.

When legendary Alabama head coach Nick Saban met with Hurley on a recruiting trip, he told Charlie that his son was "hydroponically developed."

———

In a Palo Alto business park, just off the 101, Steve Young sits in a corner office and looks at the autographed helmets on the shelves, from almost every quarterback in the Hall of Fame. Each year, roughly 16,000 boys are high school starting quarterbacks in America. About 858 start in college, including 136 in Division I FBS, the highest level. On this day, 751 have started at least one game in modern NFL history. One-hundred seventy-eight have reached a Pro Bowl. Sixty-three have started a Super Bowl. Thirty-five are in the Hall of Fame. Young is one of them. Each summer he attends the annual Ray Nitschke Luncheon in Canton, Ohio, an event exclusive for those with gold jackets and bronze busts. He surveys the quarterbacks, his peers and heroes, the only ones in the world who know what this life, their life, is like, unspoken but acknowledged, the only ones who've survived a merciless winnowing—"There are *filters* to get to that place," Young says—men who know what it's like to win MVPs, to lead the league in passing, to have their choice of endorsements and movies, who come to realize that the frills and perils, the transient asides that accompany professional and cultural thin air, aren't why they wanted to do this job and why they miss it so when it's over.

"No one that plays for a long time at quarterback plays it for the glory," he says. "It's too cheap. The reason to do it is the holy hell. It is everything a human being can be thrown into."

He stares past me, then out the office window, to the campuses of Silicon Valley, led by people who changed the world by refusing to acknowledge limits.

"No one else understands," he says.

I've mostly covered professional football for almost a quarter century at ESPN, which means I've mostly covered quarterbacks. You know why. I've come to realize that Young is the only great quarterback who knows how great quarterbacks are made, who can, without overdoing it and without veering into its Wharton-like technocratic aspects, articulate certain skills. No, *powers*. "The Force," Young says. Dan Marino knew no other way through life than being able to throw where he wanted when he wanted. Young is different. He was born a great athlete but wasn't born a great quarterback. Strange to say, but he starred at Greenwich High in Connecticut and got a scholarship to the country's greatest passing college of the eighties—Brigham Young, named after a distant relative—without knowing how to throw. Young was a multimillion-aire and years into his professional career before he learned how to be a *quarterback*. He had to be taught. He's proof that quarterback *can* be taught.

How?

And why is it so hard?

Young and I tend to geek out. He thinks we view the job in the same way: intense, concentrated, intimate, communal, a space where anything can happen and often does. "Spiritual," he says. I wanted to be this thing because it felt larger than life. Young knows that it is indeed larger than life—and also smaller. He approaches it not with the certitude and knowingness of a first-ballot Hall of Famer but from a place of curiosity and wonder, as if he's still trying to figure out his wiring, a quarterback's wiring. When Young was a backup at BYU, starter Jim McMahon once drove him home after a game. McMahon would go on to win a Super Bowl with the Chicago Bears. He had gall and then some. In the car, Young stared at McMahon's radio dial, figuring that McMahon listened to a *special* station, unavailable to mere mortals. He was relieved that it was just normal classic rock.

There's an inviting aspect to the way Young tells stories like that, enough to make me feel not like we're peers but co-travelers on a journey. People say the word *quarterback* as if it's one thing. Young knows that it's dozens. A high school quarterback is not a college quarterback. A college quarterback is not an NFL quarterback. An NFL quarterback is not a great NFL quarterback, and a great NFL quarterback is not a generational one . . . yet, they're all connected. All must indulge and nurture the voice somewhere deep inside that tells them that they're better than those around them. Not a better quarterback. A superior human. Smarter, tougher, more gifted, more blessed. At the highest levels, the symbolic dimensions of the job, to say nothing of the comforts and luxuries of stardom, require it: *You're a general, matinee idol, spokesman for a multibillion-dollar organization, prop, civic treasure, student, teacher, psychologist, conductor, instrument of momentum, avatar of debate, dream-maker, dream-wrecker, master manipulator, magician, earnest cheerleader, astonishing asshole, social force, and lest anyone forget, distributor of footballs into slimming windows that few can see, much less exploit.*

Young will remind you: There's one guy—and only one. He is a multifarious thinker, but he always ends up in a ruthless place, zero-sum and binary. The defining features of his own story are when he was Joe Montana's backup and when he was Joe Montana's successor. Decades ago, Young would attend crowded parties with Montana. Young saw clustered masses and activity, igniting an anxiety in his chest that he had tried to throttle since he was a boy. Montana would float through, gladhanding and chatting—but that wasn't the thing. What Young remembers, decades later, is when the party was over. Montana could remember a distinctive trait about each person, their socks or jacket or manner or location, even people with whom he didn't speak. That was unique. Magical, even. And so as Young carries on in his office, tossing out ideas and theories and truths about what distinguishes the immortals, confluences of arrogance and humility, of desperately trying to answer personal questions through a very public forum, of discovering mysteries, reveling in them, of existential longing—and never saying "size" or "speed" or "arm"—I can feel him wrestling with two versions of the same thing, of a gear he transcended and what he wants to help others transcend.

Young was a quarterback. Montana was an *artist*.

The next Joe Willie wasn't ready. John Elway started his first season at Granada as a backup. He first saw the field against El Camino Real High: ten attempts, four completions, a bad interception on fourth-and-goal. Of course, Elway and I aren't talking about whether he was ready, because we know what happened next. We're talking about a kind of lens, a tool for discovering and learning, of going beneath surfaces and beyond perceptions and assumptions. Elway says that those moments, those rare failures, were the start of something that no other position in sports offered, a certain freedom and trust. The coaches let him do more than throw. They let him *think*. Asked him to call plays, wanting him to own what transpired. At the same time, Elway started to grow: four inches before his junior year, joints stretched so thin that it hurt his knees to sit in a car for more than twenty minutes. He was still skinny, but the ball came out of his hand hot. His hips naturally locked into place after years of batting practice, propelling his arm forward, one of the cleanest throwing motions in quarterback history in its infancy.

In his second career start, against Carson High in 1977, Granada entered the fourth quarter trailing 16–0. But then something precious shifted in Elway, an ethic and a virtue fastening for good. He rallied his team back, throwing for 256 yards and three touchdowns, the last of which gave Granada a 19–16 lead that they held on to for a win. A few weeks later, against San Fernando High with 9,000 in the stands, Elway did it again. In that game, he got the ball in the shotgun—way back, nine yards rather than the standard five, making it look like he was lining up to punt. As soon as he got the ball, he drifted back even farther. Pressure came from the backside, which was inevitable because his line had no chance to block anyone with all of Elway's moving around. He spun free, then faded back left. At this point, he was 20 yards behind the line of scrimmage. From his own 10-yard line, he finally threw, downfield, so far that the cameraman lost the ball and focused on the deepest receiver, waiting for action. Elway threw it from his 10 to San Fernando's 10—80 yards—and it was caught for a touchdown. He threw another with 13 seconds left, the game-winner.

If Elway had failed in those two comebacks, at that precious, formative age—like I did, like most do—would I be sitting across from him right now at this bar? A botched comeback can haunt everything that is to come. All Elway knew was that when his team was down and the clock was low, he loosened up rather than tightened. Years later, Elway got beers with a quarterback named Sean Salisbury, who played for USC in the eighties and in the NFL for a decade. Salisbury was buddies with Elway, and in awe of him. He asked how Elway made these two-minute drives look routine. He was hoping for a deep dive, full of technical aspects and psychology and something transferrable. Elway simply said, "I did it once. Then it happened a second time. So by the third time everyone just expected it to happen, regardless of how the game had unfolded before the last drive, so I began to feel the same way."

What Elway was the first of—the first top-ranked quarterback out of high school to be the first overall draft pick to be a first-ballot Hall of Famer, first to *live up* to it and later figure out what it built and stripped within him—started with those rallies. It was the beginning of "never worrying about how I was going to play," he tells me.

"Why?"

"Because it was gonna pan out."

———————

First drive, first game, Arch saw something. What it was is not essential to the story—details are irrelevant to mythmaking—but it was a spring game against Archbishop Shaw High. He was in eighth grade. He stood near the line of scrimmage. He scanned the defense, like he had been trained to do, trying to decipher it, decode it, looking for keys, subtle tells. The right cornerback was in tight coverage against wide receiver Jarmone Sutherland. Newman had a slant route called, but this was inviting. Sutherland turned to Arch, wondering what to do. Arch gently tugged his face mask, signaling him to go deep. What happened next—well, now that's when those watching him witnessed a familiar, and familial, magic.

Arch had already shown promise at the essential thing: throwing the ball. That was evident from the start, when he was playing flag football in fifth grade. "He had a good throwing motion," Uncle Eli says. But what stood out to Eli is that "it made sense to him. Some people, they pick up a ball, and it just *works*." It happens to be the rarest thing in sports, but many families have it in the bloodstream: the Carrs, the Huards, the Detmers, the McCoys, the McCowns, the Vicks, the Hasselbecks, the Tagovailoas, the Bootys, the Murrays, the Palmers. The Mannings exist in a different orbit, of course, with roots dating back seventy years. As a child in Drew, Archie was the quarterback on the playground. He never announced it; everyone *knew*. Quarterback was how he saw himself. The Mannings lived across the street from the school. His father, Buddy, was friends with the teachers, and he knew that money was scarce for them, so he always went out of his way to help where he could. He had access to a big truck to help them move or farm. The teachers, especially the gym teachers, reciprocated with a soft spot for Archie. He spent hours on those fields.

You know the phrase *gym rat*? "I was a *yard rat*," Archie says.

Coaches gave him minor tips, but Archie knew how to throw, a little sidearm, but accurately. When he was in fifth grade, he had his quarterback heroes: first Charlie Conerly at Ole Miss and later of the New York Giants; then Jake Gibbs at Ole Miss, an All-American in football and baseball who went on to play for the Yankees; and, always, an eighth-grader named James Hobson. "My idol," Archie says. "Greatest athlete I ever saw!" When Archie reached sixth grade, he played organized football. A coach moved him to receiver. "I was just brokenhearted," he tells me, unaware that I *know*. Buddy told him the same thing my father told me: "Be patient." But quarterbacks are uniquely ill-suited for patience. Archie still doesn't know what happened, but he suspects players told the coach that Archie *is* our quarterback.

Even when Archie was playing basketball and baseball, he always stuck out his chest a little because of his fall job. "I loved the status that came with it," he says. From the time he was ten, he wanted one thing: to be the Ole Miss quarterback. He wasn't heavily recruited out of high school and knew that if he decided to go to Mississippi, he'd compete with seven other passers. The biggest pressure of his life was when he won the starting job as a sophomore, which nobody had previously done at Ole Miss. After his epic Alabama performance a year later, lives changed forever. His, and others'. When Archie returned home to Drew, he needed to make a call, so he called collect. He had to give his name. "I'll bet you really feel big saying that," the operator replied.

It was the start of a dynasty. Ask Peyton how he became a quarterback, and you might expect him to go back to childhood, when a local television reporter asked him if he was going to be a football player when he grew up, just like his dad, and he nodded and said, "Mmm-hmm." But Peyton starts with the arm, just like his dad. He had a throwing motion unlike any other quarterback, one that the quarterback gurus felt was inefficient. He held the ball high, at his ear. Most tell you to hold the ball at your chin or shade slightly to your throwing-side pec. One day, a coach gave Peyton a few throwing tips. Archie stepped in, for the only time in Peyton's life. "Don't let anyone touch your arm," he said. Too many horror stories. Archie was broadcasting Saints games on the radio, and so Peyton would go to work with his dad, standing on the field, watching visiting passers warm up. Joe Montana, all grace. John Elway, all power. Troy Aikman, all efficiency, a five-step drop with quick feet and no wasted motion. And Dan Marino. He was Peyton's favorite. The way he was in charge and then, my god, how he threw. His arm snapped. The ball was up and *gone*.

Peyton played baseball and basketball, but there was something different about quarterback. It was the hardest position in sports. The quarterback needed to understand every position, on offense and defense, and if possible, every assignment on offense and defense. You were under constant constraints, from time to throw to a pass rush to the defensive schemes to crowd noise. Weather was a factor in a way that it wasn't in other sports. That's what made it cool. Peyton loved the *pressure* of it all. Cooper was a receiver at Newman, and on weekend offseason mornings needed an arm to throw to him and the other wideouts. Peyton volunteered. Archie would show up to coach not Peyton, but the pass-catchers. "My dad took great pride in that," Peyton says. "He helped four all-state receivers." That was another lesson Peyton learned: A quarterback should be able to coach wideouts.

Peyton became the starter at Isidore Newman as a sophomore, and against Riverside High, a rival, he threw a post route to Cooper for a touchdown. They developed their own system of hand signals, of getting to the line of scrimmage, seeing how the defense lined up, and changing the route based on what they saw. Peyton realized the potency of that idea. It became his thing. In the NFL, he operated without a huddle—called the hurry-up or tempo—to hustle to the line of scrimmage and prevent the defense from substituting personnel or designing elaborate blitzes. He was not the first quarterback to use a hurry-up offense for most of the game—Boomer Esiason did it in Cincinnati in the late eighties, and Jim Kelly did it with his K-Gun offense in Buffalo in the early nineties—but he was the first to use it to *not* call the play quickly. He used the hurry-up to take his time, to look at the defense, to run the play when *he* wanted. He was the first quarterback to understand the inherent leverage in a basic thing: that he controlled when the ball was snapped. Jim Sorgi, Manning's longtime backup in Indianapolis, would half-jokingly offer reporters a peek at the Colts' playbook. It was filled with simple plays. Manning was the device that turned them into confusion for the defense, opportunity for the offense, and expansion for the idea of a quarterback. Peyton was blessed with height—six-foot-five—and a suitable arm, and a last name that provided the twin gifts of leverage and expectation. But his strength was that he could throw *and* think, that he was willing to be weighed down. He would use any one or a combination of tricks, like formation or motion or matchup or, most devilishly, his eyes and hands, to force the defense into declaring its intent, and then with hand signals and code words switch to a play designed to exploit it. While most quarterbacks had lockers around other quarterbacks, Peyton always wanted his near his offensive linemen's, so that it was easier to discuss audible mechanisms. Friday afternoons were Signal Meetings with his receivers. If he pretended to shovel or called the word *Crane*, for instance, it told the receiver to run a dig route.

At first, it was annoying to watch. Something about it played into a know-it-all veneer and reputation he had cultivated. But year after year, as Peyton improved upon his own impossible standards, and it became clear that we were witnessing a rarity—beyond his championships, his five MVP awards, his seven-time All-Pro nods, his growing list of records, a kind of football brilliance.

Eli was in fifth grade when he took on this role. He played flag and at recess, first for whatever team divvied up with him, and then, once it was clear that "it was just unfair," he says, he became the all-time quarterback. That's a fun title, I remember: *all-time quarterback*. Eli took to the job. "I was like, 'All right, this works.'" What he had to think most about was not being Archie's third son, but Peyton's younger brother. Every aspiring quarterback must decide at some point: Are you about this world? Are you willing to do what it takes? Do you want to leave the old version of yourself behind? Do you possess all of the strange traits—talent, smarts, drive, luck, the combination of broken in the right places and healed in the right places—to do it? There's a chrysalis, a metamorphosis that takes place. It happened to Peyton and Eli. Both faced choices about what they were willing to sacrifice. As boys, these men dedicated their lives to this job.

Arch Manning is the heir to something, not just the job but a knowledge of what it looks like to arrive at the destination, to become and to be the thing, to live and work as the one who calls the plays and delivers a spiral. Archie and Cooper and Peyton and Eli all tried to shield Arch. They wanted football to be fun. In flag football, Arch loved throwing touchdowns to his friends. But when Cooper took him to games, NFL or college, Arch barely said a word. He silently studied what was taking place on the field. "Like he was taking a class," Cooper says. He'd constantly ask Cooper to throw with him in the den, and after a few passes whizzed too close to Ellen's head, she ordered them outside. One time, the family had a layover in Miami, and Arch had a ball, because he almost always had a ball, and he threw in the terminal. Cooper took Arch to camp at LSU. People started to notice, because of course, and Arch was offered a scholarship on the spot.

But he hadn't actually done the thing. Not yet. In the Archbishop Shaw High game, he got the ball and took a few steps back. He looked left, then center, preternaturally calm, then turned right and threw with zip and touch deep down the right sideline. It landed over Sutherland's outside shoulder, perfect placement, for a touchdown—and the beginning of something beyond anyone's control. He invoked a feeling, reminding those who saw it of what they felt the first time they witnessed it, and showed them what it looked like now.

In the stands, Cooper and his longtime friend Richard Montgomery turned to each other. "Shit!" Montgomery said.

Cooper replied with a look that said *Here we go*.

———

Great quarterbacks tend to be loners, and the parts of the job Warren Moon grew to love were the moments when it was just himself and a ball, progressions and evolutions that nobody saw, much less knew about. Take spirals. Few quarterbacks in history threw a prettier ball. That wasn't by accident. Throwing a football not only gave him something to feel good about as a kid, not only gave him a sense of purpose, providing license to order people around, but also gave him something to master. "You were always looking for the perfect throw," he says. "That was my thing. . . . If it didn't spin, I wasn't happy." Moon wore his fingernails long, for a measure of extra control, and threw so many footballs that the ball developed a tiny divot, a branding of sorts. He wanted to be known for his spirals, an artistic quality to quarterbacking, before he knew the responsibilities of the position or of adulthood.

As Moon neared high school, he saw people beat up or even killed over trivial matters. He wanted to go to a safe school. That ruled out the two schools in his zone, Los Angeles High and Dorsey High. Warren had a friend who attended Hamilton High, an hour northwest. He visited, liked it. Pat knew someone who lived in the Hamilton attendance zone who allowed her to use her address as a backdoor way in. Moon commuted to school on a city bus. If he missed it, he waited for another. He took school seriously, often wearing a coat and tie. Another Hamilton student named Felicia Hendricks thought he was cute and nerdy. They dated, the beginning of their lives being intertwined. Moon thrived in every way except quarterback. He was the backup on the sophomore team. The starter had a powerful father. It felt political. He considered leaving. The spring of his sophomore year, he threw a deep ball and missed it over his receiver. Jack Epstein, the varsity coach, approached him. Moon worried that his career was over before it had a chance to begin. But Epstein knew he had seen something rare. He put his arm around Moon. "Warren, you're gonna be my starting varsity quarterback next year."

Those words, about *him*, from a coach—from a *man*—changed Moon's life. "I had some hope. Somebody believed in me."

By his senior season in 1973, Moon was renowned enough to draw threats on his life. Before a high school game against Crenshaw High, he was warned, not by an opposing player but by a gang member, that if he led Hamilton to victory, "You're gonna get killed right after the game is over."

Moon told his mom and Epstein. He hid his car. But he played, well enough for Hamilton to win. Epstein asked some players to hang close to Moon after the game, a security detail. Moon was eighteen years old and learning about talent and the world and consequences in ways that make the plights of other great quarterbacks—say, stories about lack of recruiting interest out of high school—seem trivial. He was targeted because of who he was, and he was also spared because of who he was. Many times, he did something innocuous—stepping on someone's foot by accident at a party—that would have gotten anyone else jumped, but was shown mercy. "The thing that saved me was the fact that they would recognize me," Moon says. He stopped going to parties after a fight broke out and guns were drawn. He and Felicia ran—she left one of her shoes behind—and as they sprinted down the street to his car, shots rang out. They hit the pavement.

Moon tells me this with a kind of professionally processed reflection. He's worked on and through things, trauma received and inflicted, rising above heights—physically, psychologically, emotionally—that felt anything but inevitable. He *took* quarterback, and people tried to take it from him. Colleges started to call, but as a Black quarterback who wanted to continue as one at a time when few were playing at major programs, and even fewer were operating passing offenses, Moon found he needed to sell himself to them. Moon committed to Arizona State, which ran a pro-style offense. But then the Sun Devils recruited two other quarterbacks, named Dennis Sproul and Bruce Hardy, two names that would be seared into Moon's soul. Quarterbacks never forget those who a coach felt was better. Moon de-committed.

Running out of options, Moon enrolled at West Los Angeles Junior College. He was angry at the world. One of the few people who knew what he was going through happened to work just up the

110 freeway, at Los Angeles Coliseum. He had gotten death threats, too. He was a Black quarterback, too. And he was an excellent one, gracing the cover of *Sports Illustrated*, the magazine of record, after leading the Los Angeles Rams to the playoffs. His name was James Harris. Everyone called him Shack. At the exact time when Moon saw Harris as living proof of what was possible, Harris had a condo near the junior college, overlooking the practice fields, and he would sometimes look out his window and marvel at the kid under center, throwing perfect spirals.

On a sunny morning in 2022, James Harris meets me at a suburban Orlando diner to tell me a story about a young man and a tree. Harris is seventy-seven on this day, a few wrinkles, a wobbly gait common to NFL players from the seventies, pro football's most barbaric era. He takes me back to the end of gym class one day at Carroll High in Monroe, Louisiana, early 1960s. The class played football. Harris threw, of course. He had watched Johnny Unitas on television, number 19 in Baltimore Colts blue, with a crew cut and iconic black high-tops, marveling at his command and control. Harris tried to emulate Unitas in gym, directing receivers to go to the tree and turn right, or the ditch and cut left, or head for the corner after ten yards. The teacher spotted something rare. After class, he asked Harris if he wanted to play quarterback for the team that fall.

Not really, Harris said.

Even as a teenager, Harris had a mild defeatist streak. He was a sharecropper's son. He saw crosses burned on lawns. He knew not to look at certain people. He drank out of a different water fountain and rode at the back of the bus. Harris played basketball, a sport with few racial complications. But something about the offer of being a quarterback stuck with him. He had listened to Martin Luther King's speech in the shadow of the Lincoln Memorial, and it inspired him just enough to give it a shot. Sophomore year, he led Carroll to a regional championship. Life changed. Girls wanted to walk off the field with him. Quarterback had all kinds of surprising perks, such as helping teammates. The local paper wrote game stories for white schools; for places like Carroll, it only ran box scores. This job afforded Harris the chance to call plays that got his friends in the end zone. "Get 'em that chance to score, get their name in the paper," he says. By senior year, he had won thirty-nine straight games.

Harris tells me that one night, Grambling State University head coach Eddie Robinson showed up at his house. At the time, Robinson was merely a great coach and not yet a legend. He arrived at Harris's house *pissed*. Earlier that day, Robinson had joined Howard Cosell on a radio show. *When is Grambling going to produce an NFL quarterback?* Cosell had asked. That question—and the intentional obtuseness of it—enraged Robinson. He knew that Harris was being recruited by Michigan State. His suspicions mirrored Harris's: that Michigan State would probably move him to tight end. What nobody knew at the time was that Harris might've gotten a fair shot; Jimmy Raye II, a Black quarterback out of North Carolina, would lead the Spartans to a national title in 1966. Robinson looked Harris in the eye. "Damn to hellcat"—hellcat was one of his catchphrases—"Howard Cosell had the nerve to ask me when I'm gonna produce a quarterback. You can play."

Harris liked Robinson's cranky optimism, which offset Harris's hardwired urge to walk away. But he really liked how Coach saw him as something bigger, a unique force, the latest in a lineage begin-ning with Frederick Douglass "Fritz" Pollard, who on October 7, 1923, playing for the Hammond (Indiana) Pros against the Dayton Triangles, became the first Black man to start at quarterback in an NFL game. Harris enrolled at Grambling, with NFL quarterback as the goal. Robinson invested in Harris like he had for no other player. He asked Grambling alums in the NFL to share their playbooks so that Harris could learn pro-style offenses. In the mid-sixties, Bart Starr of the Green Bay Packers was the game's preeminent winner. Robinson gave Harris a copy of Starr's book *Quarterbacking*. He sent him to speech class, so that he could learn how to be the face of an organization. Robinson was asking Harris to change, in the hopes of becoming a different kind of Black quarterback. He asked him to play the game by its rules, to conform and adapt, knowing full well that Harris was conditioned to believe the system was fun-damentally wrong. "Coach Rob can sure wave the flag," Harris told teammates.

Four years later, in 1969, Harris had an NFL-ready résumé. He had led Grambling to three Southwestern Athletic Conference championships. He won a game at Yankee Stadium, a career high-light, and was named All-America. He was six-foot-four and 210 pounds, with a fluid and high release. Not for nothing, Shack Harris was a cool quarterback name. And with it all, he was prepared to be a high school teacher. Would he get a chance to play in the NFL? Did he *want* one? In 1953, Willie Thrower got one drive as a Chicago Bear—and was pulled after he did the dirty work of moving the team into scoring position. Charlie "Choo Choo" Brackins played in a single game for the Packers in 1955. In 1968, Harris watched Marlin "The Magician" Briscoe of the Denver Broncos become the first Black quarterback to start in a modern pro football game.

Briscoe played well, all but inventing the idea of a quarterback as a scrambler—and then he was benched and moved to receiver.

If the league didn't want a Black quarterback, why fight?

On the day of the draft, Harris went to the Grambling football offices to listen to it on the radio. If he got drafted in the first three rounds, he thought, he'd have a shot. Three rounds passed. He didn't get drafted. He went home.

"It's not meant to be," he said.

Robinson asked him to meet at the stadium. They sat in the stands.

"Why bother?" Harris asked.

"I know you can play quarterback," Robinson said. "And if guys like you don't go, it's gonna be that much harder for people to make it."

Robinson wasn't done, not that Harris was in the mood to hear it. "The decision is yours. But I know you can play. And if you decide to go, don't come back and say the reason you didn't make it is because you are Black. You know before you leave, it's not gonna be fair. You got to be better."

Robinson let those words simmer.

"You got to be better."

The Buffalo Bills drafted Harris in the eighth round, pick number 192. Days before he was set to leave for Buffalo, Harris was in a dark headspace. He didn't want to go. Harris tells me how all of this led him to Bernstein Park in Monroe, an unlikely site for one of the most important moments in quarterback history.

He was alone, carrying a football. He needed to throw. He saw a large tree, about 20 yards away.

Coaches always talked about the deep out as an NFL quarterback litmus test. Harris could throw it with ease. He decided to blindfold himself and throw at the tree. If he hit it, he figured, he was ready, and he would go. He took a handkerchief, damp with sweat, and wrapped it over his eyes. He dropped back and threw as hard as he could, waiting to hear the thud of the ball hitting the tree as he followed through. . . .

Nothing.

He lifted his rag. The ball was bouncing past the tree. He walked to get it.

Was that it? Was he going to go home? If he had left, he would have spared himself the indignity of the Bills housing him at the YMCA rather than a team hotel, where the white quarterbacks stayed. He wouldn't have had to work in the equipment room between practices, handing out socks, and he wouldn't have gotten "fan" mail of drawings of himself hanging from a tree. He also would have never become the first Black quarterback to start a season opener. He would have never, in 1974 against the San Francisco 49ers, earned a perfect passer efficiency rating in the NFL's one-year-old system of trying to quantify quarterbacks, when he completed 12 of 15 passes for 276 yards and three touchdowns and a 158.3 rating. He wouldn't have become the first Black quarterback to start and win a playoff game, or to play in the Pro Bowl and to be named Pro Bowl MVP, or work in the NFL as an executive and operate the Historically Black College and University Legacy Bowl, or stand at Eddie G. Robinson Memorial Stadium in 2023 as the field was named in honor of him. He would have never inspired not only an LA-area high school quarterback named Warren Moon, but also Doug Williams, who would follow Harris to Grambling five years later and then become the first Black quarterback to win a Super Bowl and win MVP of that game, and in the coming years and decades, he would never have spawned an entire admiration society of Black quarterbacks, a kind of club, from Michael Vick to Lamar Jackson, who appreciate and understand one another. Patrick Mahomes, the NFL's greatest quarterback today—the only debate is by how many magnitudes and if he's the greatest *ever*—can recite Shack's accolades as if they are his own. "He's someone who kind of made that step, that transition, for guys like me to come in now and play." One of the wonderful things about this space is that quarterbacks beget quarterbacks. Nobody else is to be trusted.

Harris gave it one more shot. Two out of three. Put on the blindfold, dropped back, opened toward the tree, and threw.

This time, he heard a thud.

He lifted the rag off his eyes and saw the ball bouncing back toward him.

I'm ready, he thought.

———

When Caleb Williams was in fifth grade, he missed a practice before a tournament. He was a running back. As punishment, the coach refused to call his number in the game. Caleb cried after the loss— cried like he "had not since he'd been spanked," his father, Carl, remembers. He wanted to switch to quarterback. Even as a boy, Caleb saw the job as a fix, a kind of instrument. "I want to spread the ball to everybody," he told his dad. "Give everybody a chance."

"So you want to play quarterback?" Carl said a little later. "That'll be fun, right?"

"No, you don't understand. I want to be the greatest quarterback that ever played."

Carl didn't see this as a chance to raise a generational passer. Not at first. He wanted to leverage his son's ambition as a tool to force better habits. Go to bed earlier, Carl told him. No more fast food, Carl told him. But Caleb was obsessed. Soon he was throwing one hundred passes a day. Carl saw it as a duty to nurture this interest, to channel it. That journey began at a gym on the end of a suburban Washington, DC, strip mall, not far from the Williamses' home in Maryland. Caleb had an entire infrastructure: Russell Thomas and Mark McCain, two of his youth football coaches, and Carl.

They give me a tour on an early fall day in 2023, during Caleb's junior season at USC. Thomas leads me to an area with resistance bands clipped to the floor. An area designed for quarterbacks. I would have loved it.

"This is important for my QBs," Thomas says. Caleb would hook the resistance bands—"*patented* resistance bands," Thomas says—to his wrist and bicep, trying to strengthen not just the forearm but the area from the elbow to the fingertip. "That is the last part of the whip," he says. He wanted his quarterbacks to have thick forearms and strong wrists and fingers, rather than only working on biceps and shoulders, like most did. Caleb was Thomas's test case with these bands.

At the time of our meeting, Caleb is playing well and USC is winning. The Trojans have just beaten Colorado. In the first half Williams made a throw that went viral on social media, the type of throw that supposedly only great NFL quarterbacks pull off, the type of throw that makes people believe. He stood in the pocket, bouncing on his toes, waiting for an open receiver, and he eventually felt pressure and fled left. Fading and without set feet—"off platform," in quarterback parlance—Williams threw sidearm and long to a receiver alone for a 71-yard touchdown, one of six touchdown passes Williams threw that afternoon. Conversation at the table with Carl, McCain, and Russell turns to that throw. I offer that, while impressive in terms of pure arm skill, it wasn't an NFL throw. For one thing, Williams had an astounding 7.42 seconds in the pocket. That doesn't happen in the pros. After the game, NFL Next Gen Stats calculated that Patrick Mahomes had at least 7.42 seconds to throw on only 17 of his 3,136 career attempts—about one half of one percent of them. For another, Williams also didn't fit the ball into a tight window. His receiver didn't have any defenders within 11 yards of him; space closes before it can open at the next level.

I expect pushback—especially from Carl. If Caleb is CEO of his multimillion-dollar enterprise, Carl is board chair. He protects, and *projects*, his son, unafraid to speak of Caleb in similar language to how Earl Woods once spoke of Tiger, as a cultural tentpole—as a voice, presence, entity, force. His sincerity makes his ambitions endearing.

But Carl and the others agree with me about the Colorado throw. What's more, they think Caleb screwed up on it. It was third down-and-three. Rather than make a safe throw and move the sticks, Caleb looked deep. Thomas reads the table a text he sent Caleb after the game: "Fuck, you need only three yards—why go seventy?"

Caleb's 2023 goals are to win a national championship, lead the nation in passing, and snag another Heisman. Carl's goals are different. He has spent years thinking about the NFL Draft, and he wants his son to rewrite rules, exploit loopholes, maximize leverage, and most of all, assert a measure of control over his career that other cherished American professions—even in other professional sports—take for granted: He wants Caleb to have a measure of say in his future employer. Football is totalitarian. Players are drafted. The worst teams hold the top picks. Rookies have no real leverage.

Unlike basketball or hockey, they can't play professionally overseas. College football is the league's primary development league and competitor, although NFL Commissioner Roger Goodell has told confidants that it's not a real threat. Nothing can touch the NFL, and so there's little reason to change, unless profits are at stake. Its system affects all players, but hits the game's most vital and complicated job hardest. The franchises that pick first usually do so for a reason: sorry infrastructure, sorry coaches, sorry talent. Carl knows the math: Since 2000, sixty-nine quarterbacks have been drafted in the first round. At least thirty-seven failed. Blame the player or the team, it doesn't matter to Carl. He can't allow his son to be next.

Why it's so hard to predict how a college quarterback will play in the NFL is not a new question, but I still always ask it, if only for the theories. The evaluations are often personal to the evaluators, a reflection of taste. Bill Parcells used to have a minimum experience requirement of twenty college starts. Rick Gosselin, a veteran NFL writer who was so obsessed with the draft that NFL teams called him for advice and gossip, had a soft rule that a quarterback with a minimum of 1,300 college attempts often had a better chance of success, fully aware that it would have disqualified Hall of Famers like Kurt Warner and Tom Brady. Bill Walsh, a man who developed two Hall of Famer passers, invented the West Coast Offense, and won three Super Bowls, produced a 1,000-word scouting guide on quarterbacks, noting everything from the "inventory" of passes a signal caller must be able to complete to a "spontaneous genius" to make the right decision at the most crucial time. In the 2000 draft, Walsh used that guide to pass over Brady in favor of Giovanni Carmazzi, who never played a snap in the NFL. Eight-time champion Bill Belichick whittled his evaluations down to two factors: decision-making and accuracy. He won the lottery by drafting Brady in the sixth round in 2000, but in 2020, after six Super Bowls, opened the door for him to leave the New England Patriots, convinced that he was done. It was one of the worst personnel judgments in NFL history. Brady went to Tampa Bay and won another Super Bowl. Belichick never found a true replacement—he drafted six quarterbacks in twenty-nine years as a head coach; all but Brady struggled—and was fired in 2024. The career of the Super Bowl era's greatest coach was bookended with sports' greatest mystery.

Carl Williams is surveying lawyers for ways around what he sees as a system rigged against young men like his son, a product of an owner-friendly, ten-year collective bargaining agreement that the NFL Players Association signed in 2020. He doesn't care if Caleb is picked first overall in the NFL Draft. Tell the truth, he would prefer Caleb to go undrafted. That way, he could pick his team, rather than risk a bad team ruining him. At the time of our meeting, the Bears are tied for the league's worst record, which, if it holds, would land them the first overall pick. An iconic franchise had whiffed for decades at the most iconic job. Carl is worried. Worried and scared, with history on his side.

"Chicago," he says, "is the place quarterbacks go to die."

———

Colin Hurley was recruited by Louisiana State, Ohio State, Alabama, Florida, Georgia, and Miami. In February 2022, LSU coaches wanted to close the deal. They brought him to Tiger Stadium. It was cold and empty and near midnight. Spaces are sacred for quarterbacks, whether it's in the backyard with a tree and tire or the Horseshoe or the Big House or Lambeau or Anchorage Football Stadium, a modest field in midtown, cased by short bleachers, where all the local schools played during my years, where I walked after my high school graduation, unable to let go of my choices. Hurley had visited Baton Rouge a handful of times, but he had never been inside the nearly century-old stadium, seventh-largest in the world, with a capacity of 102,231 people. He walked through tunnels, dank and concrete, toward the field. The sky opened. Purple and yellow lights flashed. The grass was cut low and tight. It was soft, not frozen. Hurley could almost hear rumbles and echoes. It was not just a venue; it was a blank canvas, holding promise and peril, a cathedral to be celebrated in and to conquer. On the big screen was a picture of a smiling quarterback under big hair. Colin's picture. There was a name. His name. A team. Their team.

"Dad, turn around," Colin said. "Just turn around."

Charlie was not behind him. He was back at the tunnel. This was Colin's walk, not theirs. Charlie pointed his iPhone camera at his son, then started to weep. At midfield, Colin was officially offered a scholarship to be a quarterback at Louisiana State University. He was fourteen.

Playing at LSU was such a grand idea that Colin wanted it sooner. Preparing for his junior year at Trinity, Colin asked for a moment with Charlie. "Dad," he said, "I want to reclassify." That was American sports jargon for graduating high school early. There's a trend in the quarterback world of holding kids back a year so that they're more physically developed than the other players, giving them more of a leg up than any kind of illegal growth hormone can provide. Colin wanted the opposite. He wanted to try to pile two years of schooling into one year, entering college in January 2024, at age sixteen, accelerating an already accelerated path.

"Why?" Charlie asked. He saw mostly downside. Even if Colin

was ready to be a college quarterback at sixteen, was he ready to be a college student?

"I want to be with people who take football more seriously."

"That's not enough."

But it needed to be, because of the reality of quarterbacking now. The days of winning and improving and improvising and grinding and the chance of it all is long gone. Once you choose the machine, the machine owns you. In New Orleans, Arch Manning felt the same urges. The most frustrating moments of his high school career were when he saw the disparity between himself and his teammates not in talent, but in ambition. Most of Newman's kids knew that their careers would end on the final game of senior year. They partied the night before games, when Arch went to bed early. Arch didn't hold it against them; it was just a matter of circumstance. He was at the beginning of something; others were at the end.

Stories of burned-out prodigies are well-known, and well-worn, but Colin kept arguing his case. As if to play the role, he was going to have to keep stepping out on his own. Charlie was worried, but he wanted to allow his son some rope—to let him make decisions and own them. Colin promised Charlie that he would take classes six days a week. He called LSU and asked if they'd accept him as a '24 rather than a '25.

The Tigers said yes. Charlie relented.

Colin committed.

———

The notion of reclassifying wasn't a thing when Warren Moon was in high school. Neither was the idea of an accelerated path. He was forging his own road, with little guidance, yet a recurring theme of his career, of having to unnecessarily wait, had started to emerge.

A year at West Los Angeles Junior College got Moon to the University of Washington in 1975, and he arrived in Seattle as something of a savior. It was an era in which USC's John McKay owned college football west of the Mississippi. For a quarterback like Moon to want to play in a place like Seattle, outside in the rain, felt like a lightning strike to locals. Seattle always had a little bit of a kid-brother complex in the Pac-8, if not the country, in the decades before Microsoft altered the world. The SuperSonics had yet to win a championship. The Seahawks and Mariners were in the process of being born. Moon was the first to normalize the notion of an *elite* Black quarterback. He was expected to be great, and before he delivered in the NFL, he delivered for the Huskies. In 1975, he helped rally Washington from a 27–14 deficit in the Apple Cup against Washington State. With less than two minutes left, Moon rolled left and threw a desperation ball that bounced off one Cougars defender, skimmed past a few others laterally, and landed in the arms of Washington's Spider Gaines, who ran 40 yards for the winning touchdown. Three years later, he was the Pac-8 Player of the Year and led the Huskies to the Rose Bowl against Michigan. He completed 12 passes for 188 yards, throwing for one touchdown and running for two. Washington won, and he was named player of the game.

Moon was one of the best quarterbacks in the country, but he rarely enjoyed it. Fans called the athletic department, demanding that one of his white backups replace him. The first time he was called the N-word was at Washington. He still wonders what might have been, how much better he might have played, if not for that burden. "You just felt like you had to be perfect all the time," he says.

"If you were gonna get that opportunity, you couldn't make many mistakes. That's not a fun way to play the game." Moon was high-strung and irritable before games. His family needed to find ways to help him relax. His mother taught him how to bake. He would make cookies, using his hands in a way that required focus. "I ended up being a pretty good baker!" he says. Fridays before games, he visited with a woman who became his godmother, Thelma Payne. She would rub his forehead and ask him to breathe deeply, trying to lift away the crushing headaches. "Even when we won games," Moon says, "it was more of a relief to me than it was a celebration."

After Moon's senior year, he got a letter from a lawyer named Leigh Steinberg. Steinberg was trying to become an agent for football players. No—he wanted to be an agent for *quarterbacks*. In 1975, one of the students in his dorm at Cal Berkeley, Steve Bartkowski, the Golden Bears' quarterback, needed help. Bartkowski was due to be the first player picked in the NFL Draft, by Atlanta. He needed something more than a smart contract. He needed a friend, a counsel, a bully, an ally who would serve as a lead blocker in an exciting and dangerous new world. What Steinberg lacked in legal experience he made up for in blind confidence. When both of them touched down in Atlanta after the Falcons had drafted Bartkowski, Steinberg got his first glimpse at a mania he later found a way to exploit: hero worship on a scale with which he is still amazed, decades later, after many superstar clients. Fans waited at the airport. Local news switched to a live shot of Bartkowski—"and his agent, Leigh Steinberg." In the years that followed, Steinberg became more than the agent who authored some of the largest contracts in sports history. He created a checklist for clients, something he both expected from them and needed from them, to fulfill not only their athletic potential but also the idea of quarterback.

Before he would sign a passer, Steinberg insisted that he set up a scholarship fund at his old high school. The quarterback needed to go on a tour of his new city, meeting business and community leaders and government officials. Steinberg wanted fans to look at quarterbacks—*his* quarterbacks—and see the best version of themselves. It was a different kind of American celebrity, combining aspects of entertainment and politics and sport. Steinberg helped the quarterback become a person who could make a governor take his call. By the eighties and nineties, presidents took their calls, too. Today, presidents call *them*.

Steinberg wanted Moon. He leaned into their commonalities—both Hamilton High alums and Pac-8 guys—but he sold Moon by focusing on what Moon was going to do when his career was over. What occupied Moon's mind—whether he'd get a *shot* in the NFL, much less ever become an icon—was a given to Steinberg. The agent saw a chance to reshape America. A Black quarterback could be an icon. Nobody had ever talked to Moon in those terms before. "That was the thing that really drew me to him," he says.

First was the matter at hand: the 1978 draft. Moon wasn't going to be a top pick. At the same time, the Canadian Football League was desperate for him. Only thing was, the CFL season started before the NFL Draft. Moon needed to make a call. "Do I wanna go to the NFL and maybe not get drafted or have to play another position? Or do I wanna go to Canada where they're gonna let me play quarterback and pay me a good amount of money?" Moon wondered whether Steinberg would dump him if he went to Canada, an investment with little return. Steinberg reassured him—they were in it together, playing the long game. Moon chose Canada.

For most of his life, Moon has framed his CFL years as a detour all but mandated by racial prejudice, not because he broke through, but because of his *standard*. From 1978 to 1983, he lit up the CFL as a member of the Edmonton Eskimos, winning five Grey Cups and two league MVP awards, and setting every meaningful passing record. Those moments "erased a lot" of anger toward the NFL. But he would watch games and know he was better than most starters. In 1984, it was time. And the dynamic between him and the NFL was different. He had leverage. Scouts had flown to Canada for a glimpse of that arm in person. And Steinberg pulled off a masterful piece of agenting. A quarterback who probably would have been drafted to play another position years earlier now had Tampa Bay, New Orleans, the Giants, the Raiders, the Seahawks, and the Houston Oilers not only vying for his services, but also to make him the face of their franchises. Moon was the first huge free agent in NFL history. It came down to Seattle and Houston, and he chose the Oilers after they offered him a five-year, $6 million contract, making him the NFL's highest-paid player. His first game was against the defending Super Bowl champion Raiders. In the second quarter, Moon dropped back from the Los Angeles 10 and had to flee right. He threw back across the middle, into traffic, a throw quarterbacks are told to never try, and threaded it between two Raiders for a touchdown. Moon's relief couldn't be measured in six points. He always felt he could play in the NFL, but like all who aspire, he hadn't truly known until he did it. And of course, Moon wasn't like all who aspired. He had wondered for six years, since college. He had wondered before that, at Hamilton High. He had wondered in the first quarter against Los Angeles, when he was buried under pass rushers. Then he threw . . . a touchdown pass. It wasn't in a Super Bowl, or even a playoff game, but it was one of the most important completions in NFL history.

I can do this, he thought.

You and I can only imagine the rush. Of affirmation. Of acknowledgment. Of romance. Of something within our grasp and under our power. My god, I felt it when I threw my first touchdown. It wasn't anything special, just an out route in eighth-grade ball, but it felt miraculous. When the world sees what you saw. When it believes what you believed. You're *special*.

Peyton Manning remembers it. I ask him to list his first touchdown passes at every level, as a way of asking him when he *knew*. In youth ball: He ran the Wing T. Barely threw. Can't remember the exact play. High school: the post to Cooper, after an audible. NFL: to Marvin Harrison in a blowout loss to Miami. College is the one he goes deep on. He had arrived on campus at Tennessee. It was summer. Players weren't allowed to meet with coaches, but they were allowed to watch film. He sat down with a yellow notepad—"watching film without a pen and paper is a waste of time," he says—and grinded through every offensive play from the prior season. He was told to watch cut-ups, which was tape spliced and edited; he had never heard of a "cut-up." He felt a calling of sorts. Football wasn't a language that came naturally. School had never come easily to him. He had to study. At the time, few realized that locking yourself in a film room is as essential to great quarterbacking as throwing a comeback route. Manning normalized and even glorified it. One of Tennessee offensive coordinator David Cutcliffe's favorite plays was called 62 Meyer. It included a route called Oscar, which was an option route, where the receiver could cut a few different ways depending on the defense's alignment. Alone in that room, Manning taught himself the play—*The X runs an in route, the slot runs a little pivot, the W runs a post*—committing it to memory, not just to be good or live up to his last name and the surrounding ecosystem, but because he wanted Tennessee to never regret giving him a scholarship. "I didn't want to let them down," he says.

Third game of the season, Manning jogs onto the field in garbage time during a blowout loss to Florida. He throws a touchdown, but then notices a muted response. There's a flag. It's against the offense. No, it's against Manning—for throwing past the line of scrimmage. "You can't do that to a freshman," Peyton tells the ref, a comic and unsuccessful appeal.

A week later, Manning is in a meaningful game against Mississippi State. End of the first quarter, second down, right hashmark, he calls 65 HBO. The first read is the left receiver, far hash, running a 12-yard out route across the entire field. That's a long throw, even for the best quarterbacks. Manning is under center. The play calls for him to throw when he plants his right foot. Manning drops back and decides to gamble on the out route. The cornerback has his receiver well covered. "I wouldn't make that throw anytime in the NFL," he says. "It's too risky." But as Manning's hero Dan Marino once said, there is no defense for the perfect pass. The pass is perfect. Receiver Kendrick Jones gathers it, keeps his feet, turns upfield, and goes the distance into a box score: *Jones 76-yards pass from Manning.*

By the end of his sophomore year, Manning was one of the best players in America. One day NFL scouts were in Knoxville working out Tennessee prospects. "Are you thinking about coming out after next year?" one of them asked Manning. It jarred him. He didn't know how to answer. "I didn't know that was even an option," he tells me now, straining credulity for a man who always thought ahead and knew situation and circumstance. It was remarkable, when I considered his words: What if Peyton Manning didn't even know what was possible for Peyton Manning? It's a minor miracle when someone notices. Even for the greats. Especially for the greats.

———

After Leigh Steinberg got Warren Moon paid, Steve Young was next. Like Moon, Young had leverage, which was both earned and miraculous. He grew up as a running back, then moved to quarterback. Kneeling in the huddle and telling people what to do—it was cool, fun, addictive, and almost a disaster. During a Greenwich High junior-varsity game, Young threw six interceptions. He remembers watching one of his passes slowly flop high in the air, and the feeling of powerlessness to influence its destination, and later promised himself to do everything possible to never be left at that kind of mercy again. Young succeeded McMahon at BYU and finished second in Heisman voting in 1983. After college, he visited Joe Namath. Young was in awe, not just because Joe Willie was right there, in front of him, an actual human and not someone—*something*—that existed only on television sets and in gossip pages, but because Namath had dared to shake things up, from the Super Bowl III guarantee to spurning the NFL for the American Football League in 1965. Young faced a choice: play in the NFL or the upstart United States Football League. Namath advised him to look beyond the NFL.

The notoriety of quarterbacks had continued to increase—and for the first time since the AFL in the sixties, there was a real market, with open bidders and a fledgling league eager to land box-office draws. Steinberg was on a roll of rolls. He landed Young a contract that rocked sports: ten years, $42 million from Los Angeles Express of the USFL, a sum greater than what Magic Johnson and Wayne Gretzky earned at the time. "Two things happened," Steinberg says. "Warren Moon comes back to the NFL, and he's the first free agent at the quarterback position in his prime, and all you have to do is sign him. And then Steve Young gets the $42 million contract, and that creates headlines around the world. Dan Rather starts the evening news off with the story on Steve Young and his contract. I even have a paper from Japan, all you can read is $42,000,000. But the combination of those two sort of blew up the market. A new day was coming."

It didn't feel that way to Young. He sat terrified in a side room with Steinberg, as 100 or so journalists waited for his introductory press conference. Let's say this about quarterbacks: These men were all once boys, and those boys were connected and driven by a deep, hardwired desire to please. Coaches, fathers, teammates, girlfriends, all blurring into one. I knew that feeling, or knew how to aspire to that feeling. I knew what it felt like to have Wednesdays and every other weekend with my dad, rather than every day. I felt to the depths of my soul that if I could be the kind of quarterback that created gravity—like Young was doing—that sat at the center of a spinning solar system, it could bring just about anything. Maybe my disintegrating family could have been whole again. An arm can hold a lot together. Maybe it can heal.

When the big contract arrives, as opposed to relieving stress, or bringing the exhale of generational wealth, it is somehow a heat-seeking missile to the quarterback's most fragile and protected places, taking them back in time, back to the beginning, making them desperate to be a boy again or, as Young felt, *to get the hell out of there.*

"How am I going to be a forty-two-million-dollar quarterback?" Young says now. "I wanted to do it for free."

After thirty or so minutes, Steinberg had to almost physically pull Young up to meet the press. Young wanted to explain that the contract was a mirage, that it was actually an annuity, intended to pay out over decades. That detail was lost on fans. In one of his first games, Young threw an interception, and the crowd started to chant that he wasn't worth the contract. Young's mother, Sherry, yelled, "It's an annuity!"

Young spent two years in the USFL and then went to the Tampa Bay Buccaneers, a clown-car franchise where he looked lost. Before the 1987 season, Joe Montana was coming off back surgery. Bill Walsh, the legendary head coach of the San Francisco 49ers, was concerned that he wouldn't fully recover. He wanted to hedge his bets and trade for Young. Best case, he'd acquire a quarterback who could lead his offense to a new stratosphere. Worst case, he'd have an insurance policy. Before he did, he polled his coaching staff. Who would trade for him? It was unanimous: None of the coaches voted for the trade. Convinced otherwise, Walsh acted alone. He traded a second- and fourth-round draft pick for Young, selling him on playing time, with Montana out.

"He's had two back surgeries, Steve," Walsh said. "He will not recover from it."

First practice of 1987, Young watched Montana, thinking he was witnessing an exit and stepping into a vacancy. But Montana didn't seem injured. Looked pretty good, actually. Young turned to Walsh. "Joe looks like everything is fine." Walsh shrugged and smiled, as if to say who knew, when he knew all along.

If Young looked at Montana with wonder, then he looked at Bill Walsh with amusement and annoyance. By the mid-eighties, Walsh's West Coast Offense had won two Super Bowls, but had yet to fully revolutionize football, had yet to turn average quarterbacks into good ones and good ones into exceptional ones, had yet to be so proficient as to, for the first time, introduce the idea of a quarterback-centric offense where the individual quarterback is somewhat disposable. It was a major tentpole in the unending quest for coaches to amass control at the expense of the game's preeminent job. All Young knew was that many West Coast Offense tenets made little sense. Walsh would tell the quarterbacks that on a particular route, the ball had to be a foot and a half in front of the receiver. Montana got it; executed it. Young would nitpick, over-intellectualizing rather than doing as he was told. He'd throw it a foot-and-a-quarter in front of the receiver and Walsh would shake his head. "Is that not good enough?" Young said. Montana was wary of Walsh's seemingly steadfast desire to replace him, but he wanted to be coached hard. He wanted to be challenged. Young seemed most comfortable challenging Walsh. He'd watch how Walsh videotaped every team meeting. *Who does he think he is? Lincoln?* But what he later realized was that Walsh was creating an offensive system—"a tool kit," Young says—that would outlast him, based on timing and progressions, designed to be durable and transferrable—and to revolutionize the job and idea of quarterback.

Young recognized that his job was strange: to replace one of the greatest ever in an offense *designed* to be quarterback agnostic. He was contributing to the death of what he loved most. But he wanted it, wanted the stage, and he had one edge, in his mind: He was faster than Montana. *Can I drop back faster than Joe? Can I go through my reads faster? I know I can escape faster.* I remember the same feelings, in my own little world. Being fast is a blessing and a curse. You become addicted to escaping, when quarterbacking is supposed to be a patient, in-the-pocket game. The sooner you realize it the better. And if you don't realize it, you won't last long. Sometimes it requires lying to yourself, or tricking yourself into believing that the rush isn't getting through when it is. Or just ignoring it. If you suspect the pocket is collapsing, you speed up your eyes and move your feet too fast—and play into the defense's hands. Montana knew when to react quickly and when to let it unfold. "You don't understand," Walsh told Young. "You're hurting yourself. You're competing in the wrong places."

Montana knew the fragility of his craft in a way his backup did not. Young was a prodigy, even if inside he felt deep insecurity. Montana knew he could do the thing, but every coach of his career had wanted to replace him, dating back to high school. Montana never knew why. It bothered him for life. He could be ruthless, vindictive, petty, but there was also a tenderness to him, a vulnerability. In one game, Montana turned the ball over. On the sideline, he found Ronnie Lott, San Francisco's Hall of Fame safety.

"Hey, man," he said. "I'm so sorry you had to go back on the field."

"What?" Lott said.

"I'm sorry that you had to go back on the field, man. I should have protected the ball better."

That moment stayed with Lott for years, of how caring and sensitive of a teammate Montana was, how he was willing not only to sacrifice body and ego, but assume a level of responsibility that stretched beyond the huddle and the offense. "The hardest part in life is, you're in pain and you're not feeling good, and yet, you're going to show everybody, 'I'm going to fight through this,'" Lott says. "There's not a lot of guys that can live in a category of 'I'm willing to go to the dark side.' And the reason why they're willing to go to the dark side is that there is something in my soul that tells me, 'I got to go there because nobody else can do it.'"

All the greats go there. Late in Tom Brady's career, he watched younger quarterbacks like Patrick Mahomes battle during games then pose for pictures with one another afterward. Brady was offended, an affront to how he had conditioned himself. "It's not the killer instinct," he says. "It's just not." Michael Jordan, Kobe Bryant, Tiger Woods—they weren't smiling a lot during and after competitions. Brady didn't have true friends on other teams, not even Peyton Manning, even though they'd hang out in the off-season, talking shop and convincing uninformed witnesses that deep down they were pulling for each other. "He couldn't be my friend," Brady says. When he was a boy, Brady would throw fits on the golf course, sometimes forcing his dad to end a round. That fire stayed with him as he aged; after a bad series he would throw cups and scream. Anger, rage, darkness—all of them were good. So good that he found ways to manufacture them, twisting an opponent's public comments into something that would piss him off. "I had to create something," he once said, later adding: "I was doing a job. I wasn't the father, I wasn't the dad out there, I wasn't the husband out there. I was the *quarterback* out there on the field. . . . Nothing was going to get in the way of that. . . . I had to draw on a part of me that was emotional, aggressive, angry, decisive, irrational. All those things."

All of Montana's things were subtle, based on cunning patience. Watch his game-winning drive against the Bengals in Super Bowl XXIII now, Walsh's final game as the 49ers' head coach, and it's remarkable for its mundanity. It doesn't look like a brilliant drive, and not just because Montana famously spotted John Candy look-ing on and pointed it out to his teammates, a thrill to him that eased everyone else. He always tried to remain the same, first or fourth quarter, with his voice and eyes, because teammates would notice if he seemed hyper or tense. "The minute you change," he once said, "they change." He conditioned himself to *not* change so masterfully that none of his teammates could tell that in the middle of the drive against the Bengals, he was the opposite of calm and collected: He was hyperventilating. He kept trying to call time-out; Walsh kept waving him off, unaware that his quarterback was struggling to breathe. Montana had built a mask so complete that what followed was one of the highest evolutions of his craft, even if it appeared ordinary. He took what the defense gave him, a bevy of soft flares, before a strike to Jerry Rice for 27 yards over the middle put San Francisco in position to win. He knew the secret to two-minute drives: Move the chains, then hit one big play. Just one. That's all you need.

Montana sounded kind of dumb when he'd say it, just as Tom Brady would decades later when he'd say it. Quarterbacking *is* that simple, no matter how much we want to complicate it. And of course it isn't, because we know.

Young knows—although before he figured it out, he provided some of the greatest moments in NFL history. For the first half of his career, his most famous moment was a 49-yard run that beat the Vikings in 1988. He dropped back straight and looked left. He pump-faked, then saw danger. Montana would have held firm, eyes downfield. Young ducked, then spun right, escaping trouble, then cut left. A block from fullback Tom Rathman sent three Vikings flailing. Young slipped away from a fourth Viking, then dodged a fifth. He neared the left sideline, then used it to his advantage. Defenses usually expect quarterbacks to run out of bounds, so they slow down. Young bent back inside. He was losing steam. What legs he had left, he emptied right there, accelerating between the 30-yard line and the 10. He stumbled before falling over the goal line for a touchdown. It wasn't magical. It wasn't laborious, either. It was human, extraordinary, and as Young says, "desperate."

In 1992, a coach named Mike Shanahan was hired as the 49ers' offensive coordinator. He had been a rising star in the NFL, but was also in something of a morass, having been fired twice, by the Raiders as head coach and by Denver as offensive coordinator. Shanahan asked to meet all of the 49ers' quarterbacks individually. He visited Montana first. Montana was battling various injuries and hadn't played football since he'd been knocked out of the 1990 NFC Championship Game, a loss to the New York Giants that cost the 49ers a chance at three consecutive championships. Walsh was long gone; he was burned out and retired in 1989, after winning his third Super Bowl. His replacement, George Seifert, seemed intent on replacing Montana with Young, who had learned and studied and felt ready, after almost five years primarily as a backup. Shanahan spent two days with Montana, then two with Young. At the end, Shanahan was mystified. Young and Montana ran the same offense in completely opposite ways. Young ran it by the book, as Walsh had designed it: by progressing through options in order, receivers one through five. Montana was different. He narrowed his choices to two on every play, skipping through chaos and sequence. Shanahan called Montana back into his office.

"Joe, you gotta tell me why none of these guys think like you."

"Yeah," Montana said, "I was hoping you wouldn't catch on to that."

Montana made Shanahan promise: What was said next had to stay in the room. Trust around the building was low. Shanahan gave his word.

Others, including Young, thought Montana made magic, had supernatural powers. But Montana saw himself engaged in craft. He simplified options by process of elimination. There may have been something special in the speed with which he read through options, but for him the practice itself was elementary. He had seen enough defenses to know which receivers would be covered before the snap, so he would rejigger his progressions. Rather than starting with one, two, and three, he would go straight to three, then back to one, then to four. Receivers were open early, or not at all. When you study quarterbacks, when you want to be one, you wonder how they see themselves and each other. Young studied Montana and aspired to a transcendence in Joe's approach that he felt he lacked, a dazzle and magic that overwhelmed the senses. Joe was meanwhile thinking in more practical terms, even as he looked remarkable and racked up remarkable results. He saw himself as a pragmatist. The more ownership he took over his check-downs— the more pressure he put on himself to make the key decisions in real time—the freer he played. "If you missed perfect," he once said, "you wound up with great." Often it's easy to imagine which essential quality all quarterbacks share. Call it aspiration—to be great, to win at the highest levels, to again and again outperform the guy aiming for your job. But you find, too, that the shape that drive takes isn't necessarily shared, or similarly understood or tamed or expressed, even by two Hall of Famers in the same locker room.

The problem for Montana was that he had fully mastered his

craft as his body was near its end. He injured his elbow over the summer in 1991 and missed most of the next two seasons. Young took over for good. Shanahan kept his word to Montana—until the legend was traded to the Kansas City Chiefs in 1993. In one of his first meetings with Young, Shanahan told him that the offense was going to be redesigned to reflect Montana's ingenuity, tailored to Young's strengths.

"We're never going to go the one, two, three, four, five again," Shanahan said.

Jack Elway's expectations for his son started to turn into the expectations of a nation. In 1978, a twenty-three-year-old young man from Chicago named Tom Lemming launched a publication called *Prep Football Report*, which would profile the best high school football players. Nothing of its sort existed. Lemming had never seen anyone like John, with an arm so powerful combined with an otherworldly ability to escape. Journalists covered him almost daily. Elway even covered himself: He kept a diary for the *Los Angeles Daily News* about his recruiting experience. He was so good that there were no naysayers, just opposing schools, who taunted him and dimmed the stadium lights on Friday nights to make it harder for his receivers to see.

Jack saw creeping danger in the life he had helped engineer. He didn't want his son to become an asshole, even if being a situational asshole is one of the requirements of quarterback. John was getting put on a pedestal. Somewhere inside, Jack, and John for that matter, knew that he belonged there. But John tried to use his own hype not to lower expectations, but to prove people *right*. "It was more motivation than fear," he says.

The Elways' home phone became a symbol of what John had become, and all the dangers waiting for him outside those walls. Constantly ringing with college coaches—sixty schools offered him a scholarship—and girls. For football matters, a coach got to John through Jack. For everything else, it was Jan. When girls called, Jan would answer and hang up for him. "You're not talking to girls at home," she told her son. But these forces were beyond her control. During Elway's senior year, when he was the consensus top player in the country, he got sixty-six Christmas cards from sixty-six University of Missouri cheerleaders. One had an especially suggestive note: "We don't sleep with teddy bears. We only sleep with Missouri Tigers." Jan failed to see the humor. Elway wasn't going to Mizzou.

Elway felt most comfortable around his friends, goofing around. They'd throw water balloons out of John's Datsun B210, until it died and John inherited a beige '61 LeSabre, which was so ugly that his twin sister, Jana, refused to be seen in it. After Granada won the city league championship, John celebrated too hard, pounding drinks for the first time in his life. World spinning, he knew if he entered in the front door his mom would discover him in this sloppy state, so he tried to hop the fence and sneak in through the back. He broke the fence. The next day—"sicker than a dog," he says—Jan forced him to fix it.

But the power of something unprecedented rolling out before everyone's eyes made John's life different. Family life revolved around his games. He was always pushing harder, even harder than Jack did, just to see how much he could do, throwing with his guys, dominating offseason passing leagues before that was even a thing, talking ball with Jack over pizza, just the two of them, motivated not by a nagging question of whether he could do it but how far he could take it. Before he left for Stanford, John played in a local all-star football game. The game was broadcast on TV, with USC coach John Robinson doing color. Elway did his thing, throwing heaters all over, and 363 yards and four touchdowns later, Robinson said on air that Elway was the greatest high school quarterback he'd ever seen. Some scouts thought baseball was Elway's premier sport, with his best future. He once struck out Darryl Strawberry. One day, the Kansas City Royals asked Elway to field grounders and take batting practice in Anaheim before a game. Future Hall of Fame third baseman George Brett looked on and said, "I hope this fucker plays football." In 1979, the Royals drafted both Elway and a kid out of Pittsburgh named Danny Marino, who at age thirteen would stand outside his family's home, waiting for the buses to pass—"Every twenty minutes," he later said—and, with a football in hand, "pick a spot and nail that sucker every time."

Sitting with me, Elway shares that he learned to be *on* all the time. No course or road map existed. "You just get used to it," he says. He—like all greats—had no choice. Neither Jack nor Jan tolerated whining, especially with the opportunities before their son. John's screwups would be bigger than someone else's screwups. I want to know why. Not why for him. Why for quarterbacks. Elway entered high school in 1976, a year brightened with the bicentennial celebration and anxiety over America's changing place in the world, and four years later, he emerged as one of the patient zeroes in that changing country. A kid playing a kid's games with adult rules and scrutiny. Only later would he really understand how much the ground had shifted beneath his feet during those critical years. He couldn't see a brave new world, couldn't articulate its borders and barriers, but he could *feel* it.

Elway picked a jersey number when he arrived at Stanford. Eleven, which he wore in high school, was unavailable. He had to choose: 7 or 12. The latter was common. Too common. Nobody wore 7—except one of the guys who had inspired Elway, among others, a man who at a different moment in history had helped quarterbacks, who had changed the calculus of what was possible, who had pushed beyond the kind of parochial boundaries of sport into a seductive and celebrity realm, and thus an American one.

Bob Waterfield wore number 7.

II

QUARTER-BACK TO QUARTERBACK

A Northwest Montana ranch is a strange place for a self-constructed monument to almost everything that's happened to the country since the early 1940s. But that's where it is, in one of the last pieces of mythic America: Stevensville, Montana, the state's first settlement, a town an hour outside Missoula. I wind through the Bitterroot Valley, with views of the Sapphire Mountains, and near the top of the development line, there's a two-level brown home, cased with racks of antlers and stacked logs. A weathered floor mat greets you:

THE WATERFIELDS

Buck and Etta invite me in. They're in their sixties now, California transplants. They met through his parents: Bob

Waterfield and Jane Russell—the country's best quarterback and most famous pinup actress in the 1940s, a unit, an archetype, nicknamed RussField, a power couple before the idea existed.

Buck leads me through the living room to a hallway downstairs. Walls are lined with posters of Jane's movies and Bob's games, a testament to what they were and what they meant. *Gentlemen Prefer Blondes*, with Russell and Marilyn Monroe; the *Cleveland Plain Dealer* from December 17, 1945, Waterfield's rookie year, when he won league MVP and an NFL championship. Russell's most famous photograph, from *The Outlaw*, lying in hay with her blouse draped off her shoulder, sultry and dangerous; the family surrounding Waterfield's bust at his Hall of Fame induction.

Their life was something out of a lost America. Dad and Mom would pile Buck and his two older siblings into the car and drive into Hollywood, which was quickly emerging as America's eye candy, and get the best table at every restaurant—especially at Charley Brown's Steakhouse, their favorite. The earliest iterations of paparazzi would wait outside. Bob and Jane didn't ask to be treated differently; the world did it out of obligation and recognition. Fame was changing. Gossip columns were not new—they date back to the nineteenth century—but were gaining popularity. Back then, photographers asked permission to take a shot. Most of the time Waterfield said yes. Sometimes he said no. The photographers were polite. Bob had a temper. Everyone knew it. After dinner they'd drive home, curving up and over Benedict Canyon, with its roller coaster quality, to 14888 Round Valley Drive in Sherman Oaks, perched high up, just off Mulholland, west of Beverly Glen, about a mile and a half from the town deli. The design of Jane and Bob's house was of that era, intended to feel weightless, floating above and looking over. "A house in the clouds," in Bob's words. Once home, Buck says, the night started. Friends rolled in, from football and film. Clark Gable. Gene Autry. Judy Garland. Bob Hope. Mickey Rooney. Robert Mitchum. Bing Crosby. John Wayne. People who changed America with black-and-white images and stories. A young Rams public relations staffer named Pete Rozelle once attended a Waterfield party. He played pool with Jane, and later called it the highlight of his early professional years. Buck became accustomed to the smells of booze and smoke, of falling asleep to the sound of adults laughing. He knew why his mom was famous. She was on billboards and in magazines and theaters. His dad was different. Bob was quiet, rarely talking about himself or what he did for a living. Buck had to hear about his dad's exploits—his legend—from others, but a hint was as basic as his name. At Rams practice, Waterfield could throw a football into a bucket across the field. That earned him a nickname: Buckets. His youngest son was named after him.

Buck, for short.

———

One day, Waterfield was walking the hallways of Van Nuys High, decades before it became Hollywood's default shooting location for school scenes. He was a senior, class of 1938, monitoring the halls. He stopped a group of girls.

"Where's your pass?"

"Here," Jane Russell said, showing it to him.

She knew his face, that face: dark wavy hair, a low brow over gray-green eyes, a face without doubt. He was slim and maybe six feet. She was a freshman. She had seen him before, at a house party a few weeks earlier. He had been leaning in a doorway at the party, unbothered and cool, and over the course of the night, what Jane saw was the profile of many star quarterbacks in the coming eighty years: He disappeared frequently into a bedroom, each time with a different girl.

"Oh," Bob, said, looking at Jane's pass. "How about a date?"

"That depends."

"On what?"

"On where, when, and why."

"Oh," he said with a smirk.

Two years later, she was at the beach, and there he was. He was a student at UCLA, on a gymnastics scholarship. After hours he'd sneak over to watch the Bruins football team practice, imagining himself out there. He eventually tried out for football in 1941 and made the team. His gifts were evident. He could run, kick, punt, cover—and, by god, throw. By '42, he was a star. Robert not only noticed Jane at the beach, he remembered her. Something about his presence flummoxed her, a feeling that never faded. She felt "hypnotized by a green-eyed snake." She wrote in her diary that she'd met "B.W." and that night, Jane saw him again. They sat together in his car. He put his arm over her shoulder, then moved in for a kiss, provoking a sensation in her that "stayed with me for more than twenty years."

It wasn't that way for him. He liked her, sure, eventually loved her, if he admitted it, which he often would not. He was obsessed with winning and losing, even in casual conversation. If he saw her hurt, if he made her cry, some savage and ruthless instinct kicked in, and he would see how deep he could cut. Waterfield was born in Elmira, New York, on June 21, 1920, but the family moved to the San Fernando Valley when he was an infant. His dad, Stanton, owned and operated a storage company, until heart problems took him in 1930. Bob was nine years old, and he learned how to survive by certain codes: Never discuss loss. Show zero emotion. And win. Jane noticed that he was spoiled. He lived at home with his mother, Frances. Jane's father had died too—when she was in high school. She later wondered if that was why they were drawn to each other, two broken kids who sought careers where success depended on limitless love and approval from strangers. Knowing who they were about to become, it's remarkable to picture them as two young people looking for something as basic as to love and be loved, and to be able to commiserate with someone who understood. But of course, that's what they were doing. Robert—she was the only one who called him by his full name—had leverage over her by virtue of his job. If things didn't work out between them, even for only a night, he had options. She knew it. So did he.

———

On December 12, 1942, Waterfield's UCLA Bruins played USC, a crosstown rivalry with a Rose Bowl at stake. Week leading up, the game dominated headlines, alongside and even eclipsing the war. News broke in a gossip column that a relationship between Jane Russell and actor John Payne was over. "Looks like John Payne is plumb out of luck romantically," while Russell was set to "resume with her one-time sweetiepie, Bob Waterfield!"

Pearl Harbor had closed out 1941. The country was in a "survival war," in Franklin Roosevelt's words, in both the Atlantic and Pacific. Most Americans were being asked to contribute to the country with their lives or jobs or time. University of Kentucky professor

Tracy Campbell noted in his 2020 book, *The Year of Peril: America in 1942*, that the word *democracy* was used more often in printed material in 1942 than any other year in our history, even after 9/11. The country was desperate for good news—and for people to fall in love with. The transformation of Los Angeles, from a destination for people in need of a fresh start into a place of glamour, was in its infancy. UCLA was having its best season, led by its first-team all-conference quarterback. Waterfield threw for 1,033 yards and 12 touchdowns, and he platooned on defense, too, playing in 557 out of 600 minutes during the ten-game season. Week of the USC game, the *Los Angeles Evening Herald and Express* splashed Waterfield's photo on its front page, wearing number 7, and wrote that USC was "sleepless" over Waterfield's passing. In the *Examiner* was a feature titled "Snapped From Every Angle": Waterfield surrounded by five cameramen as he posed, ready to fire. Russell was attending two drama schools, modeling, and working as a receptionist. Howard Hughes and his assistants sifted through a stack of photos of models, looking for a heroine for his next film, a western called *The Outlaw*. "Give this Jane Russell a test," he said. She passed. Hughes paid a photographer $2,500 to spend an afternoon photographing Jane rolling around on a stack of hay, holding a pistol, blouse straps at her arms, revealing just enough. *LIFE* magazine published the photo in advance of the film. Jane Russell was famous, and even though the film itself was mired in a censorship battle, she was one of America's first sex symbols, a movie star before she had even appeared on-screen.

Waterfield and Russell were engaged for most of 1942, under the strain of youth and fame and ambition. Robert had side girls. Jane decided that if he was going have flings, she would too, and so she found Payne, a noir film actor. One day Russell realized that she was late. Neither she nor Waterfield wanted a child. They weren't married and were just beginning their careers. Robert drove Jane to a nondescript clinic in the Valley. She entered, "cold turkey—no anesthetic—into hell," she later said. And it didn't take. The second one left her unable to conceive.

Waterfield rarely visited her as she recovered; when he did, he said little and left quickly. She dumped him, telling him that they both knew he was happiest alone. She gave him his ring back. He chucked it.

But they ended up back together, two people who were experiencing a certain kind of life at warp speed with no time to think or consider. The day of the UCLA–USC game, Jane was walking through the Los Angeles Coliseum parking lot. She saw Bobby Robertson. He was USC's quarterback and one of her boyfriends—she had a type. Robertson waved to her.

"Hi," Jane replied. "Good luck, but I hope *we* win."

Her allegiances were clear. Waterfield ran for one touchdown and passed for another in a victory, sending the Bruins to their first Rose Bowl. The next day, the front page of the *Herald and Express* blared "BRUINS WIN 14–7," above the latest news from World War II. Football and war had already been linked. Now *quarterback*—which had originated as two words, then was hyphenated, then made whole, made iconic—was synonymous with fame and sex appeal. It was now a job to covet. It was now a thing that was not just about what happened between the lines. And it now came with pressure.

———

Oxford English Dictionary, 1879.

quarter back (*n*): A player station between the forwards and
halfbacks, by whom the team's play is coordinated and
directed.

———

One afternoon in the archives wing of the Pro Football Hall of Fame
in Canton, Ohio, I wander through the library. I've come looking
for the first language to describe quarterbacks. More than that, I've
come looking for a single game. I stop at a shelf filled with what at
first glance appear to be rows of nondescript books: thin and small
and uniform, burgundy covers with gold type, and ordered chron-
ologically, like miniature encyclopedias. *Spalding's Official Foot
Ball Guide*, beginning in 1871. I pick the book from 1906, knowing
that it's different. The banner on the cover says THE NEW RULES.
I rifle through it, the paper worn and smelling like old stock. On
page ninety-five, I find a new rule—and as it turns out, an American
revolution.

> One forward pass shall be allowed to each scrimmage,
> provided such pass be made by a player who was behind
> the line of scrimmage when the ball was put into play, and
> provided the ball, after being passed forward, does not touch
> the ground before being touched by a player on either side.

Like most innovations, the forward pass had numerous false
starts and new iterations, and inspired many people to try and
grab credit. College football legalized it in December 1905 after

eighteen players died, a last resort after University of Chicago Divinity School dean Shailer Mathews called football "boy-killing, man-mutilating" violence. The National Intercollegiate Football Conference tasked a seven-member rules committee with making the game safer. Of the six rule changes implemented was the legalization of the forward pass. The rule change didn't launch the idea of the forward pass so much as unleash it.

Spalding's Official Foot Ball Guide was written by Walter Camp, one of football's fathers. He looked like most American innovators of the era, photographed in black-and-white, mustached and staring at the camera with a visionary glare. In the football world, Camp is as influential as any coach, even though he was never a paid coach, and as powerful as any executive, even though he never worked full-time in football, and as authoritative as any gridiron writer, even though he was not a journalist. He was born in 1859, and entered Yale in 1876. He played halfback. After Camp graduated, he successfully pushed through a rule that allowed for a snap from the line of scrimmage.

The player who received the ball, Camp proposed, would be a new position, nearest the center: a *quarter back*.

It was a fundamentally different position from the others, set apart from the start, requiring new assets and skills and gifts. Camp saw the quarter back, which quickly became hyphenated to *quarter-back*, as an extension of a coach's ethos and mind, more than a typical player. Michael Oriard, a professor and former college football player, noted in his 1993 book *Reading Football* that Camp's ideal quarterback "was no bloodless intellectual" but instead "a man whose charismatic personality was more powerful than mere physical strength." And so from the outset, with a brutal game born in the Gilded Age entering the Progressive Era, an expansion of American land and technology and values and perceived purity, to say nothing of the addictive identity associated with winning and the practitioners of it, *quarter-back* was the promise of something romantic and mysterious, idealistic and graceful, courageous and daring.

On a spring day, I drive through New Haven to what's left of some Greek Doric columns, a few miles east of Yale's campus. It reads THE WALTER CAMP FIELD, in faded letters. Across the street is Yale's track-and-field stadium. Football was played there in the late nineteenth and early twentieth centuries, when it was called Yale Field. The goalposts are still up.

On October 3, 1906, Wesleyan played Yale here. Wesleyan quarterback Sam Moore took the ball and faded back. The precise location, down, and distance are lost to history. Two receivers ran long. They were decoys. Moore stared deep, then threw to halfback Irwin van Tassel underneath for 18 yards. He was tackled immediately. At first, the crowd was silent. One writer in attendance called it a "breathless stillness." It was the thrill of something unorthodox and unexpected. And then there was a roar, as if everyone were celebrating the same thing at the same time. "Such an ovation as scarcely ever before greeted a visiting team at Yale," the journalist wrote.

Anyone could throw a football. Only a quarterback could make people cheer.

Before John Elway, there was Bob Waterfield. But before Bob Waterfield, there was Bo McMillin. On October 23, 1920, Centre College of Danville, Kentucky, played Harvard at Soldiers Field in Cambridge. Both teams were undefeated. Harvard was at the top of the college football world, a year after winning its first Rose Bowl. Centre, meanwhile, was a school of 100 located in the middle of the Southern sticks. But Centre had something intangible. Alvin Nugent "Bo" McMillin was a three-time All-American, and his face was in newspaper photos and honorific cartoons, touting his heroism, not just because he left school for a year to serve in the navy during World War I, but because he did this strange, relatively new job of leading a football team by throwing the ball. Like most quarterbacks who seem flawless to the public, McMillin had a hidden devious side. He had a proclivity for dressing like a bum, entering pool halls the night before games, and hunting for drunks and duping them into giving him favorable odds for Centre's next game.

Against Harvard that October, McMillin passed for 131 yards and ran for 151 in a 31–14 loss. His passing was so dominant that Harvard offered him the game ball. McMillin declined it, saying that Centre would "be back next year to take it home with us."

In the 1921 rematch, McMillin knew that Harvard would key on him, so he and the coaches developed two game plans. One was full of passing plays. That was what they worked on much of the week leading up to the game, which was such an event that the *Boston Herald* sent a reporter to Danville to detail Centre's preparation. Centre allowed the reporter access, knowing that Harvard coaches would read his reports of passing plays in the paper. When Centre held a walk-through practice at Soldiers Field the day before the game, McMillin showcased an array of passes—suspecting, likely correctly, that the Crimson were spying. The other game plan was what Centre executed on game day, in front of an estimated crowd of 50,000 and with newspapers from all over the country covering it. Centre used the threat of the pass and of McMillin—used the idea of a quarterback—as a decoy, and ran the ball. After a scoreless first half, McMillin broke away for a 32-yard touchdown, the game's only points. Thousands of fans from Massachusetts Institute of Technology stormed the field and tore down the goalposts, celebrating in solidarity with Centre. McMillin was carried off the field on the shoulders of fans—and he carried off bags of money he'd won betting on himself. In 1950, the Associated Press named it the biggest sports upset of the century's first half. In 2005, the *New York Times* named it the biggest upset in college football history. In an attempt to retroactively award the Heisman Trophy to those who played before its existence in 1936, the National Football Foundation gave it to McMillin for the 1921 season.

But it was what happened when McMillin returned to Kentucky that might provide the biggest line from *quarter-back* to *quarterback*.

He held the game ball on a fire truck before a parade of thousands. He was onstage with Kentucky governor Edwin P. Morrow, who told the crowd that he'd "gladly trade places" not with Centre's other alums—which included two vice presidents of the United States, a Supreme Court justice, eight United States senators, and thirty-seven congressmen—but with McMillin. "I would rather be Bo McMillin than the governor of Kentucky," he said. Classes were canceled. A woman later saw McMillin walking past and yelled, "Tear my socks," seductive lingo of the time. When McMillin married Dorothy Mahan, it was news, not just locally but nationally. "McMILLIN MARRIES," blared the *New York Times*. Later in 1921, when Centre played a bowl game in San Diego, McMillin was given a tour of a movie studio and posed for a picture pretending to tackle film star Gloria Swanson. The basic mechanics of being a quarterback emerged into the national consciousness at the same time the myth of quarterbacks did. The hyphen was nearing its end.

———————

Oxford English Dictionary, 1927.

quarterback (*n*): one who claims special knowledge of and insight into a game or team; usually in compounds, as downtown quarterback, grandstand quarterback, etc.

———————

Benny Friedman made quarterbacking an art, giving a brutal game an alluring aesthetic. Many quarterbacks had successfully thrown a football by the time Friedman became the University of Michigan's starter in the mid-1920s. But he was probably the first to throw a consistently beautiful spiral. He had realized the key to making it spin was in the grip. It was all in the hands and wrists. As a boy, he read that baseball pitchers strengthened their fingers and forearms by squeezing and releasing tennis balls; he started to do the same. The college ball was still fat, an offspring of rugby. But it was slimming, for one reason: to make it easier to hold and throw. He positioned his hands toward the nose of the ball, rather than in the middle, and he realized the value and virtue of the laces. His fingers were strong enough to grip the ball without palming it, without squeezing it, handling it gently, like a golf club. After Friedman's first game, a win over Wisconsin, the *New York Times* wrote that Michigan had "found a new and dazzling gridiron meteor."

When Friedman became a professional, first with the Cleveland Bulldogs in 1927 and then with the Detroit Wolverines in 1928, his stature and celebrity carried the struggling National Football League. Friedman was one of the few—maybe only—players who could draw a massive crowd, even though NFL rules discouraged passing. Something needed to change. In 1929, New York Giants owner Tim Mara bought the entire Wolverines franchise to try to jumpstart his own. Friedman was the jewel. Mara signed him to a league-record $10,000 salary, hoping that Friedman's presence would elbow the Giants into the local picture, with Babe Ruth and Lou Gehrig's Yankees. A New York writer called the acquisition "a ten-strike for Mara, both from the playing and box-office points of view."

Friedman became New York's first star quarterback, and pro football's first great passer, earning first-team All-NFL honors each of his initial four seasons. He threw 20 touchdown passes in 1929, a record that stood for thirteen years. A writer for *Liberty* magazine called him the "greatest football player in the world." George Halas of the Chicago Bears would later write a column calling Friedman a "pioneer passer." He arrived when the use of *quarterback* in the American vernacular was expanding. It was now defined as a figurative noun. *TIME* used the phrase "legislative quarterback" in 1931. The *Christian Science Monitor* called President Roosevelt "quarterback of the recovery team" in 1933.

Friedman, meanwhile, realized the public's fascination with his work and wanted to let fans into his world. He hosted a radio show called *Sunday Morning Quarterback*. Wrote a book in 1930 called *The Passing Game*. Was the first quarterback to be on a box of Wheaties, one of his many endorsements. After throwing 68 career touchdowns, a record that stood for a decade, he retired in 1934— the same year that the NFL switched to a skinnier football, a ball meant for throwing. If he had played a few more years, with that new ball, his career might have resonated longer with the public. As it was, his accomplishments faded, not only from the record books, but from the conversation of the game's architects and premier quarterbacks. He was ignored by Hall of Fame voters until 2005, when he was posthumously enshrined. Author Murray Greenberg wrote in his biography of Friedman that his "bitterness spilled over into the periodic criticism of modern-era quarterbacks."

There were two exceptions, in Friedman's eyes. One was Sammy Baugh, the star out of Texas Christian University whose arm prompted Friedman to gush, "I thought I could pass—until I saw Baugh."

The other was Bob Waterfield.

Oxford English Dictionary, 1943.
quarterback (*v*), transitive: To direct or coordinate
(an operation); to lead.

Bob Waterfield and Jane Russell married in Vegas on April 23, 1943, an epic cultural collision. "ACTRESS BRIDE OF FOOTBALL STAR"; "JANE RUSSELL WEDS BOB WATERFIELD, UCLA GRID PLAYER"; "BOB WATERFIELD MARRIES BEAUTIFUL JANE RUSSELL." A few months later, there was a splashy film premiere in Hollywood. The papers ran a collage of the attending stars. Robert and Jane were at the center, he in a suit and she in a dark jacket, smiling arm in arm. The caption noted that they were a "popular twosome."

There have been other famous college quarterbacks, ones that spawned more of a regional mania, but no college quarterback ever has been in Waterfield's social circles. He was friends with Bob Hope, whom Jane adored; Frank Sinatra, who Jane thought was a gentleman; and Dean Martin, who Jane thought was an asshole. In June of 1944, after a year in the army, Waterfield got a Western Union telegram from Charles Walsh, the general manager of the NFL's Cleveland Rams. "Will pay you $4,000 to play this season plus $200 to cover traveling expenses to and from California provided you report August 12, opening date of training camp." Waterfield opted to stay in California; Russell's career was exploding. The papers called her the "most photographed woman in the world," and she earned $50,000 for a romance called *Young Widow*. But Rams owner Dan Reeves saw a flight out of orbit in Waterfield and Russell. He upped his offer. This time, Waterfield accepted. The Rams had a quarterback, but they also had something just as vital: a story. Speaking to the *Cleveland News*, Walsh acknowledged that the team had hired two stars for the price of one.

The notoriety Waterfield had received in LA prepared him for being the face of the team. Before the 1945 season, there was a cartoon of him in the paper—Big Number 7 of the Rams—and there was his face, clean and glistening, under wavy hair and wearing a perfect smile. A runner, passer, and punter, with stars and stripes and a degree, married to *her*. First game, first victory, 21–0 in exhibition over Washington, his name in every headline: "WATERFIELD PACES RAMS"; "WATERFIELD STARS AS RAMS BAG FIRST VICTORY"; "WATERFIELD BIG HERO" . . . Waterfield was creating as he went, and his throwing—he was "Mr. Forward Pass," per the *Sporting News*—shook the league, picking up from where Benny Friedman had left off.

The second game of the season, against the Chicago Bears, was hyped as a "pitchers' duel" between Sid Luckman and Waterfield. In 1927, as an eleven-year-old boy in Brooklyn, Luckman had received his first football, a gift from his dad, who had told him that being a quarterback "could set a boy apart." One day, Sid found the nerve to approach his hero: Friedman, who, of course, showed him how to grip the ball. Luckman practiced, first at Alexander Hamilton High upstate in Elmsford, then to Columbia, then to the Bears, who drafted him with the second overall pick in 1939.

Along with coaches George Halas, Clark Shaughnessy, and Ralph Jones, Luckman was a pioneer in the T Formation motion, with three running backs lined up behind the quarterback and a man shifting laterally and behind the line of scrimmage. Like most of football's evolutions, it originated somewhere other than the professional leagues, its earliest iterations from Walter Camp in late 1882. Author Murray Olderman argued in his book *The Pro Quarterback* that the modern T Formation came out of the National Recovery Administration in 1933, one of several inventions intended to create excitement and lift the country out of the Depression. Don Faurot, Missouri's head coach, turned the T into the Split T, origin of the option play. The Split T was first used three months before Pearl Harbor and sixteen months after Germany changed military tactics forever by rushing across France and Europe. It was designed to turn the quarterback into something of a general. When Luckman arrived in Chicago, the Bears playbook had hundreds of designs from the T Formation, with hundreds of variations in the playbook and seemingly hundreds more in the imagination. Luckman loved the formation, not only because it was innovative and blessed the quarterback with the gift of decision-making, but because it protected him better than other offenses. Using it, Chicago won the NFL championship 73–0 over Washington in 1940. Three years later, Luckman threw seven touchdowns in one game and had 13.9 percent of his passes go for six for the entire season, a mark that still stands. In all, he won four championships.

Facing Luckman in 1945, Waterfield threw two touchdown passes and kicked a field goal, embarrassing Luckman at Wrigley Field: 17–0. It was the beginning of something. For the season, Waterfield completed 52 percent of his passes for 1,609 yards, with 14 touchdown passes and another five on bootlegs, a play he had invented in college, where he faked a run and tucked the ball at his hip. He threw for more yards and touchdowns than Sammy Baugh, with fewer completions and attempts. He led the league in punting and kicking and even played a game at defensive end. He was named Rookie of the Year and All-Pro.

But it was them, this couple—Waterfield and Russell, living at the St. Regis in Cleveland—that swept through the nation's consciousness. Headlines read: "MRS. ROBERT WATERFIELD (JANE RUSSELL OF MOVIES) IS TOPS IN HOUSEWIFE ROLE" . . . "AT HOME WITH THE WATERFIELDS" . . . where writers, in unironic prose, noted him teaching her how to grip a football and hold a placekick, where she cooked on a three-burner stove, helped him shave, and lit his pipe, where he planted "a dreamy kiss on a domesticated Jane, who nevertheless keeps a steady hand in pouring out the coffee." The stories quoted her more than him. Jane called Robert Old Stone Face. Years later, when Jane was cast in a stoic role in *The Paleface*, intentionally ironic to combat her voluptuous persona, she didn't look for inspiration beyond the other side of the bed. "I just made up my mind that I was going to be a female Bob Waterfield, because all the lines were flat and dry."

But when weekends rolled around, Waterfield expressed himself like few could. "Courage in the Clutch: That's Rams' Waterfield," the *Cleveland News* wrote. The Rams reached the 1945 championship, where they faced Washington—Waterfield versus Baugh—at Cleveland Municipal Stadium. Before the game started, Waterfield signed a new three-year contract worth $20,000 annually, making him football's highest-paid player. It was two degrees when players warmed up. Waterfield had plenty of two of the essential qualities for a great quarterback in a big game: skill and luck. Late in the first half, with Washington up 7–2, he faked a handoff and faded deep into the pocket, drifting as much as dropping back. When he hit his back foot, he threw long and over the middle to receiver Jim Benton for a 37-yard touchdown. Waterfield's extra point was deflected, flopping low toward the uprights. It hit the crossbar—and bounced over. Waterfield would throw another touchdown pass in the second half, but that kick ended up as the difference in a 15–14 win.

After the game, Waterfield drove all night to meet Jane in Los Angeles for Christmas. Once there, he received a telegraph announcing that he had won league MVP. Photographers snapped a shot of Robert and Jane jointly holding the letter and looking at each other.

Imagine, for a moment, how incredible it must have felt, to be him, her, to be them, beautiful and young and envied, what it must have been like to be the Rams, and the city of Cleveland, on top of the world. Nothing could be better . . . and yet, it wasn't enough. Rams owner Dan Reeves saw the rise of something—and wanted to monetize it. The team had lost money since he purchased it in

1941. By 1945, with the All-America Football Conference planning to put a team in Cleveland, Reeves had his sights on relocating to Los Angeles or Dallas. Other NFL team owners were wary of expanding west due to travel costs. Reeves convinced his skeptical and budget-strapped fellow owners to allow the move the classic way: by throwing a rich man's fit. He left an owners' meeting in a hissy, stomped to the bathroom, and threatened to sell the Rams if they blocked his move. In January 1946, less than a month after the Rams' championship victory, they relocated to Los Angeles, becoming the first major professional sports team located west of the Mississippi and breaking the seal for baseball's Brooklyn Dodgers and New York Giants to follow twelve years later. Clevelanders, angry at losing their team—though little did they know, it would not be the last time—blamed not only Reeves and the NFL, but *her*. "If Dan Reeves wanted Robert Waterfield," one columnist wrote, "and he did, he'd have to please his wife, Jane Russell, and bring the team to Los Angeles."

Jane read those words and thought, *As if!*

No single decision did more for *quarterback*, and professional football, from billboards to dark film rooms, than the Rams' move to Los Angeles. Waterfield was a handsome idol returning home with a championship to a movie star wife, in the golden age of Hollywood. In Cleveland, a void needed to be filled. An Ohio coach named Paul Brown moved into the market with his All-America Football Conference franchise, first named the Panthers, then when confronted with a patent issue, changed to the favorite in fan polls, which happened to be his own name: the Browns. He liked challenging norms, a rare independent thinker in a profession full of glorified gym teachers. He was the first to use film to scout opponents, first to hire a full coaching staff, first to try to apply military psychological testing to football players, first to introduce the face mask, which ended up offering the head as a target and as a weapon. Brown was the first coach to try to control every facet of the game—first to believe that the game *could be* controlled. His writings of what he wanted from the game's most important position were prescient: "an artist throwing the ball; a particular kind of guy; a quick thinker; a finesse man." He found him in Otto Graham, a star out of Northwestern. In 1946, Graham produced a 112.1 passer rating, a record that stood until Joe Montana broke it in 1989, and he won the first of four straight AAFC championships. The team was absorbed by the NFL, and Brown and Graham—or Graham and Brown, depending on where you lean—reached ten straight title games and won seven championships, the league's first dynasty, a legacy eclipsed only by the legacy of all dynasties: of fighting over legacy.

Like Walter Camp did at the turn of the century, Brown both elevated the quarterback position and chipped away at it, trying to keep it in its place. Graham once said that he'd "rather risk losing games by, say, 35–28 and have the fans on their feet with excitement" than win 3–0. Brown was the opposite. He emasculated Graham, first by stripping play-calling from him, then by questioning his toughness. During one game, Graham felt the pass rush and fled the pocket; Brown had ordered him to stay in it, no matter what. Brown benched him, which wasn't enough: He told an assistant coach, knowing that Graham was within an earshot, "Now at least we have a quarterback playing who has the guts to stay in the pocket."

"If I had a gun," Graham later said, "I'd shoot him."

Instead, Graham walked away in 1955, after another championship. A fight for credit ensued. The two central questions that would dominate all NFL dynasties, from the Steelers to the 49ers to the New England Patriots, were unleashed at the same moment: Coach or quarterback? System or player? What makes for genuine creativity and success? Is the relationship between two people with the same goal collaborative or combative? Does a coach possess the power to make a quarterback? Way, way, way, *way* down the ballot, could many of those who failed, including me, have done a little more with the right playbook? To be truly great, a team needs both, but only one is essential, which coaches tend to learn the hard way. Brown replaced Graham with a man named Milt Plum. He produced a stellar passer rating of 110.4. The Browns reached the playoffs in 1957 and 1958. They never won another title.

Brown blamed the quarterback. Of course.

An image was coming into focus out west, of glamour and wonder and beauty. Here was RussField exiting a black limo at the Ambassador Hotel, in a gown and tux, photographers clamoring for a shot. Once, at an awards show, Jane decided to do something rare, and sang "Buttons and Bows." She flubbed a line but pulled it off. Waterfield was so proud that when Jane returned to her seat, he squeezed through the aisle, banging knees, making a spectacle of it, and kissed her, for the audience and papers, to applause and flashes, two people who occasionally played for the cameras, but who, for a moment, owned what was becoming America's most important city. In post-internment Los Angeles, with longstanding segregation and Bloody Christmas around the corner, Waterfield tried to transcend racial and ethnic lines. The Rams signed running back Kenny Washington in 1946, Jackie Robinson's backfield teammate at UCLA, the first Black player to be a member of an NFL team since it had segregated during the Great Depression, owners not wanting Black men to *take* jobs over white men. Once on the road in Chicago, Waterfield noticed that Washington wasn't at the team hotel. He tracked him down at a Count Basie performance at a Black hotel. Waterfield asked Washington to stay with the rest of the Rams. Washington was, in Waterfield's words, "the best football player I ever saw"—and briefly was the Rams' backup quarterback. In 1946, he became the first modern Black quarterback to complete a pass in an NFL game.

Back home, Waterfield's fame kept rising. He liked most of Jane's Hollywood friends, and in the later years especially enjoyed Joe DiMaggio and Marilyn Monroe. Bob and Joe liked to talk sports, often analyzing statistics deep into the night. "Birds of a feather," Jane said to Marilyn. "The most egotistical people in the world." But there was also an undeniable appeal. Bob, in her words, "was sexy, dynamic, opinionated, extremely bright, witty, and as stubborn as they come. You either find that kind of man irresistible and exciting or you don't understand him and can't tolerate him for a moment."

Jane wrote about a dark side of Robert's personality in her 1985 autobiography, *My Path and My Detours*, describing herself as a battered woman. The struggle to cope with pain and pressure too often meant anger, drinking, and violence between them. As Jane told it, she and Robert were in Vegas at a comedy show. As the drinks went down, mutual irritation rose. At one point at the table, Jane ran a fork down the side of Robert's face, leaving red lines, humiliating him. When they returned to their hotel room, Jane approached and apologized, but something in Robert snapped: He slapped her face. She slapped back. Her face swelled up—like a "purple cantaloupe," she later said. Photographers noticed it the next day, behind her huge sunglasses. Her management team cooked up a story about her getting hit by a car door in a windstorm.

"I'm so sorry I could die," Robert said later, according to Jane. "I'll never hit you again as long as I live."

They both swore off drinking—Jane lasted three years; it's unclear how long he did—but eventually started up again. It was too much a part of their public lives and too critical a painkiller in private.

Waterfield was named All-Pro again in the Rams' first year in LA, leading the league with 17 touchdown passes. He played a fictionalized version of himself in the 1948 football movie *Triple Threat*. Two years after the move to LA, on October 4, 1948, the Rams fell behind the eventual champion Philadelphia Eagles 28–0 in the third quarter. Waterfield was reduced to that familiar challenge of any quarterback: The opponent knows you must throw, and you've got to figure out how to do it. Waterfield passed: 27 yards to Jack Zilly on a corner route for a touchdown, then a short bullet on a tight end crosser at the goal line for a three-yard score, then a handoff for six, then Zilly again on a fly for 20 yards. The game ended in a 28–28 tie. The *Los Angeles Examiner* wrote that Waterfield "led the Rams with the surety of Churchill, and the quiet dignity of Ed Murrow."

By 1950, a man who knew how to navigate many American

spectacles found himself in a new one: a quarterback controversy, the country's latest version of the broadsheet debate over who should play centerfield for the Yankees. A year earlier, the Rams had brought in a star out of Oregon named Norm Van Brocklin—teammates called him the Dutchman—to compete for snaps. Essential to any quarterback controversy is that the players have competing styles, and the first one was no different. Waterfield was a triple threat, a thrower and runner and kicker, whose passes arrived with a soft touch. Van Brocklin was a straight-up pocket passer, strong-armed and lethal. The press dissected them with a fervor normally reserved for presidential candidates. In Buckets and the Dutchman, the Rams had a dream scenario: the aging veteran and the precocious understudy. During the four years when the Rams roughly split quarterback snaps, their statistics were staggeringly equal, and the Rams won division or conference titles each year. In 1951, Waterfield led the league in passing and was named Player of the Year. That same year Van Brocklin threw for 554 yards against New York, an NFL record that nobody—not Marino or Moon or Manning or Brady or Mahomes—has broken. The Rams averaged 38.8 points a game in 1950, another record that still stands.

In December of 1951, Waterfield, Van Brocklin, and Otto Graham—three future Hall of Famers—met in the NFL Championship Game, the Rams against the Browns. Twelve years after an NFL game was first shown on television in a period of fear of war and triumph in war, the championship game itself was broadcast across the country for the first time. The first images viewers saw were the introductions of the coaches and quarterbacks for each side, generals and lieutenants, twin pillars of the franchises. Almost 60,000 people showed up at the Coliseum. Tied at 17 in the fourth quarter, Van Brocklin hit receiver Tom Fears for a game-deciding 73-yard touchdown. After the win, Rams players celebrated in a huge huddle at midfield. Waterfield stood outside the group, distancing himself and feeling distanced. He was almost thirty-one years old. A doctor diagnosed him with a duodenal ulcer, and told Russell that what made Robert a great quarterback—that he took victories and failures so personally—might seriously erode his health if he didn't walk away. He added that Waterfield's need for friction and tension, the desire for a winner and a loser in all facets of life—essential elements of a quarterback—was making him miserable. Waterfield stayed on for one more year, starred in his first major film role, *Jungle Manhunt,* and on December 1, 1952, he retired. A newspaper ran a cartoon of him, touting his accomplishments and statistics and his changing of the calculus of what was possible, being tackled from behind by a familiar old man: "Pop Time."

Soon after Bob Waterfield retired, in the summer of 1953, Henry Luce looked at a proposal for what was called Project X, a top-secret document accessed by only seven people at Time Inc. Luce's title was editor-in-chief for all the empire's magazines. Inside the file was a plan for an "experimental sports magazine," a full-color weekly that would cover sports for fans both casual and intense. Nothing of its sort existed, and not by accident. Few Time Inc. executives believed there was a market. Something about sports seemed like a bad bet.

Author Michael MacCambridge noted in his 1997 book *The Franchise: A History of* Sports Illustrated *Magazine* that most analysts believed the rise of television would destroy spectator sports, rather than enhance them and expand their audience. Bert Bell, the NFL's commissioner, once said that if the league ever started "valuing the TV audience more than the paying public, we'll be in trouble." But they had little choice but to embrace it. From 1948 to 1952, the percentage of American homes with televisions rose from a quarter of one percent to thirty-four percent.

Luce greenlit the project. In August of 1954, *Sports Illustrated* debuted. In its fifteenth issue, dated November 22, the editors decided to put an NFL player on the cover for the first time. The San Francisco 49ers were hot, led by the Million Dollar Backfield, four future Hall of Famers. Only one of them was on the cover. It was an isolated shot of his face, behind a big clear plastic face mask, staring into the camera as if you were in his huddle. His name wasn't on the cover. You knew.

Y. A. Tittle was the quarterback.

———

One afternoon in 2013, Tittle showed me that *SI* cover. It was in a side room on the ground floor of his house in Atherton, California, proudly displayed on a wall filled to the brim with trophies and portraits. A wall that makes you stop and stare and feel what it's telling you, even if the items lost their shine long ago. He was in his late eighties. He couldn't walk without help, but he didn't look much different than during his playing days six decades earlier, a man who seemed old even when he was young: bald head, blue eyes that glowed from deep sockets, ears he had still not grown into. He wore a navy blazer, khakis, a light blue shirt, and a Hall of Fame ring on his left hand. It was shaped like a stadium, with gold trim, blue casing, and a 1.75-carat diamond football inside. He later let me try it on. It forced you to imagine an alternate reality. It also made you feel like you were test-driving a car that you had no business looking at.

"I'm sorry. What's your name again? Seth Wickersham?! That's worse than Yelberton Abraham Tittle!"

His daughter, Dianne de Laet, sat nearby. Something about her dad's presence had always changed the air. She noticed it from a young age, in the Bay Area and New York in the late fifties and early sixties, her early imprints of the world and its values: Her little brothers, otherwise irascible, would wait until she left the room to ask Dad about work. Other parents got strange around him, asking for autographs, or for a picture, or for a handshake. She grew up with people knowing her before she knew herself. Whenever the family went to a restaurant, people surrounded them before they were seated. And her dad loved it. The rest of the family got used to standing around as Dad chatted, constrained by neither time nor circumstance. That was the thing with her dad: He was on a first-name basis with the world.

All this for an insurance salesman. That's what Dianne thought her daddy did for work, those early years of her life. Y. A. Tittle & Associates. The office was right down the road from their Menlo Park home. The firm offered insurance and later developed real estate in Silicon Valley, getting in early on land that eventually became as expensive as any America had to offer. Y.A.'s father, a rural East Texas postman who developed land on the side and owned grocery stores and pressing shops during the Depression, had taught him to stay busy.

But there were hints why people really wanted to talk to her dad. One time he was between meetings, on a field in a military base, in a jacket and tie. Dianne was with him. Some kids had a football and one yelled, "Can you throw it back to me?"

"Sure, start running," he said, taking off his jacket.

With a ball in his hand, her dad transformed, the look and shape of someone who was suddenly centered and knew what to do. He waited a few beats, long enough for his target to exceed an ordinary man's range, then he whipped back. The ball shot out unlike anything Dianne had ever seen, long and exquisite and capable of reshaping a person in the eyes of those around him. He slipped between mortal and immortal and then mortal again. Tittle didn't linger to watch. He had picked up his jacket and briefcase. He knew where the ball would land. The greats always do.

Dianne was six when she opened a book about Greek mythology and saw a picture of Perseus holding the Gorgon's head. An image that would have horrified most kids, she found captivating. A man, knee bent, in perfect harmony with himself, relaxed as he was holding a severed head. She remembers thinking it was about losing things, about things ending, and says she knew even then there was a kind of beauty in that, a kind of dignity. She cheered her father in the cold fog of the San Francisco hills when he was a 49er, and later in Yankee Stadium when he was a Giant, her voice carrying down to the field, as fans around her screamed. Sometimes people would boo him, even when he was down and barely moving. In 1964, a photographer captured an image of her dad on his knees, his helmet ripped off, blood snaking down his bald head. It would become one of the most famous photos in sports history. "The Blood Picture," Tittle called it. Her dad had powers and he was strong, but he was not invincible. He couldn't make fairy tales real.

———

Y. A. Tittle is famous for losing. He won a lot of games, a lot of big games, a lot of miraculous games, but not *the* game.

One afternoon at Y.A.'s house, Dianne held a scrapbook, wondering if something in it would unearth one of her father's memories, buried by time and disease.

"I wanted to show you, Dad. Do you remember this letter?"

"Go on," he says.

She hands him a piece of paper. June 26, in the 1950s—it's hard to tell the year—on his insurance stationery, her misspellings in cute child handwriting.

Dear Daddy,

Every one knows that you are a great foot ball player. And even when you don't win every champion chip game—

Dianne laughs at "champion chip."

it will always be that way around our house. I can hardly whet until you come home it will be a thrill to all of us. I love you more any thing in the world.

Love,
Dianne

"So you wrote this?" Y.A. says. "You wrote this to me when?"

"I don't know—'57, '56, '55?"

As a senior at LSU playing both offense and defense, Tittle had tripped while returning an interception against Ole Miss because his pants ripped and fell down, costing him a touchdown and the

Tigers a Sugar Bowl. But he seemed carved out of the type of rock that Dianne studied in Greece. Tittle was drafted by the Detroit Lions in 1948 but didn't want to play there, so he joined the Baltimore Colts of the All-America Football Conference. He won Rookie of the Year. Quarterbacks, and football, were changing in those years, becoming more intellectual. Defenses were learning how to play together, an eleven-man blanket, rather than as individuals, and had realized that they didn't need to stop all eleven players on offense. They needed to stop one, the *one*, the quarterback.

They did it with confusion and pain, messing with the quarterback's head and testing his heart. Tittle thought to combat it he needed to make fast decisions. He decided where to go with the ball before the snap, then figured out how to get it there. "It was always me and one receiver against the defense," he said. Quarterbacking is easy to overthink. Sometimes, the best of it is a kind of radical simplification. For Tittle, the perfect math was two-on-eleven.

Tom Brady understood this too, I think. Down by ten points in the fourth quarter against the Seattle Seahawks in Super Bowl XLIX, he faced one of the greatest defenses ever in a known throwing situation. He completed dagger after dagger, using relatively simple arithmetic. At the snap and from the shotgun formation, Brady first looked to see how many pass rushers Seattle was sending. If the Seahawks rushed five men, Brady knew that it was man-to-man defense, not zone. Once he diagnosed that, all he had to do was find the player with the biggest mismatch.

In 1953, Y. A. Tittle's first season as a starter, he threw 20 touchdown passes and was selected to the Pro Bowl. The 49ers led the league in scoring. The better Tittle reduced the game to manageable terms, the more brilliant everyone thought he was. Sometimes, he would try to answer reporters' questions earnestly, in technical shorthand, if not occasionally with a hillbilly flair. *Say the tight end was split out four yards from the tackle. The linebacker should be out there with him, but if he wasn't, if he was shaded a little inside, it was a tell that he was probably going to blitz. Or say the weak-side safety was shadowing the tailback. Instead of being relaxed or at ease, the safety might be crouched, focused, maybe unconsciously drifting down to the line of scrimmage. That was a giveaway. That would be a blitz—not from the safety, but from the weak-side linebacker, the guy who would normally cover the tailback. You know to get rid of the ball quickly.*

Other times, he described what happened as if quarterbacking was beyond explanation. "You can't answer the questions," he said. "There isn't any answer. It's a matter of *feel*."

Six of the 49ers' eight wins in 1957 were comebacks; in 152 career starts, Tittle led an astounding twenty-three game-winning drives. Once, during a sloppy practice, the rush broke free and hit him hard one too many times. Tittle was pissed and so fuck it, he threw the ball high and looping, a pass designed to send a message. Receiver R. C. Owens, a tall and lanky former basketball player, outleaped everyone for the ball, snaring it two feet above traffic. Something clicked for Tittle. Why not throw it up a few times a game and let Owens snag it? Players on the sideline called the play the Alley Oop, which later morphed into the Hail Mary when Roger Staubach called the same play on the last down of a Cowboys playoff game and said a prayer as the ball descended. A routine play with Tittle was an act of desperation for others.

In 1957, Tittle completed 63.1 percent of his passes, an accuracy that took the best quarterbacks four decades to approach. He accounted for 19 touchdowns. United Press named him Player of the Year, and he was also All-Pro. The 49ers made the playoffs, and in the second half of their first postseason game led Detroit 27–7. A win would send them to the NFL Championship Game. But something started to slip. The Lions came back, scoring twenty-one straight points. With the game on the line, the 49ers failed to score a touchdown on four downs from inside the Lions' 10-yard line. Detroit won 31–27. The 49ers lost. Tittle lost. There was a winning and a losing *quarterback*. His teams won almost 60 percent of their regular season games throughout his career, but he didn't win a title. And that's what we remember.

Not because he wasn't great. Not because he didn't have skills and creativity and fire in his belly, insatiable and irrational. Not because he wasn't valiant in the attempt. But because another quarterback, on the other side of the country, walked into Yankee Stadium in December 1958, with the nation watching on television, and made winning a championship the only thing that mattered.

Some Americans become ideas. In a long line of legendary quarterbacks, Johnny Unitas has always seemed different, a multidimensional enterprise. What he molded and shaped in the city of Baltimore, if not beyond, inherited and nurtured, remains in spirit but is mostly gone. Baltimore is still a pub city, a union city, a place where it feels like you clock in and out. But outside of a statue at the Baltimore Ravens' downtown stadium, there are few acknowledgments of one of its most iconic citizens. The venue where he played—Municipal Stadium—on Thirty-Third Street, north of the harbor, where the Colts would walk across the street in full uniform to enter, was leveled decades ago. Golden Arm, his local bar, is long closed. If you want to feel his presence most, drive with me to the opposite of what he invokes: a nondescript suburban apartment complex, surrounded by chain restaurants and box stores and markings of sprawl. At the entrance, there's an electronic keypad, where you punch in the resident's last name.

U . . .

Independent of us.

N . . .

Yet belonging to us.

I . . .

His name, *that* name, the greatest quarterback name of all time.

T . . .

A standard and a template.

A . . .

Jonunitis was the family name when they came over on the boat from Lithuania. They removed the *Jon* when they arrived at the Port of Baltimore.

S . . .

Unite-us, that elusive American prayer.

His name pops up on an LCD screen, telling you to press the call button. I stare at it for a second, mildly amused. His name, reduced to this . . . And like *that*, the screen goes blank. I didn't press call fast enough. Classic Johnny U: He gave instructions *once*.

━━━━━━━━

Upstairs, in a small apartment, Sandy Unitas greets me. Her husband has been gone for more than two decades. He never resided here—they mostly lived on a farm outside of town with their three kids—but this place is a shrine to him. A bronze bust by the kitchen. Framed magazine covers near the bedroom. A box of home movies, stuff that the family hasn't gotten around to digitizing. A booklet a friend of Johnny's wrote and self-published is on a coffee table. A portrait of Unitas hangs over the couch, of him in full uniform, standing tall, in his black high-tops, in a blue Colts long-sleeve jersey with number 19 on the back, and no last name. No need.

"He's everywhere," she says. "I miss him."

Sandy will auction most of this stuff a few months from now at the Super Bowl. What she misses most about John is his hands, big and soft and safe. Unitas as a quarterback and an idea is a dusty door to something most of us can't imagine. As a boy in Western Pennsylvania, he was forced to grow up young. His father, Francis—who Johnny said could grab a truck by the bed and lift it off the ground—died of pneumonia when he was five. His mother, Helen, worked multiple jobs to support the family. People told Johnny that he was just like his old man, but he had no idea what that meant. He remembered that his dad smelled like coal, so he wanted the same smell for himself. Every morning Helen left their house on William Street in the Mount Washington area of Pittsburgh, south of where the Ohio and Monongahela Rivers kiss, with written tasks for Johnny and his brother, Leonard. There was only one hard rule: Helen better not come home to a cold house. That meant keeping the furnace full, which usually fell to Johnny.

He became a quarterback for the same primal reason as many others: to impress girls. Unitas being Unitas, he aimed high. A substitute teacher named Mrs. O'Connor captivated him. "Boy,

I had a bad crush on her," he later said. She asked students what they wanted to be when they grew up. John's answer set his life in motion. His throwing mechanics were pure and of the era, high and behind the ear, like a statue of a quarterback. What he loved most was calling plays. It was an extension of his personality, tactical and clever and rebellious within the confines of Catholicism. Unitas was jarringly small and thin, but he gained notoriety at St. Justin's High.

In December 1950, an assistant football coach at Louisville named Frank Gitschier was in Pittsburgh recruiting players and decided to stop by Unitas's house. As he walked up the stairs to knock on the door, Gitschier saw a burlap bag at the top, with a black hole at the bottom. He recognized a world in that torn bag. Gitschier was a Pennsylvania kid himself. His dad would give him fifty cents to collect "slack"—coal that had fallen off the truck. He would fill a burlap bag and drag it home, wearing out the bottom until there was a hole. Johnny had built his forearms by shoveling coal as a kid in Pittsburgh, giving him old-man strength as a young man—the kind of forearm strength that Benny Friedman built squeezing tennis balls and Caleb Williams wrought from bands. Gitschier offered Johnny a scholarship that night.

Gitschier didn't know, of course, that with that offer he was setting in motion something that would change the country. He did know, however, that John Unitas, with a boy's arm and a man's toughness, would carry a certain perception and expectation, of self and those in the huddle.

And Unitas became the archetypical quarterback by becoming the first truly great one to come out of nowhere, in possession of a kind of genius that nobody saw. At Louisville, he played single-wing tailback and safety and returned kicks and punts and once, against

Florida State, showed off by throwing a pass under his legs, completing it for 15 yards. He battled injuries as a senior and slipped to the ninth round of the NFL Draft. The Steelers picked him and released him before the season began. He worked construction and played quarterback on weekends for a semipro team called the Bloomfield Rams. In 1956, he borrowed money to join a teammate in traveling to Baltimore to try out for the Colts. He made the team as a backup. In his first game, he threw two passes; one of them was intercepted. In his second game, his first pass was picked off and returned for a touchdown. Unitas had a mix of ruthlessness, talent, and audacity, and a combination of both delusional and earned confidence. He refused to quit. By the end of 1956, he had completed 55 percent of his passes, a record for rookies, and in the final game of the year, he threw a touchdown pass, beginning a streak that lasted a record forty-seven games. In 1957, his first full season as a starter, he won the first of his three league MVP awards. He not only became a purveyor of miracles. He was one himself.

Every piece of exceptional quarterbacking before 1958 was prelude to the NFL Championship Game that year, Baltimore Colts against the New York Giants at Yankee Stadium. Broadcast on NBC, an estimated 45 million people tuned in, at the time the NFL's largest-ever viewing audience. Live television wasn't just a technological innovation, bringing worlds into living rooms; it was an answer to a market inefficiency, something that Hollywood studios could not do. This matchup later would be called the greatest game in NFL history, which Unitas thought was funny. There were *six* combined turnovers in the first half. But an era was winding down. Our country projected cool and calm but had rebellion bubbling underneath, all in the middle of a Cold War, with a field general as president and in need of symbolic field generals elsewhere. Eighty-three percent of the country owned televisions, many watching in the comfort of suburban living rooms, the plight of white families abandoning cities from perceived threats, after Jackie Robinson had inspired many people and terrified others by demanding meritocracy.

In the fourth quarter, Colts down 17–14 and 86 yards away from the end zone, Unitas got the ball. Whatever the *Oxford English Dictionary* definition of a quarterback was at the time—by then, it included the abbreviated "QB"—he proceeded to expand it beyond words and into collective imagination. Third-and-10, with 2:20 left, Unitas threw outside to Lenny Moore for 11. He then gashed New York inside, hitting Raymond Berry over the middle for 25 yards. Unitas threw inside again to Berry with less than a minute left for 15 yards. The Giants adjusted by packing the middle of the field. Unitas told Berry to find space and turn around near the sideline, a simple buttonhook. That gained 22 yards, down to the 13-yard line. By now, the Giants were getting used to the PA announcer saying, "Unitas to Berry, Unitas to Berry, Unitas to Berry . . ." The Colts kicked a field goal to tie it with seven seconds left.

In overtime, Unitas called a huddle and said something that few men can pull off, even those who can throw a beautiful pass: "We're going to take the ball and we're going to score." Unitas always got away with it, not just because of his vaguely supernatural presence, but because he was about to toy with grown-ass men on the opposite team. A flare outside for eight yards, converting a third-and-15 to Berry. A slant inside to Berry that gave Baltimore a first-and-goal. Another short pass inside, moving the ball near the goal line. "You couldn't outthink Unitas," Sam Huff, the Giants' Hall of Fame linebacker, later said. "When you thought run, he passed. When you thought pass, he ran. When you thought conventional, he was unconventional. It made me dizzy." After Berry caught his final pass, millions at home saw their TV screens turn to snow. The stadium shook so hard that the broadcast cables had unplugged. A drunken fan ran onto the field, screaming, "God-dog number nineteen!" A master of efficiency, Unitas decided that the game needed to end so that he could get the hell off the field. Colts running back Alan Ameche scored from a yard out. But Johnny Unitas, quarterback, had won it, the first of consecutive championships.

A fulcrum was invented that night, whether or not you tuned in, a new idea of command, control, inevitability, competence, a new standard of what the right man with the laces at his fingers could do. Discussing the game decades later, with the benefit of time and perspective, Huff added up the future Hall of Famers on that field: twelve players, three coaches, including a Giants assistant named Vince Lombardi . . .

"And one master," Huff said. "Unitas was the master."

———

Everyone remembers Unitas's greatness. Tittle's is mostly lost. In 1961, he was traded to the New York Giants, becoming the city's first superstar quarterback. Tittle, not Unitas, was the NFL's best—and frankly, it wasn't close. But there was a subtle difference between the two men, beyond legend and hardware, as earnest and sincere and pure as the way both went about their work. Lenny Moore played with Tittle in a Pro Bowl, giving him a chance to compare and contrast the game's premier quarterbacks. Tittle would enter the huddle and suggest a play as much as call it. "The way he puts it," Moore said, "you're convinced it's a good idea and maybe it'll work." Unitas, as Moore put it, "tells you what the defense was going to do, what he was going to do, and what he wants you to do." Maybe myth matters, more than anyone wants to admit.

But even if Tittle had plateaued at mere future Hall of Fame status, he was still in New York during a good time to be the best of something in New York. He would go out with Frank Gifford and Sam Huff, all these legends who became as known for losing championships as their peers on the Yankees—with whom they shared a stadium, a city, and many rounds of drinks, at Toots Shor's or P.J. Clarke's—became renowned for winning them. Tittle loved raising a vodka with his teammates and saying, "*We* did it." In 1961, his first year in New York, Tittle won the Jim Thorpe Award and an MVP award voted on by the players, his peers. The Giants reached the NFL Championship Game, and were shut out by the Packers, 37–0. In 1962, Tittle was even better. On October 28 against Washington, he had the greatest game a quarterback had ever played, one destined to live forever in black-and-white photos in commemorative coffee table books.

Tittle owned one of those books. One day in 2014, he sat with Dianne and sifted through it. She hoped it would trigger memories; instead, he read with wonder. One touchdown pass in the first quarter. Two more in the second. Three in the third quarter, and another to start the fourth. He had thrown seven in about forty-five minutes, tying the NFL record.

"Did you know I threw seven touchdowns in one game?"

She nods.

"I didn't know I was that good."

So good, in fact, that he could have broken the record. Up 49–20, the Giants got into the red zone. Gifford, the Giants halfback, urged

Tittle to call a pass. But Tittle refused. The game was in hand; it seemed in poor taste. Gifford was angry for years. Tittle never regretted it—mostly. He kept rolling, throwing six touchdown passes in the two weeks that followed the Washington game, and six in the regular season finale against Dallas. That gave him 33 touchdown passes for the season, a record. The Associated Press named him MVP. He won the Howard Clothes Award as the most popular Giant, voted by fans, for which he was given a yacht that he had no idea how to operate. New York hosted the NFL Championship Game at Yankee Stadium, once again against the Packers. Green Bay won, 16–7. The Giants lost again—no, *Tittle* lost again. He had vowed that 1962 would be his final year. But he couldn't go out, not like that.

A year later, the 1963 NFL Championship Game: Giants against Bears, December 29 at Wrigley Field. Four degrees, wind chill minus 11. Jet engines blew hot air on the field. George Halas, the Bears' legendary coach, was worried most about Tittle, who had thrown 36 touchdown passes in thirteen games, breaking his own record—and setting a new mark that lasted 21 years, until Dan Marino broke it in 1984 during a sixteen-game season. Tittle was busy in the week leading up to the game, a reflection of status. He appeared as the celebrity guest on the hit TV show *What's My Line?* He had been featured on CBS, and the segment mentioned that he lived in Eastchester. Fans rang his doorbell and called his home at all hours, wishing him luck. One morning he saw a parking ticket on his car, but it was from a cop who had written, "Forget the ticket,

Y. A., just beat the Bears!" Nuns at the local Catholic school said the rosary for him every day that week.

Tittle warmed up in a Yankees ballcap and short sleeves, a superstition. He threw a touchdown pass to Frank Gifford in the first quarter. It looked like today would be different. The Bears fumbled minutes later. Tittle dropped back and faced rushers from the front and side. Someone gripped him at the waist, but Tittle, never agile, slipped free, and he saw his best receiver, Del Shofner, alone in the end zone. He made the throw that would have won the game, the type of pass that becomes lore, the capstone of a Hall of Fame career. The ball hit Shofner in the hands. He dropped it. That's how close Tittle was to an inarguable immortality. "There are moments in a lifetime," Dianne says now. "And lifetimes in a moment." Decades later, Tittle wrote a chapter about the Bears game in his autobiography. He mentioned his own shortcomings, and not Shofner's drop. He couldn't do that to a teammate. Always a quarterback.

In the second quarter, Tittle was hit twice on his left knee. He felt a twinge; he had torn a ligament. The knee started to stiffen. "I hope I can last this out," he told running back Kyle Rote on the sideline. At halftime, game tied 7–7, doctors put the decision to continue playing in Tittle's hands. He was thirty-seven years old. It felt like his last chance.

"It could be worse," he told the coaches. "Let me give it a whirl."

Dianne watched her dad take the field in the third quarter, struggling to walk, and saw a storybook ending, higher powers at work. But the second half was among the worst of Tittle's career, interception after interception. With ten seconds left, down 14–10, he dropped back and threw down the left sideline. Four Bears waited. It was picked off, his fifth. Tittle ripped off his helmet and slammed it to the ground, cracking it in half, a line splitting the NY on the side. It's now in the Hall of Fame, with a kind of epitaph: *Title Eluded Y. A. Tittle . . .*

Dianne, her brothers, and their mom and Tittle's wife, Minnette, went to a room under the stadium. Y.A.'s devastation was atmospheric. Someone gave him an ice bag, and Tittle placed it in a shelf in his locker. He answered questions from reporters, trying to explain that the injury left him with no lateral movement. A few feet away, Francis Sweeney, the team doctor, said, "It takes guts to do what Tittle did. He's a great old warrior." Tittle hated pity almost more than losing. He told himself stories to help make sense of it all, of how those who mocked him had watched the championship games at home, while he was the one playing in them. He seethed at the cosmic unfairness of how a great career could be defined by failures at the highest altitude. "He paid dearly for the luxury and privilege of trying to win it all," Dianne says. He returned for the 1964 season, hoping for one more chance at a ring. Instead an iconic photo defined him forever.

Quarterbacks tend to fall off a cliff. The game becomes too fast, obvious to everyone but themselves. Y.A. knew at the start of the 1964 season that he had stayed too long. Second week of the season, against Pittsburgh, Tittle was in the act of throwing when a 270-pound defensive lineman named John Baker launched into him, colliding between his arm and ribs, a sweet spot for pass rushers, cracking his sternum, dislodging his helmet, driving him into the ground as the ball flopped into the air and was intercepted and returned for a touchdown.

Tittle rolled onto his knees and tried to straighten his back. Blood trickled down the topography of his forehead and cheek, curling near his ear. Swollen hands rested on his thigh pads, his eyes fixed on the grass. He couldn't breathe. A photographer for the *Pittsburgh Post-Gazette* named Morris Berman collected a series of photos of the play. Berman was previously a war photographer; before this day, his most famous photo was of Mussolini and his mistress, both punctured with bullets. A photo that didn't even make the sports section—the editor wanted action shots—ended up as one of the most iconic pictures in sports history. It framed Tittle as the embodiment of a broken warrior—and romanticized NFL players as broken warriors. Tittle hated the image. Hated how it painted him as a wounded loser, down on his knees. Dianne saw something noble, not unlike what she saw when she first looked at the picture of the Gorgon, of suffering and striving. She was the only one.

Tittle returned to play during the 1964 season, but it was one of his worst, with 22 interceptions thrown—and punctuated by another photograph. This one was in the season finale. In it, Tittle is suffering a fate worse than physical pain. He's benched. His head is down, back slumped over less like an injured athlete and more like an old man. His jersey is muddied. His hands are wrapped in a towel. Only a few hours earlier, Tittle had stood with Frank Gifford on the steps of the Yankee Stadium dugout, moments before the game kicked off, as the crowd arrived under the iconic copper friezes. "Frank, this is what I loved more than anything else," Tittle said. At the end of the third quarter, the Browns led 45–7. Tittle left the huddle for good. The photo ran in the *New York Times*, captioned "Quarterback's Last Game."

Not *Tittle's* last game. *Quarterback's*.

───────

On January 22, 1965, Tittle made it official, at a press conference at Mama Leone's on West Forty-Fourth in midtown Manhattan. Giants owner Wellington Mara announced that the team would retire Tittle's number 14. Coach Allie Sherman called him the "greatest passer of our time." Legendary New York columnist Jimmy Cannon wrote that "Y. A. Tittle beat this town, and how many can claim that? . . . Some of New York will always be Tittle's. What he did so well for three years will survive in the small talk of men killing time in saloons." Cannon didn't know at the time that only the first part would be true.

On the same day, a few hours later and a few blocks away at Toots Shor's, New York officially met Joe Namath. The time and location was no accident. The idea was to make it easy on the press, both logistically and narratively. One myth died, another was born. Namath was the opposite of Tittle, beyond the fact of his hair: He was new, young, and, though he hadn't done anything yet, seemed *limitless*. He was a product as much as a quarterback, an acquisition of an entertainment executive named Sonny Werblin. Werblin owned the New York Jets of the American Football League, and he knew what the team—what the upstart new league—was missing was not great players, or even great quarterbacks, but *stars*. Werblin didn't know if this kid would be a good quarterback, but he awarded him a $400,000 contract, the largest in American sports history, an investment and advertisement. He knew a secret about America: Money makes people more interesting.

Joe Willie Namath existed to blur all distinctions between his art and life, stature and status, between athletic celebrity and the celebrity we celebrate most. But soon after he moved to New York, Namath asked a friend, "Man, how do you meet girls here?"

"Three touchdowns," the friend replied. "They'll be lined up out the door."

———

When Joe Namath arrived, only seven years after Johnny Unitas reinvented the job and the game, he made both look *ancient*.

Money. Bulky, dangerous hair. Fur coats. Transparent indulgence. Indifference to convention. An Upper East Side pad with a llama rug and mirrors above the bed. Game-day breakfast of coffee and a dip. And finally, the purity and authority—pure authority— with which he snapped the ball into the air, shoulders back and hips forward, a release modern and natural . . . all of it inspired some and scared the shit out of others. There are only so many faces in America like his, so ingrained in culture as to be immune to age, and there are only so many American faces like his, famous for more than sixty years strong, prominently placed on dozens of books and hundreds of magazine covers, of multipart documentaries, of gossip pages and red carpets, the face of a man smiling by the pool in the Florida sun days before Super Bowl III, cool and carefree and tan, stating that he *guarantees it*—well no, he actually said it at a reception from behind a podium—a face chin-up when arriving at the Academy Awards with Raquel Welch, or on Broadway with Barbra Streisand, or on set with Ann-Margret, or at a commercial shoot with Farrah Fawcett, or at an event with Margaux Hemingway. A face drunk on national television in 2003, offering to kiss an interviewer.

Namath isn't classically handsome. If he had never been gifted with the ability to throw a football in a way that altered our collective axis, his face wouldn't have meant anything, just another from a Pennsylvania town. As it was, his face redefined notions of what's possible. Joe Willie, Broadway Joe—he was the first to offer quarterback as a lifestyle. He forced the team, coaches, press, fans, country—forced *us*—to accept him. He told American boys that this universe could be theirs. There were better quarterbacks than him, more efficient and less turnover-prone. But nobody had *it* like Joe did. Nobody dared to be the envy of so many men *and* women. He not only partied like a rock star; he was sort of built like one, more so than a quarterback, rounded at the shoulders, not small but not hulking, either. With his soft and strange accent, demons that became public long after his playing days, and bad knees, he was vulnerable while being the desire of the world. He first numbed life with scotch whisky—"I like my Johnnie Walker red and my women blonde!"—then vodka. He was one of the most mortal figures in the pantheon of legendary American men, but he is undeniably one of them.

Look at his jersey, number 12, an iconic number in American sports and among quarterbacks. Luminaries have worn it—Roger Staubach, Terry Bradshaw, Jim Kelly, Tom Brady—but 12 is not *theirs*. Namath authored a vision, not only of what a football could look like cutting through air, but of what throwing it so beautifully could get you. Even if you chose to believe those who insist that his cutaneous pursuits were overstated—"Everything you hear about Namath's personal life, divide it," Jets receiver Don Maynard once said. "Everything you hear about his professional life, multiply it."—he still had lived enough life to write an autobiography at age twenty-six, and still possessed the gall to title it *I Can't Wait Until Tomorrow 'Cause I Get Better-Looking Every Day*.

The upbringings of Unitas and Namath were similar. One boy's coal was another's steel. Little money, single-parent homes, quarterback as a means of escape. Namath's parents divorced when he was young, and his mother, like Unitas's, worked several jobs to support the family. As a teenager, Namath blew money at a pool hall that he was supposed to give to his mother, and he felt so ashamed that he later wondered if that was why he wasn't in a serious relationship with a woman until his early forties.

But unlike Unitas, Namath was never under the radar. He attended Alabama, where Bear Bryant scolded him once for not knowing the playbook and suspended him for partying; where teammates called him the N-word because he was friends with Black players; where he claimed to have slept with 300 women; where he was elected team captain, which he considered his greatest athletic honor. Unitas looked like an old man even as a young man. Namath always looked young, but his body had started to fall apart before he even played professionally. Bad knees, tight hamstrings, to say nothing of tectonic hangovers, all conspired against him. Unitas was a better quarterback at every stage of his career, and he once told his wife that if he had played in New York, he could have made as much money as Namath. But women screamed for Namath; teammates noticed how he had different types of groupies, depending on the city. He hung with Elvis, and Dean Martin, and Mickey Mantle. Macy's introduced the Broadway Joe Namath doll, with twelve different clothing combinations, including "touchdown outfit," "bachelor outfit," and "maximum effort outfit."

Namath was the first quarterback famous for doing the job before he did it well, and so in 1968, the year the country broke culturally, when things started to click for him on the field, catching up to his performance off it, it felt like another cultural shift. The rebellious New York Jets of the cartoon AFL reached Super Bowl III in Miami and squared off against the flat-topped Colts. They were not Unitas's Colts, not exactly—he was a backup that season, older and nursing an injured elbow—but two ideas and ideals clashed. The Colts were 19.5-point favorites. Namath offered his guarantee.

Once it kicked off, both men hovered over the game. Colts starting quarterback Earl Morrall failed to see a wide-open receiver for what would have been an easy touchdown and instead threw an interception. Namath dominated, not because of his passing—he was efficient, hitting 17 of 28 throws, for 206 yards, with no touchdowns and no turnovers—but because he executed a game plan with the command and tact of his hero on the other sideline. He called his own plays; what was once a right for quarterbacks was becoming a scarce privilege. Colts head coach Don Shula had not only demoted Unitas but stripped his quarterbacks of play-calling duties, a loss of identity as much as an assertion of control, another episode in the power shift toward the headset and away from the helmet. With the Jets up 16–0, Unitas came off the bench. Namath said a prayer, then he called runs to drain the clock and shorten the game. Unitas's rally fell short. The Jets' 16–7 win was the most famous upset in American sports history. Probably still.

Super Bowl III felt like another rebellion against the staid

America of the early Cold War. The sixties had challenged almost every American institution, except football. Its rules had been as absolute and unbreachable as the military. Namath breached them. And then he walked off the field with his right index finger lifted to the sky, the first time in his life he had done so, an image so lasting that decades later, when a company named McFarlane started making figurines of star quarterbacks, all of them were in the act of throwing or running—except Joe Willie Namath. He had his finger raised.

Go down a YouTube rabbit hole on quarterbacks, as one does, and a funny thing happens, after the algorithm serves up Springsteen videos and something on Rubik's Cubes. You might catch some of the old-timers, superstars, Hall of Famers, carve up defenses with roundhouse throwing motions and in grainy black-and-white footage, or worse, that dull computerized color, and wonder....

Could they actually do it? Could they actually play? Could they actually throw? Or did they throw well relative to the 1940s and '50s, with and against mostly white men lumbering in the dirt . . . ?

We'll never know. Prejudice didn't allow for natural order. But in any given generation, then or now, there are only a handful of truly transcendent arms. These guys are born, not made. Back then, offensive schemes weren't sophisticated enough to mask marginal talent. There was no technique, no progressive passing offense, no basic tenets. Those jump-rope throwing motions got the job done. And then there's the games. Most look foreign, plodding, unimaginative, of an era, with one glaring exception: September 24, 1972, Jets against the Colts at Memorial Stadium in Baltimore. It was the first true time that Joe Willie and Johnny U faced off. They had played against each other before, but never for a full game.

What happens when we encounter phase shifts? For as long as the game's been around, the best quarterback has symbolically passed the torch to the next one when one legend's time is over and another's begins. Few of these transitions were as jarring as Unitas to Namath. Before then, and even since—maybe until Tom Brady gave way to Patrick Mahomes—quarterbacks had resembled one another, a stylistic and artistic evolution if not next step. As the sixties became the seventies, the country changed, and both Unitas and Namath changed into something closer to one another. Unitas grew his hair out a little, blanketing his forehead; his family later told me that he stopped going to his regular barber after it turned out that the shop was a front for a money-laundering scheme. Namath was still shaggy, but less threatening, even though he was on President Richard Nixon's enemies list. And they were both playing a fundamentally different game than everyone else.

On this day, Namath and Unitas combined for an astounding 872 passing yards and eight touchdowns, but topline stats neither explain nor do justice to what transpired. Namath, in the seventies Jets road whites—coolest uniforms ever—threw deep all game with that brief motion that still seems to defy basic physics: a 65-yard touchdown to start the game, followed by a 67-yarder, two tight, short ones—of 28 and 10 yards—and then back to airing it out, 79- and 80-yarders in the fourth quarter. Unitas, precise and patient and piecing together what he had left, threw touchdown passes of 40 and 21 yards. His final touchdown pass closed the Jets' lead to 37–34. Namath answered by calling a pass play with three options. He dropped back and saw something inviting: a clean Colts jersey, covering Jets tight end Rich Caster. That meant that the cornerback—in this case, Rex Kern—was new, entering the game fresh in a critical situation. "I knew that's where I was going to go," Namath later said. He threw deep and across the field to Caster, who was open by three steps, for the decisive touchdown and final points: 44–34, Jets. This game lacked the symbolic gravity of Super Bowl III. It didn't change America. What it did was show the timelessness of the perfect forward pass. There was no defense for it then. Or now.

Less than a month after that game, in the middle of a presidential election, *TIME* magazine put on its cover an illustration of six quarterbacks. Namath was in the middle, bigger than the rest, sending a clear message: This *thing* revolved around him. The magazine assigned a foreign correspondent and former bureau chief of Saigon and Jerusalem, Marsh Clark, to interview Namath for the fawning five-page story. The NFL was a $130 million annual business. The Quarterback was iconic. Nixon and Watergate could wait.

A year later, in 1973, Unitas was traded to the San Diego Chargers. The image of Unitas fumbling around in pastel uniforms, overwhelmed by football's pace and power, is as unappealing, if not appalling, now as it was then. But he enjoyed living in San Diego, where he was no longer Johnny U, was just another California journeyman. He had separated from his first wife, Dorothy, and fallen for a flight attendant he had met named Sandy Lemon. If his proposal to Sandy was classic Unitas, on bended knee—"Do ya or don't ya? Hurry up!"—their wedding was peak Unitas efficiency. John and Sandy moved to Nevada for six weeks because of its expedient matrimony laws, and he divorced and married within a thirty-minute span.

In San Diego, Unitas started to hate football, unable to handle teammates who took the craft less seriously, who failed not only to aspire to his standard but to understand it, a curse of the exceptional, the same affliction that in 2000 drove Troy Aikman into retirement after only twelve years and three Super Bowls with the Cowboys. But life felt lighter in Southern California. Sandy never asked him to go to Tijuana or Disneyland or into the Pacific Ocean—"John hated water," she says—but there was a little beachside hotel in Coronado that they loved. She was soon pregnant with the first of her three kids. John accompanied her to Lamaze classes, cold beer in hand. He lost three out of his four starts with the Chargers before giving way to a rookie named Dan Fouts, who took what Unitas had taught him and elevated it when Don Coryell became head coach in 1978, matching design with fluency and becoming a first-ballot Hall of Famer. Unitas retired after eighteen years, with every meaningful NFL passing record. He and Sandy went home, buying the barn outside of Baltimore, reestablishing roots and expanding on what he'd already built, allowing him to be Johnny U forever.

———

Namath wanted to be Joe Willie for a little longer, even if he sometimes hated what it had wrought. More than any other quarterback, he was and is defined by a single moment, one forty-eight-hour window of guaranteeing victory to seeing it through. And remarkably, sometimes blessedly, maybe sometimes cruelly, he lived a long life before and beyond that moment. He remained set apart.

When Lou Holtz became the Jets' coach in 1976, he asked a secretary for Namath's number. She didn't have it. In fact, nobody in the Jets front office had it. "Classified information," the secretary told him. Holtz called Jimmy Walsh, Namath's agent and lawyer. Walsh replied that he couldn't give out the number. If Holtz wanted to speak with Joe, this was the only way it would go: Walsh could take down Holtz's number and pass it on. If Namath wanted to speak with his new head coach, *he* would call.

After the 1976 season, the Jets released Namath, at age thirty-three. He signed with the Los Angeles Rams, which made all and no sense. It wasn't just that Namath had been in three feature films and four television series. It was that Namath was older—and knew it. One day at practice, he yawned. He'd rarely done that in New York, even when hungover. Right then, he knew it was time to go. He wanted a wife, kids, and a house; he wanted, after a life that regular guys aspired to, the life of a regular guy. He retired to Florida, not only because doctors told him that warm weather would be better for his knees, but because he wasn't Broadway Joe in Fort Lauderdale.

Namath was not the best quarterback in New York football history. That's an argument between Y. A. Tittle, Eli Manning, Benny Friedman, and maybe Charlie Conerly. But Namath's myth was so potent that when the *New York Times* called him to write about his retirement, he couldn't help but mythologize himself. He was, in his words, a "father of a revolution." When asked what he brought to the game, Namath cited not his watershed contract, not the Guarantee, not his pure release; he cited nothing that concerned being a mere quarterback and everything that had to do with being the first *modern* quarterback:

"I think I was a helluva entertainer."

III

LEVERAGE

Early summer 2016, John Elway and I are in his office. He's the general manager of the Broncos, the defending champs. We are talking quarterbacks, about him, sure, but also the ones he needs to lead his team *now*. He has just traded up to draft one in the first round, from Memphis, a kid named Paxton Lynch. Elway likes Lynch; Denver's head coach at the time, Gary Kubiak, really likes him. Lynch will end up an epic bust, lasting only two years and 128 attempted passes in Denver. But at the time, Elway feels pretty good, and he's riffing about his former profession, what makes certain guys special and insufferable, and why. . . .

"They don't ever admit *anything*," Elway says.

He says it with a knowing smile, vaguely donnish. Of course, *they* is him. By then, he knew himself well enough to recognize the familiar survival mechanisms. What he was really saying is that they—he—have to know and internalize, if not prepare an answer to, all of their weaknesses, yet also cannot concede an inch. Not to flaws, faults, realities, not to anything that fails to fit inside a fragile but glorified ecosystem. You cannot have any doubt when you step on the field, even if deep down, it exists. You must be able to hold those contradictory forces in your head and heart. That's why Elway says great quarterbacks always bounce back from poor games. Because they refuse to acknowledge that the performances were poor in the first place, regardless of what they knew deep down to be true.

Imagine everything that it takes to admit nothing. Imagine coursing through life that way, from home to huddle, the allure and callousness of it all. And imagine that behavior permitted and encouraged, even celebrated.

———

Search YouTube, not for Elway's dynamic throws, but for the story of Elway discovering that this thing he felt on the field could also translate to control over his life. Click on a press conference from a Bay Area hotel on April 26, 1983. It was the day of the NFL Draft, and he had just been picked first overall by the Baltimore Colts. What should have been one of the best days of his life was an epic mess of his own making.

After four years at Stanford, scouts called him the greatest quarterback prospect in NFL history, another greatest something, which was now how John was experiencing the world. Consensus All-America, rewrote Pac-10 passing records, single-handedly led upsets of Washington and Ohio State, earned $150,000 for a summer of baseball at the Yankees Class-A team, graduated in economics. All the shenanigans Elway pulled in high school had not only transferred to college, but seemed *suited* for it: Against USC, he scrambled back and forth and backward, making people miss, driving his coaches nuts, seemingly compounding disaster, until he let one fly 65 yards over the head of the safety, who was convinced that no human could throw a ball that far, and hit his receiver in the numbers a few yards into the end zone. Gil Brandt, the future Hall of Fame personnel executive for the Dallas Cowboys, a man who would revolutionize football scouting with a sliding grade scale for prospects, said, "If we already had Danny White, Dan Fouts, and Joe Montana—*and* we had the first pick in the draft—I'd *still* take John Elway."

Not bad for twenty-two years old. Yet here he was in the video, standing before the cameras in a red rugby shirt, feigning command and control as he prepared to tell the press why he was refusing to play for the Colts—an unstable organization—and was planning to play baseball for the Yankees for a year and re-enter the NFL Draft in 1984. No quarterback had tried to pull a power play like this before. His father, Jack, was with him, of course, standing at the podium, with his dark wavy hair and checkered blazer, the architect of this thing. John was behind him, scared at how this was playing out. Jack meant well, like Archie Manning would mean well when he helped lead-block for Eli to be traded from the Chargers to the Giants in 2004, after Eli expressed concerns with the orga-nization and told them to "please" not draft him, a fanciful request, and like Carl Williams would mean well, too. Jack wanted his son to land where he could thrive and, maybe more, wanted to pre-serve his son's love of quarterbacking. Elway was already famous nationally; he was going to be rich regardless of whatever NFL team—whatever professional sports team—he played for. But Jack knew football would be a job, and the job would be a job, more than it already was. The game had to be an escape, a fundamental joy. "That's where he'll find his greatness," Jack told a friend.

An aspiring young agent named Marvin Demoff was aligned with Jack's vision. Months before the draft, his pitch to the Elways was simple: "You don't have to play for the Colts."

"What?" Jack said.

"You know, when I got out of law school, I didn't get drafted by a law firm in Des Moines. I got to do what I wanted to do. Your situation is sort of made for you having a choice. And that's what baseball provides for you."

"Wow," John said.

Nobody had ever blown up the draft before, but the Elways were sold. Demoff and Jack Elway met with Colts general manager Ernie Accorsi and head coach Frank Kush before the draft, and believed they'd reached a quiet agreement: Baltimore would agree to trade Elway before the draft, and Elway wouldn't go to war publicly against the team. Well, no: Accorsi never signed on to it. He had a stiff asking price for the best prospect he'd ever seen: three number one picks, including one in the top five or six of the loaded 1983 draft, and two number twos. He was determined to hold firm. Elway was worth it. Accorsi's friend Johnny Unitas believed he wasn't, and encouraged him to draft another Demoff client, Pittsburgh's Dan Marino.

"You're just saying Marino because he's a Western Pennsylvanian," Accorsi said.

"I'm just saying Marino because he's the best passer of the lot," Unitas said.

The draft arrived. Accorsi was determined to sit tight and withstand the storm, knowing that someone—Elway, or another

NFL team—was going to blink. At 11 p.m. the night before the draft, Demoff called the Elways with good news: The Raiders had a three-way trade ironed out with the Bears and Colts. Elway was ecstatic: He'd be in LA, on a team with a Super Bowl roster. Then, at 6 a.m. the day of the draft, Demoff had another update: "Looks like the trade's off." The Raiders, Bears, and Demoff believed that NFL Commissioner Pete Rozelle killed it, not wanting the optics of a renegade owner like Al Davis landing Elway.

"Shit," Elway said, and the Colts picked him.

The first round would forever be known for its famous Class of '83 quarterbacks, a group that elevated and evolved the position's status and power and potency. Kansas City picked Penn State's Todd Blackledge, Buffalo picked Miami's Jim Kelly, New England took Illinois's Tony Eason, the Jets picked Cal-Davis's Ken O'Brien, and Miami grabbed Marino toward the end of the first round, with the twenty-seventh pick.

The Elways had to do something, so they called a press conference. Jack insisted that he and his son were not "challenging the draft," but the entire spectacle reeked of bravado and condescension. Jack blanked on Accorsi's name as he spoke. He reminded the room that the Colts had "earned the right to pick first," then rolled his eyes.

A reporter asked John, "Did you call Frank Kush after the draft this morning?"

"He called *me*," Elway said, correcting the record and, not for nothing, clarifying status.

"What did you say?"

"I said, 'Mr. Kush, I don't want to be a jerk or anything, but we've been telling you for three months that I'm not going to play in Baltimore, and right now you have nothing.' And then I hung the phone up."

A reporter asked how Elway's desire to play in warm weather squared with choosing to play baseball in New York.

"They play baseball in the summertime."

Reporters laughed, a little too hard. It wasn't funny. Elway knew it. He was coming off like a toothy, preening prick. Watch closely, like Elway does when he pulls up the clip, and you see that for a split second he glances down. He knew this wasn't going well. An iconic football city hated him, the establishment couldn't stand him—Terry Bradshaw *really* hated him—and he hadn't even taken a snap yet.

When Elway and I discuss the press conference, he notices how nervous he was, how naïve, how pissed off. But—and maybe this is what Archie Manning and Carl Williams were thinking of—it worked out. A week after the draft, Elway and his buddies were watching *All My Children*—it was their thing—when Demoff called and told him to get on a plane to Denver, and bring a suit. The Broncos snared Elway for tackle Chris Hinton, a backup quarterback named Mark Herrmann, and a 1984 first-round pick. It would go down among the most lopsided trades in league history. A few years later at Elway's charity golf tournament, John's wife, Janet, told Hinton, "I don't know what to say—I'm sorry or thank you."

Elway's introductory press conference was carried live in Denver. As he stepped offstage, he turned to a Broncos PR man and said, naïve at both self and situation and what it would mean down the line, "Wow! I'm glad I'll never have to go through *that* again."

It was easy to get swept up in Arch and all the buzz, his every act being viewed through the prisms of precociousness and prelude, even for coach Nelson Stewart. As a freshman, Arch threw 38 touchdowns in eleven games. There was one game where Arch struggled, throwing a few interceptions, which is memorable to Stewart not only because it was the exception but because of what he saw. Stewart looked at Arch's eyes as he came off the field. How the Mannings react to interceptions has become a kind of sport within a sport. Archie was the angriest: He hated interceptions. Peyton had an entire palette of reactions, which Bill Simmons, then of ESPN, termed "Manning Face": "the look of someone who has just faced up to a sobering fact: I am in complete control of this offense. I prepare for games like no other quarterback in the NFL. I am in the best shape of my life. I have done everything I can to succeed—and I'm losing." Eli had his own Manning Faces, but he took pride in appearing untroubled, lest he give the New York press any fodder. Arch was overwhelmed and stressed and looked . . . *young*. "I had to remind myself that he's just a kid," Stewart says.

Was it already too late? A documentary crew had already called Cooper and asked if Arch wanted to be featured alongside some of the game's legends, including Elway. Cooper loved the idea but couldn't do that to his kid—couldn't allow him to be in a project alongside an all-timer. Archie created headlines when he told a reporter that his grandson was "a little ahead of" his sons when they were freshmen. What was intended as a simple observation of fact—neither Peyton nor Eli had started on varsity as freshmen— became a family member upping the hype and went viral, not just on recruiting sites and college message boards, but on actual news outlets. Predictable backlash followed, anonymous whispers from college coaches who saw Arch as a good kid and good player, but probably not a top recruit if his last name were different—not the most desired player in America from the 2023 class. The entire episode was proof that Arch hadn't done anything other than play quarterback, yet this stuff—these forces—were his problem, and almost didn't need him to exist. One day, Joe Brady, then the offensive coordinator for LSU, visited Newman's campus. He saw Arch, who was fourteen years old at the time. Brady rushed to him. "I just want to shake your hand! Damn good to meet you!"

Cooper and Stewart had a question: How seriously should they take this stuff? In one sense, it was just a boy throwing a ball. In another, it was national news, and there was an entire modern media ecosystem that seemed reverse engineered to drive traffic off the next Manning. When Arch was a sophomore, Stewart and Cooper met to lay out a plan. Both men felt like they were staring at a tsunami taking form in the distance.

"What do we want this to look like?" Stewart asked Cooper.

"We're gonna do a 1975 recruitment," Cooper said.

Cooper wanted the impossible: an environment where Arch could thrive as a quarterback, but also what Jack Elway wanted for his son—for him to not fall out of love with the game, and the job. John was twenty-two years old when Jack felt the need to draw those lines; Arch was fifteen. Jack was worried about a professional football team; Cooper wanted to get his kid through high school. Both Stewart and Cooper knew that a cocoon—or a pretense of one—seemed beyond reach, but worth trying for.

Cooper's own recruitment was straightforward. He was a wide receiver, and he went to Ole Miss, the family school. Spinal stenosis cut his career short, but he nonetheless managed to become a legend—"a social legend," in Peyton's words. Peyton honored Cooper by switching his number from 16 to 18, which his older brother had worn at Newman. Cooper was in college in 1993, when Peyton was one of the nation's top recruits. Peyton had a full desk of letters and bins, organized by school, sixty in all. Olivia helped file paperwork. Recruiting websites, chat boards, social media, transfer portals, rumors filed by the minute—none of those existed. Peyton handled the process himself, wanted it all on his shoulders, classic quarterback stuff. The Manning family installed a second home phone line just for Peyton's recruitment. On the first day that NCAA rules permitted coaches to call, it rang twenty-three times from twenty-two different schools. Over the course of a year Peyton spoke to each school that recruited him, even if he had little intention of going there, out of respect and due diligence. Joe Paterno visited Newman. So did Bobby Bowden, and he even handwrote a letter; Peyton smeared the ink because he couldn't believe it was real. Stewart would ask Peyton in the weight room what it was like to visit Notre Dame and touch the famous PLAY LIKE A CHAMPION sign in the stadium tunnel. Michigan badly wanted Peyton, and if he'd gone there, a lanky quarterback from San Mateo named Tom Brady might have gone elsewhere. *Sports Illustrated* wrote a long feature on Peyton and Archie and the entire Manning Southern thing.

There was a presumption that Peyton would attend Ole Miss. "I thought Ole Miss was the only school that ever *existed*," he later said. If Archie had told him that he wanted him to go to Ole Miss, Peyton would have listened. The school sent Peyton a letter of the Top Ten Advantages of Becoming a Rebel. Most were garden variety temptations, of legacy and lore, but one of the items cut to the chase: "At Ole Miss, you would be exposed to a perennial top-ten school in America for beautiful women." But after a weekend in Knoxville—it snowed, narrowing entertainment options to vast consumption of moonshine—Peyton picked Tennessee. He wanted to play for offensive coordinator David Cutcliffe—who knew how to talk Quarterback, who ran a progressive passing offense, who would become a lifelong mentor and friend. Eli followed the same formula when he picked Ole Miss, where Cutcliffe became the head coach. It was Cooper's legacy: The football life could end at any moment.

"I want you to run point," Cooper told Stewart. "Very old-school."

Very old-school meant that Cooper wanted Stewart to be his son's gatekeeper, organizer, spokesman, confidant, security guard, evangelist, strategist, and of course, head coach of what the family expected to be the most sophisticated high school offense in the country. And one more condition:

"No offers," Cooper said.

"What does that mean?" Stewart asked.

"No offers. No talking to the media if we can."

Scholarship offers are a barometer for top recruits, a tangible way to measure demand. Offers are also a way for college coaches to mark territory. What happens to a boy when so many people want to tell him where to do this, with whom to do it with, when so many people make decisions for him, when there's no way to know what the right choice is, with potentially catastrophic consequences? "Nothing you're doing as a freshman or sophomore is gonna be relevant in the big picture," Cooper told Arch. This is where the last name came in handy. They could afford to run an atypical process, to be a little *special* in a way that, say, dozens of other top prep quarterbacks like Colin Hurley could not. Cooper didn't want Arch to have to continually post on social media how blessed and humbled he was to receive offers.

"We're not doing that crap," Cooper said.

"All right," Stewart said.

The plan quickly faced its first test. One day Stewart returned to his office after teaching class to see Ole Miss head coach Lane Kiffin sitting in his chair. He had already offered a quarterback in Jacksonville named Colin Hurley, but nonetheless, he told Stewart, "I have to offer this kid."

"I don't know how to tell you this," Stewart said. "But we're not, you know . . ."

Kiffin was confused. But he, and other college coaches, eventually appreciated it. It was one less thing they had to monitor. Still, Kiffin wanted his world, the world of college coaches and of recruiting junkies, to know that he was already staking his claim. Kiffin took a selfie at Stewart's desk and posted it on social media.

It was on.

Word about Carl Williams had started to spread in NFL circles. That he was a combination of Marv Marinovich, the poster boy for out-of-control quarterback dads. That he was Jack Elway, or Archie Manning, only with a less talented son. Bill Belichick, who had won eight Super Bowls in large part because of his talent for designing defenses that exposed quarterbacks for what they were and, especially, what they *weren't*, watched film of Caleb Williams and was unimpressed. Too quick to leave the pocket. Too slow to see open receivers. And that was separate from the baggage of his entire enterprise. "The dad . . ." team executives would utter when Caleb's name came up, leaving the ellipses to do the talking. Carl took it as a compliment. Archie, Marvin Demoff, even a famous labor lawyer named Jeffrey Kessler—those guys were who Carl wanted to learn from. They had taken on the system, in varying degrees of magnitude, and won. How could Carl do it?

When Carl and I chat about owners and coaches, I tell him that once, over beers, a longtime NFL team executive referred to clubs as "billion-dollar lemonade stands." Why? I asked. "Multimillion-dollar decisions are made with almost no thought," he said. I thanked the executive for giving me a title for a future book.

Carl nodded his head and took it a level deeper, how a bad owner—who doesn't invest in the team, who hires and fires cheap—can ruin the game's most important position, killing a guy's career before he has a chance. Carl believed, not irrationally, that his son was better at his job than most NFL people were at theirs. Carl could live with anonymous scouts ripping him; he refused to be haunted for life if his son failed to reach his potential because some team bad enough to hold the first overall pick ruined him.

"There's organizational support, then there's coaching," Carl says.

There was also actual leverage and *perceived* leverage. Over the summer of 2023, Carl and Caleb—mostly Carl—spitballed what a power play would look like. If Williams didn't want to play for the team picking first, the easiest option was to return to USC—and another seven- or eight-figure NIL windfall. Two other schools called Carl, asking what it would take for Caleb to transfer there for his senior year. The answer: tens of millions. Problem was, that would delay what NFL players want most: a second contract. That's when they usually cash in. As if there weren't enough NFL landmines—bad coaches and worse owners—there was a collectively bargained rookie wage cap. It was instituted because for a few years after the turn of the century, a team's highest-paid player was often not just its quarterback, but its *rookie* quarterback: six years, $49.5 million for Alex Smith in 2006 to $78 million for Sam Bradford in 2010. For context, Tom Brady spent most of those years on a four-year, $42.8 million contract.

Those rookie contracts wrecked teams, both within the structures of the salary cap, leaving teams with less to spend on surrounding talent, and culturally, where a guy who had yet to take a snap was compensated as much or better than future Hall of Famers. The dominos would fall. The quarterback, without good teammates, would struggle. Coaches would be fired; new coaches would come in and start over, with new belief systems and playbooks. Alex Smith had seven offensive coordinators in seven years in San Francisco. JaMarcus Russell had two head coaches in three years with the Raiders. Of the quarterbacks that signed those monstrous rookie deals, only two—Atlanta's Matt Ryan and Detroit's Matthew Stafford—became true franchise quarterbacks.

Carl knew that Caleb likely would be drafted by a team that chose him, not the reverse. He'd sign a four-year contract, in a preordained $39 million range. If he panned out, the team would exercise an option to keep him for a fifth year. By the end of the fifth year, Williams would be twenty-seven years old—and a free agent in name only. He would not be able to test the market for his value. The team that drafts a player can block them from free agency by designating them with what's called the franchise tag, under which the team is obligated to pay them the average salary of a sliding scale of the top earners at a given position. Teams are allowed to tag a player for three straight years. If that happened, Caleb would be forced into below-market deals for eight years, until he was thirty. Carl saw loss of income at anywhere from $200 to $400 million.

"The rookie cap is just unconstitutional," he tells me, later adding that the CBA is the "worst piece of shit I've ever read. It's the worst in sports history."

Carl called Archie. He called Demoff. He called labor lawyers. He spoke with agents. He visited with a billionaire in LA named Dennis Gilbert, who was a former agent to a bevy of Hall of Fame baseball players. All said versions of the same thing: The league had closed all the loopholes, maybe out of concern that NFL players would try to form super teams like LeBron James and others in the NBA had managed. Options were limited. One of them, within the context of getting in line, was to seek an equity stake in the team that drafted him. If a franchise quarterback could help increase value of a club, why not have a piece of it? Williams's representatives started to ask about it. So did Aaron Rodgers. Owners shut it down by voting to prohibit nonfamily employees from taking equity in NFL teams just before the 2023 season. That left father and son, like it was with Jack and John Elway or Archie and Eli Manning, to force a trade.

Carl was willing to go there. Caleb was nervous. "He's worried about me taking bullets," Carl says. "I don't care. I just don't agree with this shit, you know? I'm more interested in making sure that he can do what he wants to do."

I've been wrestling with a feeling about Caleb, and many young quarterbacks, that as products of a machine, they are now *what came after*. But I'm coming from an artistic and cultural lineage. Carl saw his son as *what came after* from a financial one. As a product, an entity, with a compensation ceiling out of step with demand. From sports to entertainment to business, he's watched our romance with stars become a shield for economics that screw over the most vulnerable. I'm the guy with a notebook in my hand; I can be theoretical. Carl is the guy with a quarterback in his hand; he can't.

Caleb is the guy with a football in his hand—and he's figuring out how to be, both in our world and his own. I ask Carl how aware Caleb is of the bind he's about to be in.

"Very."

———

Slouched in the front seat of his dad's pickup as they slide into a parking lot on a December morning, Colin Hurley yawns and stares at his phone. It's the offseason, school is virtual, so today is every day: drills, weights, drills, weights, drills. . . . A dozen or so people are on a turf field in this complex outside of Jacksonville. Most are professional baseball players, Colin's workout friends. He feels sluggish. "My gumbo last night?" Charlie says with a laugh.

Colin grabs a bag with his cleats and walks to the field, where the others stretch and throw, the pop of baseballs hitting mitts, like machine-gun fire. When the Hurleys reach the white sideline, Colin keeps walking. Charlie stops.

"This is where I stand. I stay out of the way. I'm Dad."

Will Hewlett works with Colin for the next hour, on a variety of lower-body resistance drills, doing the work of a private quarterback coach. What was once a luxury invented by a man named Steve Clarkson now feels essential in the quarterback industrial complex. Clarkson was a high school quarterback in Los Angeles in the late seventies. He played for Jack Elway at San Jose State, quarterbacking a team that beat John and Stanford in 1982. After a few years in the NFL and CFL, he returned to California to work in the restaurant business. It was unfulfilling, and he saw an opening: that as football's popularity grew, so would the obsession with quarterbacks. The classic role of the high school coach, as authority and teacher—what Cooper Manning asked of Nelson Stewart—seemed outdated. If you wanted to be a guitarist, there was a private tutor. If you wanted to act, there was a private tutor. Why not quarterback?

Clarkson's business started small. After his first client, a Southern California kid named Perry Klein, ended up in the NFL, Clarkson expanded, launching a passing academy. He reportedly charged $60,000 for a year of tutoring at his camps. Private coaching was reportedly $8,000 a month, not including a $3,000 two-day evaluation and travel costs. The country was ripe for this space, the fusing of ambition and wealth and obsession with the idea of spotting genius early, and the specialists knew who to target: dads. Former college coach Rick Neuheisel once said that quarterback dads were like "nomads in the desert. If you tell 'em there's water, they're gonna drink it. . . . All you have to do is tell him, 'Hey, he's got it.' And they'll keep spending. And spending. And spending."

Spending into a multimillion-dollar industry, featured in the *New York Times* and *60 Minutes*. Tom Brady considered his private coaches, first Tom Martinez and then Tom House, vital to his development and rise. Peyton and Eli Manning would spend weeks in the offseason with their personal instructor, David Cutcliffe. Bruce Feldman's 2014 book of the guru space, *The QB*, revealed many of the top names as flagrant self-promoters and immature backstabbers, if not outright hucksters, who promised results in a crapshoot of an industry. Powerful college coaches started to co-opt the gurus, turning their businesses into a funneling system. The tutors wanted to claim credit for their clients, like Ben Roethlisberger or Matt Leinart, as if *their* instruction solidified them as first-round picks. The inherent flaws in the concept—that nobody knows which quarterbacks have the goods, nobody knows how to teach it, and nobody knows how to predict it—made it even weirder, maybe more quintessentially American.

Clarkson boasted that he had trained the sons of Wayne Gretzky, Will Smith, and Snoop Dogg. None of them ended up being college quarterbacks. The gurus miss as often as college coaches or NFL general managers do—which is also to say, they're exactly as proficient as them. A recruiting book called *5-Star QB* once polled fifty top high school quarterbacks and asked how many employed a private coach. Sixty-four percent said yes. Four of those quarterbacks used *two or more*. Of those polled who had finished college, only two ended up as first-round picks. One of them—Trent Edwards—used a private coach. The other—Josh Rosen—did not. Both flamed out.

If you want a glimpse into private quarterback coaching, all the places it might take a kid, visit an Instagram account named The QB Plug. In 2023, it posted a video touting the instruction of Jeff Christensen, a quarterback coach out of Chicago. In his sixties now, Christensen played quarterback at Eastern Illinois, was a fifth-round draft pick in 1983, and spent four years in the NFL, for three different teams. He's spent much of his post-playing career tutoring a list of stellar quarterbacks, including Patrick Mahomes. In the video, Christensen is billed as a "legendary QB guru" and a "football genius" who has "a bunch of secret sauces." He's teaching a quarterback out of Arizona named Dylan Raiola, the top-rated prospect of the 2024 high school class, a cold-war rival of other quarterbacks like Colin Hurley. What follows on the clip is fairly pedantic instruction, as quarterback stuff goes: *Right toe is at the target . . . How level are his shoulders? . . . Because he throws it higher, not harder . . . Now, close your eyes. . . .* Raiola throws on air with eyes closed. He is not doing it to show off, or as a dare, like Michael Jordan once did in a game with a free throw. This is a teaching point. Christensen shouts at quarterbacks as they throw, although we don't hear what. In one of the clips, Christensen holds an iPad with the screen blurred. The sauces are too secret.

It's as easy to see why NFL coaches are dismissive about the quarterback-guru industry as it is why the industry believes that bad coaching kills quarterbacks. But quarterbacks need a support system. The team doesn't always provide one; in fact, it often doesn't. Quarterbacks need someone who answers at any hour, who will get on a plane with a day's notice, whose presence is as valuable as their pure advice, maybe more. It's a lonely job, a damn lonely one, which is what I know from experience, what I've imagined in doing it at the highest level, and what I'm learning as I study this space. Christensen is a friend, a damn good one, with singular benefits. He sees in Mahomes a kind of earnestness that he wants to nurture. "His only purpose in life is to win," he has said. "He's a very secure person." Once, Mahomes had suffered two bad ankle sprains in the middle of the season. He asked Christensen to visit him. They watched film; Mahomes asked for advice for playing with curtailed mobility.

"I think it's going to cause you to play even better," Christensen said.

"Yeah," Mahomes said. "I think you're right." What he needed in the moment was someone completely dedicated to figuring out how to make it happen. Christensen was that person. *Is* that person.

Sometimes, a quarterback coach can provide more than iron companionship. The biggest trend in throwing mechanics over the past twenty years came not from an NFL coach but from a private one: a former major league pitcher and psychology doctorate out of Southern California named Tom House. House started a practice to help pitchers and eventually moved on to quarterbacks. He started with Drew Brees, then Matt Cassel of the Patriots. That led to Tom Brady, who in 2013 was at something of a crossroads. He was the best quarterback in football, but he had stalled. A plateau at a high level was a plateau nonetheless. In Super Bowl XLVI in 2012, Brady had receiver Wes Welker open down the seam. A completion would have iced the game. Brady missed him, not by yards but by two inches. The Giants went on to win. The next year against the Broncos in the AFC Championship Game, Brady missed receiver Julian Edelman on an early throw, a pass that could have sent a message. New England lost.

Brady needed to be a few inches more accurate when it mattered most. Was it possible? House instructed Brady to keep his left, non-throwing hand firm and close to his chin, rotating *to* it, rather than swinging it open. That was relatively new. Coaches had been all over the place on what to do with a quarterback's non-throwing arm during their release. Brady, like most quarterbacks, was taught to keep his open and pull it down, a mechanism for power and torque. House opened his mind, and Brady felt a difference. He was two inches more accurate. He committed it to muscle memory, and it ended up altering his career, and then the entire quarterbacking industry. First NFL quarterbacks copied Brady's technique, then college ones, then high school. It's now accepted practice. There's no doubt that it helped a phenomenally accurate thrower, humble enough to realize he could improve on his own incredible standard, become even more phenomenally accurate. There's also no way to know whatever kid is phenomenally accurate until they prove it, first in the large windows of high school, then the narrowing ones in college, then the tight ones in the NFL, and then the impossible ones in the final minutes of a Super Bowl. Maybe four men in each generation are capable of that level of precision. Nobody can see it in teenagers. Nobody can buy it from an instructor. It's revealed, one way or another.

Will Hewlett and Tom Gormely don't have a secret sauce, and don't claim to. If a quarterback is weighing working out with them or Tom House, they'll compliment House. Like all in this space, they see The QB Plug's post and shake their heads. "Instagram quarterbacks," Colin Hurley calls them. Hewlett doesn't shout at quarterbacks as they throw. He tries to present situations and create dynamic thinking and organic reactions. For instance, like many right-handed quarterbacks, Hurley sometimes struggles with accuracy to his left. He tends to close his shoulders and hips, forcing him to deploy more arm than body. Another of Hewlett and Gormely's clients, Brock Purdy of the San Francisco 49ers, struggled with the same issue. They try to change the angle of Hurley's arm and the window of the opening until it feels natural. Then they shift the angles and windows, as long as Hurley maintains *feel*. Once he's throwing to his left with his natural mechanics, they have him throw that way until it feels committed to muscle memory. "We teach through constraints," Gormely says.

Hurley found Hewlett and Gormely before they were the *it guys* in this space, almost by accident. He was twelve, a dominant player in youth football, and needed help rehabbing an arm injury. Local high schools started to recruit him, adolescent free agency. Trinity Christian's coaches told him that he was ready for varsity. Head coach Verlon Dorminey was a local legend, in the top ten all-time in wins in Florida football history. That was enough for the Hurleys.

Trinity was forty minutes from home on a good traffic day, but this was a chance for what Colin wanted: a fast track. He was the varsity starting quarterback as a freshman despite not playing a down of middle school football. Infrastructure came next. Charlie wanted to hire a private coach but couldn't afford $50,000 a year. Hewlett was working in Jacksonville for a company called QB Collective. He became one of the best at an American craft despite not being from America. As a kid in his native Australia, he fell in love with throwing a football and he was good enough to play quarterback for Dodge City Community College in Kansas. He worked at a car dealership after graduation. It felt empty. "The position has controlled my life," he tells me as Colin works out. He started training quarterbacks, and eventually linked up with Gormely, who everyone calls Dr. Tom. They work in tandem, both on a quarterback's mind and body.

Hurley is a kind of test case for them, a quarterback who arrived raw and left molded. By the time Hurley enters LSU's campus as a freshman, Hewlett says, "most of his development will be ahead of the four-year college guy."

I ask Hewett when he can tell that a quarterback has the goods. "Normally, by seventh or eighth grade, they'll be among the top guys," he says. Hewlett senses my mental eye roll. I point out that Brady wasn't even playing football at that age. He smiles. "Nobody's got it figured out." He promises to help a quarterback improve, not put him in the Hall of Fame.

Colin stands feet away, switching between fun and business as he throws a football, formatting his mind and body. If Hewlett— and the homeschool teachers, strength and speed trainers, coaches who teach how to study film, arm-care experts, seven-on-seven tournament coaches, media trainers, nutritionists, rehab and recovery specialists, agents, coaches who work with virtual-reality software to mimic a game, motion-capture specialists, and financial advisors—can help get a kid a full scholarship, that's a good rate of return for a parent. It's also a lot of adults for a child to please.

"We prep for the NFL," Tom Gormely says. "That's our pitch."

In the years that Colin Hurley has worked with this outfit—first at a gym called Tork, then CORTX Sports Performance—Gormely has given him as much as he can handle, refusing to allow age to be a factor. When LSU coaches called Gormely and asked for Hurley's ceiling, he replied that physically Colin was already at an NFL level at age fifteen. Hurley was also an interesting test case. Working with so many pitchers over the years steeped Gormely in the art and science of arm care. He saw a massive deficiency in NFL circles. "NFL arm care is light-years behind baseball," he says. Quarterbacks tended to not suffer from arm pain so much as fatigue. His goal with Hurley was to help him reach his dreams—help him reach the NFL—while also not overdoing it.

Charlie stands to the side, on the phone with Kyle Strongin, who at the time is Colin's agent. After the 2021 Supreme Court NIL ruling, any athlete could sign with an agent. NCAA rules previously forbade it, adding to the unnecessary cesspool of college sports, as money was traded under the table. Some football observers wondered why college quarterbacks needed agents. Why high school ones did, too. But the job had long ago reached that status. Change was overdue. The Hurleys hired Strongin, who had worked for the 49ers' scouting staff and the Ole Miss football-operations department. His biggest clients were Trevor Lawrence, the Clemson quarterback whom the Jacksonville Jaguars drafted first overall in 2021, and Brock Purdy. Strongin is tall and thick, a former college quarterback, and knows the world well. In one of their first meetings, Strongin told Charlie, "Quarterback dads are fucking nuts. You're nuts too, but in a different way."

Every few months CORTX produces an assessment of Colin's strength and power and rotational development. The goal is to spot inefficiencies. Gormely refers to it as an "athlete's profile." He ran Colin through ten or so tests to measure KPIs—key performance indicators. Most drills test Colin's range of motion, from internal and external shoulder work to knees and hips. The tests produce an odd result: that Colin is more of a strong athlete than a powerful one. "Really good at putting out maximal force," Gormely says. "The position he plays requires power. He has a ton of force output, but we want to make sure he uses that force better." Gormely wants to improve Colin's shoulder and hip rotation, so he runs Colin through flexibility drills.

Shoulders and hips are not only essential to a quarterback's power, they quicken a quarterback's release, making a motion like Namath's and Marino's, once considered a generational gift, somewhat attainable. Fans marveled at how fast Namath and Marino whipped their arms, but they each had world-class hips, a trunk that thrust forward and fastened, like a great hitter's swing. The arm simply followed. Smart coaches can teach quarterbacks how to quicken their hips, commoditizing something rare—and maybe dehumanizing them as they demystify it. Working with Tom House, Tom Brady perfected a technique of rotating his shoulders twenty degrees past his hips, farther back than most quarterbacks. It helped to increase his velocity by approximately four to six miles per hour, turning his body into a slingshot. CORTX uses different measurements, but the idea is the same. Colin has a rotation speed of 3,000–4,000 degrees per second. Major league pitchers are around 7,000. That means Colin's rotation, while improving, is already exceptional. Biometric expert Chris Hess periodically runs Colin through 3D imaging, capturing rational velocity numbers, down to degrees per second, spitting out pages of code. An infrastructure can turn a kid into Marino, but can it do it without the kid occasionally feeling like a collection of levers?

Two weeks ago, Hurley received his latest throwing assessment, a breakdown of inputs ranging from Kinetics to Alignment to Sway. It was filled with jargon: *Add knee flexion after stride foot plant. This disrupts sequence timing and energy transfer from the lower to upper body. Result is late hip collision (after ball release), less rotational velocity in the trunk and compensation through higher internal shoulder rotation velocity. . . .*

Gormely puts it more succinctly: "Colin is up there with the pros."

Warren Moon didn't have a quarterback infrastructure. He was alone.

Oh sure, he had a support system in his family and in Steinberg. Even if Moon was a man apart—even if he was forced to grow up far too early, to help manage a household far too early, to have expectations and burdens of race and class far too early—he was still trying to be his idea of a man. And, of course, Moon had to be a great quarterback, too.

Those two things—two ideas and ideals—aren't always related or in concert. By the time Moon arrived in Houston in 1984, he was already considered a great man. He had already overcome so much. The press wrote about his preternatural maturity and grace. In his first two years as a starter, he had a problem: He wasn't a great quarterback, much less the first great Black quarterback. The Oilers were an awful team in general, with awful pass-catchers in particular, beautiful throws bouncing off teammates' hands.

"I'm tryin'," Moon told the coaches during a game. "I can't catch it, too."

In Moon's second season, Houston hired Jerry Glanville as head coach, and with him a pass-first offense called the Run and Shoot, a weird and gimmicky scheme, pure eighties, with funky and, to be fair, prescient tenets: four receivers on the field on every down, one running back, passing as an imperative, in any situation. The quarterback dropped back not straight, like in other offenses, but in an arc to the right or left—like, well, a quarter moon. Moon's job was to throw it on his third step. The lack of pass protection exposed the quarterback to more hits, so Moon prioritized weight training, transforming from spindly to statuesque. Moon made this offense work, like he made everything work. It's one of the things he's proudest of. He tinkered at the line of scrimmage, doing stuff

Peyton Manning later made famous. Against the Bengals in 1991, the Oilers called a screen pass to the right side. Moon started his goofy mini-rollout drop right, curving like a comma, but Cincinnati had the play covered. He reversed field, back left, and saw receiver Drew Hill streaking down the sideline. He twisted his body and let the ball fly deep. One of the things Moon had learned over the years was to never look at his long passes after he threw them. "If you wanna throw a good deep ball," his coach June Jones told him, "you can't look at it. Your eyes have to look at the receiver."

There's a beautiful split second when you can throw a ball, see it on its initial flight path, and you'll have a good idea of where it'll land. Nothing else in sports is like it. A pitch or a slapshot is too fast; a three-point shot is too uncertain. Moon did more than watch his passes; he admired them. But with this one, he tried to fix his eyes on Hill. He snuck a peek, of course, to make sure it was a good spiral. The ball landed in Hill's arms and carried him into the end zone for a 61-yard touchdown. He considers it the best throw of his career.

Moon became a national hero, putting up better numbers than Joe Montana and Dan Marino and Jim Kelly and John Elway, and he changed the national debate. The coded questions—*Can a Black quarterback not just play but* run *a sophisticated passing offense?*— receded, but didn't fully disappear. Racist chants—*Hey, Warren, throw that ball like you throw a watermelon!*—remained. He heard the N-word so often that he got used to it. By the late eighties and early nineties, Moon had heard it for most of his football life. The difference now was that he had married Felicia, his high school girlfriend, and they had started a family. Now the hate affected people beyond him. Moon was not only a public American figure, but he was a brave one, too, because not every fan in Houston cared. Many didn't care when Moon turned the Oilers into a playoff team, or when he won NFL Man of the Year in 1989, didn't care when he overcame questions in his own mind about how good he could be and became a perennial Pro Bowler.

In 1990, Moon threw for 527 yards against the Chiefs in Arrowhead, the second-best passing output ever. He lived with a general crush of expectations, layered and complicated. Work came first. He needed to float above the discourse—or at least appear to be above it. He read books about Jackie Robinson, wondering how he held himself together. Moon couldn't break, couldn't explode; those were privileges for white men and white quarterbacks. "I woulda been shipped out of town," he says. Moon's head would pound after games.

When Moon was stressed, he was quiet. More stressed, the quieter. "Never shared it with anybody," he says now. But as he aged, it was harder to bury stuff. Cracks were starting to show. He and Felicia fought more. Death threats became routine. Asking his kids if they were targeted at school seemed like a daily conversation—and that's when he was at home, focused on family. He had an image to uphold, a full-time job in itself, never saying no to an interview, to an appearance for the team, for teammates, never passing on an autograph request or picture, all the demands of his profession, as his rage built and built.

After one Oilers loss, Moon sat at his locker and looked up to see his seven-year-old son Jeffrey. He was crying. Moon asked why. Jeffrey asked, "Why are these people calling you all these names?"

"What do you mean?" Moon asked.

Moon wasn't prepared for the conversation that followed, at least not right then. He told Jeffrey, "Some people don't like your dad."

America in the eighties was a time and place for men to get rich fast. John Elway fit in. The idea of capitalism as lifestyle not only launched but became cool, touching all areas of entertainment. Namath and his agent, Mike Bite, had introduced the notion that precocious quarterbacks deserved to be compensated on the level of actors and musicians; Elway and Marvin Demoff upped that and then some, placing the profession in the realm of the best actors and entertainers when he signed a five-year, $5 million contract as a rookie in 1983, making him pro football's highest-paid player.

The difference between Elway's contract in 1983 and Namath's in 1965 was that Elway wasn't a marketing ploy. His compensation was tied to immediate expectations, not potential. His success in the NFL seemed like an inevitability. The best quarterbacks of the 1970s, like Terry Bradshaw and Roger Staubach, were well-off, but not set for life. Staubach would create a real estate empire in Texas that would push his net worth close to $1 billion, but that was years after he played—after he had established himself as a Hall of Famer. In 1983, Elway pushed quarterback into corporate economics.

And corporate battle. The *Denver Post* and *Rocky Mountain News* ran daily stories on all possible aspects of his life, including what he had for lunch at the team cafeteria. Soon the Associated Press and local television stations jumped in. When Elway reported for training camp, Broncos PR man Jim Saccomano noticed a bulletin normally reserved for heads of state: "John Elway Weighed In Today at 217 Pounds."

Denver had been home to professional sports since 1960, producing neither championships nor superstars, a brown smear of a cow town with a pile of moveable bleachers off I-25 that happened to have an all-time top-five name for a venue: Mile High Stadium. Twenty-eight reporters bunked at training camp in Greeley. Both the *Post* and *Rocky* started running daily Elway-watch columns, ratcheting up an already competitive beat. One morning brought news that Elway had enjoyed his first uninterrupted lunch since training camp had started. He ate bean soup and won a one-dollar bet with an assistant coach. On another day it was reported that someone had left him a dozen roses on his motor scooter. He also "spent some time Wednesday examining the earring Larry Evans wears under his helmet."

First week of camp, Elway realized that his hair was flopping down too far into his helmet. During a break, he left the team dorm for a barber shop.

"Where are you off to?" a reporter asked.

"I think I'm gonna get a haircut."

"Well, we'd just like to follow you around. Do you mind?"

Fame takes daily acts and turns them into unrecognizable events. From here on out, Elway would always have the best tables at restaurants, courteous and polite people waiting on him, and a strange public freakishness around his steps. He learned to live life with his patience tested, strangers at his door, people following him, with few outlets. A few days later, Saccomano called a local barber who agreed to see Elway after hours at his home. When work ended for Elway that night around ten, he hopped in an unmarked police car without anyone noticing and got a haircut. A *Washington Post* reporter covered Elway by covering how those who covered Elway covered Elway. After Elway's first preseason game, the *Denver Post* ran fourteen photos; the *Rocky* ran eight. *Sports Illustrated* put him on the cover, under the banner

LOOKING LIKE A MILLION. "He's Namath with knees, Bradshaw with brains," receiver Mike Haffner said.

Elway already wanted his rookie season to end, and it hadn't even started. In training camp, he was asked to give advice for kids who wanted to be famous. "Don't be a quarterback, don't be a first-round draft pick, and don't get traded from Baltimore," he said.

The regular season arrived, and Elway wasn't great. Or good. He was awful, completing less than half of his passes and throwing twice as many interceptions as touchdowns. He had been experiencing, in his words, "a rat race, from the time of the draft, coming into training camp, training camp, all the attention, preseason, then jump into the regular season." He lost about twenty pounds. Still, he gave a brief glimpse of the future, throwing three touchdown passes in the fourth quarter in a comeback win over the Colts.

In his second year, Elway improved, but he wasn't exceptional, wasn't unstoppable, wasn't living up to expectations of city and team and self, wasn't . . . Dan Marino, who set records with 5,084 yards and 48 touchdowns in 1984. Marino loved the feeling of eyeing a slimming gap between a receiver and a defensive back and thinking—*knowing*—that he could fit the ball in it. That was his superpower. He could throw where he wanted, when he wanted.

Elway was from the West Coast, the son of a coach, with the weight of expectations; Marino from downtown Pittsburgh, the son of a truck driver, unleashing fury on the league for doubting him. Both needed the constant dopamine hit of feeling superior. In college, Elway and Marino had gone on a press junket and argued first over who had been on the cover of more preseason magazines, then over who had been on the cover of *better* magazines. One magazine put both of them on the cover, under the banner CLASS OF THE QUARTERBACKS. "Man," Marino told him, "your release is way too low."

"Pissed me off," Elway remembers, even now.

Now Marino was making the other Class of '83 quarterbacks look worse than mortal: He was making them look like errors in judgment. He threw more touchdown passes in his first two years than the rest of the class combined. Elway had spent his formative years doing something that chose him as much as he'd chosen it, and the intensity in the NFL still caught him by surprise. The tone of the Elway Watch shifted from obsessive flattery—he was named the NFL's sexiest player, by the U.S. Sports Fan Association—to obsessive blame, hunting for why Elway might not pan out. One Denver bar promoted shots called Elways, charging five cents each. So it went, until Elway's fourth year, and he shifted, improved, not suddenly, but steadily: He led Denver to a first-round win over New England, launching a touchdown pass 60 yards through the air after he'd duped the Patriots into jumping offside, giving him a free play, a quarterback trick Elway used in order to walk so that Aaron Rodgers could run.

On January 11, 1987, in the AFC Championship Game in gray and sloppy Cleveland against the Browns, Elway knew he had to perform. "I had taken a lot of criticism up to that point and really hadn't played well coming into that. I had gotten better each year, but it wasn't to the expectations of what a lot of people had of me." The first fifty-four minutes mirrored his career: inconsistent and mortal.

Then with 5:28 left, Elway found himself down 20–13, with 98 yards to go.

Arch Manning had his own command center: Nelson Stewart's office. Only Arch wasn't in command, and for the most part, neither was Stewart. College coaches often showed up for the sake of showing up, setting up shop at Stewart's empty desk while he taught class. Some schools—Ohio State, Princeton, Texas A&M, Rutgers—stopped by once, hoping for mutual interest. But for most of 2021, there was a steady stream of fifteen or so coaches from the main contenders: Texas, Alabama, Ole Miss, and Georgia.

NCAA rules forbade them from regularly talking to Arch, so they were there to be seen by him—and to get to know the quarterback by getting to know the coach. They'd sit down and talk ball with Stewart, who would take notes and steal ideas, losing track of time and hustling off to teach. When he glanced at his phone, the screen was filled with text messages and voicemails from other coaches. Coaches would FaceTime Stewart, hoping that Arch happened to be with him, a way to sneak in actual face time. On the day of the 2020 NFL Draft, when the Bengals picked Joe Burrow first overall, LSU coaches FaceTimed Stewart, hoping Arch was in the background. He was. The message was clear: You can be next.

Arch was nominally aware and acutely oblivious to it all. He just went about his thing, existing and playing quarterback. He did both remarkably well. He was self-assured, cocky but endearing, good-natured and calm. Arch had Peyton's situational intensity, Eli's situational indifference, Cooper's situational savvy, and his own sincerity. He was a byproduct of the entire Manning infrastructure, the receptor of every aspect of quarterback intelligence that this iconic family had learned through the decades. He had a quick release, an inheritance and the result of hours of work with his uncles and coaches. He went to Tulane for arm care. He had a huge trunk, thick thighs, and a quick torso, honed from drills useless in any other field. One day Arch sat in on a meeting with New Orleans Saints coaches and scouts as they evaluated the quarterbacks in that year's draft.

Grandpa Archie seemed more engaged with his grandson's recruitment than he had been with his own kids', often leaving Stewart long voice memos. Uncle Eli was there to answer any of Arch's questions, but he knew better than to impose—he had been in Arch's shoes, as the youngest taking on this job and all that attended it. But the benefits were undeniable.

When Eli was starting at Newman, Peyton called from Tennessee with a new way of thinking about a first-day basic for quarterbacks: the three-step drop. The way it had always been taught—to me, to all—was in terms of depth. You had to get five yards deep. That meant that your first step was a long one, followed by a long crossover step. Peyton had a new way of looking at it: The point wasn't depth, it was timing—throwing when the receiver was ready. Peyton kept the first step the same, but quickened the second and third ones. "Don't do a full crossover on your second step," he told Eli. That way, he'd throw on time and from a better platform. It worked.

By the time Eli committed to Ole Miss, Peyton was in the NFL. Peyton gave him a thick notebook full of protections and plays and ideas and truths, stuff he had been jotting down on flights during the football season. It was more than a tip sheet and life guide. It was a deep expression of love, a gift of hard-earned wisdom passed down on the eve of Eli's career, full of answers and warnings. In the years that followed, Eli realized that everything Peyton had offered was prescient and prophetic. When Eli became a professional, he and Peyton spoke a few times a week. They discussed football, sometimes not even in complete sentences, just phrases, codes, verbiage, a shorthand for brothers . . .

And now a nephew.

Arch and Cooper flew from New Orleans to Denver, where Uncle Peyton lived. They worked out at the Broncos facility. Peyton also got Clyde Christensen, a longtime NFL offensive coach who'd worked with him in Indianapolis and Tom Brady in Tampa Bay, to send private videos of Brady's practices, melding the best of Manning's theories with Brady's techniques, two legends funneling into a boy. Peyton texted them to Stewart, telling him to run those drills. There were dozens of video clips. Both uncles tried not to impose, although once he was on a football field, Peyton couldn't help it if he saw Arch doing something that could be done better. But if Arch happened to *ask* for help, look out. When Arch left for college, he once texted Peyton a question about two-minute offense. Understand: You don't just text Peyton a quarterback question. Each answer is a varied universe. Peyton knew that he couldn't possibly type a reply; he had too much to say. Plus, Arch rarely texted him back. "The text response rate," Peyton says, "is not super high. It's not a great completion percentage." He deployed a device of the middle-aged man: the voice memo.

Peyton replied with a seven-minute voice memo about the hurry-up offense, about the plays that he liked and what he wanted to call. Then he hung up only to realize he'd forgotten to mention a few things. Like how defenses tended to call exotic blitzes after time-outs. That required a six-minute explanation. Then he realized he didn't touch on red-zone two-minute offense. So it went.

"I'm sure as soon as he texts me a question he regrets it," Peyton says.

Eli was different, of course. He'd watch Arch and text: *Hey, did they roll to Cover Two and you tried to force an out route, where you should've worked it to the three-receiver side?* Arch: *Yes, exactly.* It was a sacred circle.

———

Arch visited Clemson twice, Alabama four times, Georgia four times, Texas four times, Ole Miss a few times, LSU, and even Virginia. Of all places, Cooper liked Virginia for his son for one reason: It wasn't a football-crazy school. He could live under the radar. His older sister, May, was a student there. As Cooper and Arch walked through campus, the father saw an opportunity for something close to peacefulness. "You could come here, be a normal guy," Cooper told him. "No one's gonna mess with you."

They did mess with Nelson Stewart. In 2021, he had four full-time jobs: coaching football, teaching, managing Arch, and managing the Mannings, in all their iterations. All except Eli were intense, in their own way. Cooper wasn't a classic quarterback dad, but he was learning fast and wasn't afraid to be cutthroat. Peyton would sometimes hop on the phone with Stewart after games, going through play-calling, and then would follow up a day later wondering if the school needed any donations. Eli, meanwhile, would purchase thousands of dollars of equipment for Newman without telling anyone. New shoulder pads would just show up.

Stewart's own family was squeezed into the margins. He taught five classes a day. Visiting coaches learned his schedule. Tuesdays at 10 a.m., Stewart's job was to watch Newman's pre-K kids on the playground where little Arch had once played. College coaches, with nothing better to do, pitched in. Pete Golding, then Alabama's defensive coordinator, pushed kids on the swings. So did Bill O'Brien, then the Tide's offensive coordinator. Texas coach Steve Sarkisian showed Arch the play sheet from Alabama's national championship over Ohio State when he was a Crimson Tide assistant. Golding would FaceTime Sarkisian from Stewart's office, just to tweak him. Brian Polian, who was associate athletic director at LSU at the time, stopped by one day wearing Arch's number 16 jersey and reminding everyone that his dad, Hall of Fame general manager Bill, had drafted Peyton.

Arch was in the middle of a career at Newman, surrounded by a bunch of marginal Class 2A players. Good dudes and future doctors and lawyers and hedge fund managers, but not NFL players. One of the primary things he wanted out of a college was a program with top talent; he never wanted to look across the line of scrimmage and see a more talented opponent. "I want to be with guys that are really hungry, really driven," Arch said.

Only one coach was told to not waste his time: Dabo Swinney of Clemson. Stewart pulled Arch aside one day to tell him that Swinney was visiting that week. Arch looked worried; Swinney could *talk*. When Uncle Eli was being recruited, he took a different approach than Peyton: If he knew he wasn't going to go to a certain school, he told the coach right away. Better to not waste anyone's time. That night, Stewart got a call from a Clemson assistant coach.

"We're out," he said.

"What?" Stewart said.

"The kid's great, but he called me and said he didn't want Dabo to fly all the way down if he wasn't going to go there."

The Mannings didn't go out of their way to thank Stewart for the long hours, and he didn't expect them to. It was part of his job. He was a coach. But Arch was grateful.

Cops, doctors, friends, everyone wanted to know: Could Arch actually do it? Was he for real? Yes, Stewart insisted. Ever the offensive lineman, Stewart tried to protect his quarterback, lead-blocking through fans after games to get Arch to his car. Other times, the backup quarterback, Christian Sauska, would come out and claim to be Arch and pose for selfies. Never in the history of humankind has it been easier to check a face, famous or otherwise, yet people fell for it. Cooper's plan to keep Arch away from social media and the press helped keep Arch sane, but it had an accidental consequence. "He became more of an enigma," Stewart says. Who *was* Arch Manning? What was he *really* thinking?

Stewart told college coaches that he was a good guy. Whenever they tried to pull any inside information from Stewart, he would shrug. He had no idea which college Arch preferred. That left the coaches to their own devices, all of these maladjusted texting addicts. One day Golding took a photo of his dip cup on Nelson's desk and texted it to Sarkisian, his buddy: "Guess where I am?" Sark started to freak out, and with nowhere else to deposit his nerves, he rapid-texted Stewart. On another day, Sarkisian pranked Kiffin by saying that he'd spoken with Arch at least one hundred times. Sure enough, Kiffin exploded on the other end of the phone.

What they were witnessing and participating in was simply too big for any of them. One day, someone sent Stewart a link. It was for an Arch Manning autographed football. The price: $957. It was almost impossible for him to process. He showed it to Cooper, who shook his head and lamented.

"Put my last name on it . . ."

On a winter morning, the Hurleys eat breakfast at Louie's Cafe in Baton Rouge. Colin orders scrambled eggs and a biscuit, part of his 5,000-calorie daily diet, and talks about how the psychological aspect of quarterbacking will prepare him for life after football, whether that's in two or fifteen years.

"I want to be a judge," he says.

High school quarterback can be a launching pad across disciplines, except for president of the United States—none of them were ever high school quarterbacks. But all kinds of jobs are populated with those who spent a portion of high school under center. A number of things make determining the first star high school quarterback complicated and cloudy, most of all that high schools and colleges often played one another into the early twentieth century. Frank Ridley Jr. of Park High in LaGrange, Georgia, might have been the first, during the 1900 season. He ended up at University of Georgia and was elected captain two years in a row, becoming the "only middle classman ever thus honored." In 1905, he was elected president of the senior class of the Atlanta College of Physicians and Surgeons. He was the start of something.

Musicians Sam Hunt, Darius Rucker, and Scott Weiland, no strangers to leading a band, all played high school quarterback. So did politicians Jack Kemp, who was a star in the NFL, J. C. Watts, who played in the CFL, and Tommy Tuberville, who was moved to safety in college. Actor Mark Harmon, the son of a Heisman

Trophy–winning quarterback, played at Harvard-Westlake and was a two-year starter at UCLA, leading the Bruins to an upset of two-time defending national champion Nebraska. James Caan was class president and quarterback at Rhodes Prep in New York City, and played for a year at Michigan State. Phil Robertson was good enough at North Caddo High in Louisiana to become the starter at Louisiana Tech, where he later quit after an underclassman named Terry Bradshaw beat him out. Josh Duhamel was once asked if he got more women as a quarterback or in Hollywood, which he declined to answer. Mike Smith, who piloted the *Challenger*, and Admiral Richard E. Boyd, who was once named the world's top explorer and adventurer, were both high school quarterbacks. So was Jamie Foxx, who has said that he wishes that everyone could feel what it's like to be under center and have everyone love you. Taylor Swift's relationship with Travis Kelce, a dopey but charismatic future Hall of Fame tight end for the Kansas City Chiefs, makes more sense when you realize that he was a quarterback at Cleveland Heights High.

Becoming a judge is a nice idea, but Charlie's mind is on next year, when his son will enter a gauntlet on campus. Quarterback meeting rooms, where they gather and study film, have strange dynamics, seven or so kids vying for one job. All were promised something, even if just a chance to compete. It's a business, with little guidance. Quarterbacks aren't rooting for one another, and they're often taught and trained to be overly competitive, neurotic preeners in a contest to out-alpha one another at mundane tasks. In private, they often talk about how frustrating it is to be recognized everywhere—and how they seethe when they're *not* recognized. In class, some professors respect athletes, others look down on them, seeing the college football enterprise for what it is, not that it's the kids' fault. At Michigan, Tom Brady would make a point to wear nothing that indicated that he played football and would sit in the front row and introduce himself to his professors without ever mentioning that he was a quarterback. That luxury is long gone. When Colin enters LSU, he will be known.

"I want him to struggle," Charlie says. "I'm not going to be here with him in a year. He needs to learn how to handle all of that."

When Colin announced on social media that he would attend LSU, his direct messages lit up. Many were from girls. Some of the photos were so racy that Colin showed them to Charlie, prompting a laugh. "That right there is kryptonite," Charlie said. "It'll ruin everything."

"I'm not gonna ruin anything," Colin said and grinned.

But this is the way he's learning relationships. Offerings of service, in rapid succession, available at a keystroke, all for his ability to throw. Imagine if Bob Waterfield or Joe Namath had Instagram. As it was, all Namath had to do was *arrive*. "You almost start accepting it," he once said. "You almost start thinking that's the way things are now. The way it is." The fact that Hurley will enter college so young, in a state where the age of consent is defined as 17 and up, has caused the Louisiana State football staff to consider his dating options. When Colin arrives on campus, it will be the job of a football staffer to shadow him at parties until his seventeenth birthday.

All of this worries Charlie, a natural worrier. "There's no guarantee," he says.

"I'm guaranteeing myself," Colin replies.

The bones scare the hell out of John Elway. He's standing in the end zone, during what feels like the longest television time-out ever, in the 1986 AFC Championship Game in Cleveland, Broncos trailing 20–13. His left ankle aches. Denver is at the two-yard line with 5:28 left. At this moment, Elway has completed barely half of his passes. That area of Cleveland Municipal Stadium, the east end, is called the Dawg Pound. There are benches rather than seats, an area designed to be affordable, giving blue-collar fans the kind of proximity to the field that is normally reserved for the wealthy. Fans throw stuff: batteries, snowballs, ice chunks, dog bones. Every now and then, a bone hits Elway in the helmet, a ring and echo that mainlines straight to his psyche. It's Elway's fourth year in the NFL, and while he's had some success, he knows what fans know: "I hadn't done anything." It's time to deliver.

Waiting for play to resume, Elway manufactures belief the quickest and easiest way: straight to the clichés and the platitudes. *When you're behind, there's only upside.* Of course, his job would be easier if he only had to worry about himself. He has a huddle, looking at him for hope. He knows that if he doesn't believe, his teammates won't either, so he has to figure out a sequence of—let's just call it what it is—bullshit that manages to just be plausible enough to get everyone to the line of scrimmage with a semblance of confidence, or at the very least, marginally less doubt. Quarterbacks often joke about this aspect of the job: the art of stirring up hope, even outright feigning it. And now Elway gets lucky: An offensive guard does the believing—and bullshitting—for him. Keith Bishop tells the other Broncos, "We got them right where we want them."

Everyone laughs. Still, the quarterback has to say *something*.

Elway tells the guys, "We have a long way to go, so let's get going. Do whatever it takes, and something good will happen."

Whatever it takes.

——————

Something has been missing in the nine times Colin Hurley has visited LSU, even after he committed to attend: a campus tour. He has only been to the football offices. After breakfast, Colin and Charlie hop in a golf cart for a look around the school. Patrick Kelly, son of head coach Brian, is behind the wheel. As they wait at an intersection, a trolley carrying students to class passes.

"There you go, Colin," Charlie says. "I'm going to move out here and get a trolley-driver job."

"Oh hell no," Colin says.

Charlie is going to miss his kid. He knows it. In some ways, Colin already seems gone. After I told Charlie that Tom Brady Sr. saw a therapist after his son left for Michigan, Charlie signed up for counseling, twice a week, as a preemptive measure. For Christmas before Colin's final year of high school, Colin gave his dad a puppy to keep him company when the son left for college. They named him Deuce, after Colin's jersey number.

First stop on the tour: Mike the Tiger. An *actual tiger*, housed in open air, behind glass walls, right by the stadium. Colin hops out of the cart and peers in wonder through glass.

They snake through campus. Patrick parks to the side of a large white building, with tall picture windows.

"Student union," Patrick says. "There's food. You can study here. Events you can watch, seminars. It's a mall."

Girls pass, drawing Colin's eyes.

"You'll be that guy," Patrick tells Colin. "It's good for you to reach out, to be part of the student body."

For as long as quarterback has been a thing, one of the traditionally cool aspects of it is being a big man on campus. When Peyton Manning was growing up in the Garden District of New Orleans, listening to tapes of the radio calls of his dad's games, he wanted to be a *college* quarterback. He was in a rush his first three years at Tennessee, serious and driven, the fast track of the motivated, earning a degree and becoming the consensus first pick in the draft. In 1997, he could have left for the NFL, but he decided that he wanted to *remember* college. He didn't want to be forty-eight years old and not know. His senior year, the Volunteers beat Alabama, and someone asked him if he wanted to conduct the band. He had never heard that question before, never had that thought before, but he knew that it was important, and that he was in college for stuff like *this*. He hiked up the director's ladder in front of the band section of the stadium and started conducting "Rocky Top." Cameras followed. He was at the center of something fleeting and precious that existed not in high school ball, and certainly not in the NFL, and he thought he was doing a pretty good job of directing, who knows, maybe unearthing a second calling . . . until he looked down and realized that the conductor was below him, and the band was following that guy's cue.

Quarterback is so big now that maybe it's better to be a shortstop if a semblance of a classic, merely warped celebrity college experience—where you skip the lines to bars, strangers hand you drinks, and you own the school—is what you want. The complexity of the game quarterbacks need to excel at, and the sophistication of the stage on which they need to do it, has never been higher. And yet, in some fundamental way, it's never seemed less real, less instinctive, less open to improvisation, less receptive of detours, of quirks, of the virtue of these years as anything except a moving walkway.

They steer themselves toward LSU sororities, near a lake and winding roads that hug campus, streets that subtly but quickly curve and intersect, lined by oak trees old and strong.

"This is where they hold Bible study," Charlie says.

"Did I also mention the ratio on campus?" Patrick says.

"We know about it," Colin says.

Fifty-four percent women, forty-four percent men. Colin is unfazed. He knows that's the ratio for regular students.

———

First play: Elway hits running back Sammy Winder on a flair outside for a few yards. Two plays later, Denver grinds out a first down. This will go down as one of the greatest two-minute drives in NFL history, but for most of it, Denver isn't in a hurry. The Broncos huddle and chug, until midfield. An incomplete pass on first down, a sack for an eight-yard loss on second. Third-and-18, with 1:47 left. Time-out. Dan Reeves tells Elway to take a short throw if it's there, and to try to pick up the rest on fourth down, classic conservative coach fare.

That triggers something primal in Elway. He wants it all—the full eighteen. This is what he's been created for. He isn't sure how he'll do it, only that he will. It's a rare mental place, some lucid combination of evidence-based confidence—the comebacks at Granada

Hills, fourth-and-18 against Cal—with a tool kit both generational and irreducible. The play itself—3 Scat X Post Z Dagger—is only a suggested theory, a base for Elway to begin from, and it ends up a half inch from disaster: Elway sends receiver Steve Watson in motion, trying to time the motion with the silent snap count, an idea cooked up in the early eighties by legendary offensive line coach Howard Mudd to combat crowd noise. It doesn't work. Elway realizes the ball is going to be snapped a fraction of a second too soon, right into Watson. He tries to wave off the center, hoping he sees it, hoping that he'll hold off, but it's too late. The ball is snapped—and trickles off Watson's ass as he trots by. Elway gets lucky: the ball pops up, then sharply back down, but generally continues its trajectory, fluttering toward him, wounded but on track. Ball in hands, fingers finding the laces and a suitable grip, Elway sees receiver Mark Jackson holing up past the sticks. Something pure happens next, a fusion of opportunity and gift. He's coming of age before everyone's eyes. He throws a ball that must have the least arc ever for a pass of that distance, 29 yards in the air, 20 in the stat sheet, into Jackson's stomach. First down.

The throw raises a question beyond whether it's the most vital of Elway's career. Does anything else in quarterbacking matter if God gave you the ability to do *that*? What follows is an adrenaline rush, the freedom of knowing that if shit goes sideways, it won't matter. "I know how to throw," Elway tells me, recalling that moment. "I'm *supposed* to do that. You don't compare to someone else. You just think you can do it better than anybody else. When you do it, it's like, well, you expected to do it."

When Caleb Williams decided to become a quarterback—decided he would become the greatest *ever*—and participate, self-consciously so, within the context of a machinery, Carl searched YouTube. He spoke with local coaches who fashioned themselves as specialists. Something about the entire racket bothered him. He felt preyed upon. What he wanted for Caleb as much as a path was what he calls "a protective village." He found one in Russell Thomas and Mark McCain, two longtime friends opening their own training facility.

Caleb arrived for regular morning workouts at 5:30 a.m. He threw tennis balls for accuracy, pulled the resistance bands, and worked on rotational drills. Thomas and McCain coached him in youth ball and ran a passing offense. When he was effective, they encouraged him. When he was careless, they benched him. "We didn't just teach him how to play quarterback, but how to *be* a quarterback," Thomas says.

At home, Carl set the thermostat in Caleb's room to sixty-eight degrees, which he had read was the optimal temperature for proper rest. Caleb's diet consisted of clean foods. He swam for all-around strength and attended hot yoga for all-around flexibility. At one point, Caleb's mother, Dayna, signed him up for dance class to increase footspeed. Carl tried to not pressure his son, but to empower him by taking him at his word. Once, Caleb didn't want to get out of bed to go to the gym, expecting Carl to pull the blankets off as a rallying cry. Carl didn't. "Cool, I'm going back to bed," he said instead. Caleb popped up, his competitive fires lit.

Sometimes the grind wore on him. Caleb would tell Russ, "My dad gets on my nerves." But by eighth grade, local high schools started to recruit him. Carl decided on Gonzaga College High

School, four blocks north of the Capitol. Caleb wasn't tall as a freshman—five-foot-nine at the time—but his talent was evident. Gonzaga's head coach, Randy Trivers, called Carl to his office before the season. "I may lose my job over this," the coach said. "But we're gonna start Caleb as the quarterback."

Caleb gave Trivers a kind of feeling, something he felt when he watched Jeter or Jordan on television. A presence. A seeming faith in himself. A precious obliviousness and a scary intensity. Trivers knew that he had put Caleb in a tough spot. Teammates would dismiss him if he didn't have answers. Trivers told Caleb to work harder in the weight room, just so that teammates would see him trying to get stronger. He sat with Caleb in his office, going through the offense, then quizzing him on it. That way, when Trivers looked to Caleb for answers in front of the team, they both knew that he'd ace it.

Then the season started, and Caleb underwhelmed, a precocious slow starter. But in the fourth quarter of games, something would click for him. Sophomore year, Gonzaga fell behind in the conference championship game 20–0 to DeMatha. Williams helped them claw back. With four seconds left, Gonzaga was down 43–40, around midfield. Trivers called a Hail Mary. Williams dropped back, on a fractured ankle, and threw 60 yards into a pile of players. . . . It was caught, for a walk-off title. "Working his magic," Trivers says.

Colleges started to hover. But Carl entered Trivers's office one day with something bigger on his mind.

"We're trying to put him in position to be the first pick of the draft," Carl told Trivers.

Ambition, hubris, a willingness to envision a certain landscape— Carl was starting to see the whole thing like it had already happened: *Caleb Williams, national champion.*

Caleb Williams, Heisman winner.
Caleb Williams, first overall draft pick.
Caleb Williams, the future.
"Carl!" Thomas yelled at him one day. "Shut the fuck up!"

––––––––––

John Elway is inefficient, following up completions with incompletions, but he's in a realm beyond statistics and traditional measures of effectiveness. He follows the strike to Mark Jackson with a pass out of bounds to stop the clock. He connects on a screen for fourteen yards. The Browns crowd, once defiant, is now struggling to not be submissive. Elway can sense the energy drop; he'll miss that feeling decades later. First down: He takes a shot to the end zone; just wide. Second-and-10: He runs right for nine, sliding in the mud. Third-and-one, from the five-yard line, Elway calls Blitz Quick 62 Rub. It's a play designed to get a first down, a quick pass to the left flat. Maybe a touchdown, if they're lucky. Elway drops back and stares left. His first read is covered, so he dials a few degrees inside to Jackson on a slant, finally cuts off his drop and throws a strike low and away. Touchdown. What Elway has engineered will go down in history as The Drive. Denver will win in overtime. But Elway isn't merely doing his job. He's transforming, becoming something else. Browns tight end Ozzie Newsome stands on the sideline, a future Hall of Famer in his own right, and sees a kind of a device, of faith and art and optimism, of *belief*. He points to Elway and says to the staffer nearest him:

"We don't have one of *those*."

––––––––––

The circuit took Caleb and Carl across the country, costing Carl north of $80,000. He felt underwhelmed by what the quarterback machine had to offer.

They attended Football University in Atlanta. Its recommendation for Caleb: increase his football IQ and strengthen his arm. That pissed off Carl. It was vague. Plus: football IQ? Look at Caleb's low interception totals. Arm strength? "This fucker's arm was the strongest!" Carl said.

Caleb became a five-star quarterback, the highest rating given to a high school athlete. He wanted more. He and his dad were on a mission to force the world to see what they saw, to bend this strange universe to their will. Caleb would look for his name in recruiting rankings. If he wasn't listed first, he wasn't listed high enough. Carl knew that it wasn't enough to be ranked high. After all, Caleb was Black. The NFL had come a long way since Shack Harris's career had hinged on whether he hit that tree, but not far enough.

"You need all the stuff Peyton Manning does," Carl told Caleb. "All the stuff that Brady does. All the stuff these other white guys do. But you've gotta be the premier athlete. You've gotta become a different kind of athlete." Speed, power, agility, resistance, accuracy, over and over. Carl hired a local communication specialist to train Caleb for the media. Caleb watched quarterbacks he admired, mixing aspects of their game into his own. Aaron Rodgers, with his quick and powerful arm. Patrick Mahomes, how he'd contort his body and release point to account for and match the situation. Russell Wilson, how he'd run and react. Caleb watched YouTube clips of Doug Flutie scrambling around in the mid-eighties. He studied receivers and running backs, hunting for open-field moves to steal. Word spread nationally of a quarterback out of the District, a place not known for producing them. At the QB Collective camp in

Southern California, Green Bay Packers head coach Matt LaFleur watched Williams throw, turned to Will Hewlett, who was a camp counselor, and asked, "Who the fuck is *that*?"

Hewlett had worked with Williams for a few years. He thought Williams was better than Bryce Young, who was a peer on the quarterback circuit and an eventual first overall draft pick. Williams *cared*, in a way that Hewlett knew was rare. He would text Hewlett self-filmed videos of his practice throws, sometimes seventy at a time.

After QB Collective, Carl and Caleb sat in silence as they drove to the airport. Caleb blurted out, "I need more."

"More what?"

"I need more of *that*."

More of what QB Collective offered: More learning about Mike Shanahan's offense, which by then half the league was running. More instruction of how to read NFL defenses. More NFL stuff. It clarified to Caleb what mattered most. He deleted "five-star" from his social media bios. When people found him, they'd know. More than eighty college coaches visited Caleb at school. His grades suffered. Carl was livid that coaches who arrived in jets couldn't read a class schedule. He instituted a rule: Catch Caleb during lunch or not at all. "Shut that shit down," he says.

When it came time to choose a school, Caleb worked backward from the goal of greatest ever. He developed a spreadsheet called "Caleb University Criteria." He ranked fourteen schools by weighted inputs. There were four buckets, comprised of subcategories: academics, athletics, preparation, intangibles. Athletics was 45 percent. Among the categories under it were the stability of the head coach and of the offensive coordinator, the staff's relationships with NFL teams, the sophistication of its offense—"full-field reads, changing protections"—and commitment to developing quarterbacks.

Lincoln Riley, a brilliant college offensive mind who'd produced consecutive Heisman Trophy–winning quarterbacks and first over-all draft picks in Baker Mayfield and Kyler Murray, was Oklahoma's head coach. Caleb liked Riley, liked how he didn't call every day. He chose Oklahoma.

Caleb started behind Spencer Rattler as a freshman in 2021. The night before the Sooners played Texas in early October, Carl told Caleb, "I feel like tomorrow is going to be the day."

"Me too."

Rattler turned the ball over twice early, leading to two Texas touchdowns. Riley switched to Williams. Before he ran onto the field, Caleb found receiver Jalil Farooq, one of his best friends.

"The Legend of Caleb begins," he said.

Cameras greet Colin Hurley in the lobby of a Manhattan Beach hotel. He stops and a crewmember asks to wire him for sound. This week each year—mid-June—is one of the biggest events on the high school quarterback junket: the annual Elite 11 competition. Twenty finalists are here, from high schools around country. Colin is the youngest ever.

Elite 11 fashions itself as America's premier place for spotting generational talent in its infancy, a *Mickey Mouse Club* for quarter-backs. What started in 1999 as a regional competition has turned into a national rite of passage. Trent Dilfer directed the program for a few years and turned it into a reality show. A good but never great pro quarterback himself, Dilfer invented catchphrases and descriptors for the overlooked ingredients of quarterbacking prowess, like DQ—Dude Quality—and LTA—Load-to-Arrival, the split second between when a quarterback decides to throw and when the ball arrives at his target. The list of Elite 11 alumni includes impact college stars and first overall draft picks, such as Matthew Stafford and Kyler Murray. The program calls itself a "showcase," an essential part of the quarterback economy.

As with many in this circuit, Elite 11 is well-intentioned, and it's better run than most, but imprecise. It provides high school quarterbacks a platform to conduct an array of drills with no predictive value. It's noncontact; quarterbacks throw to receivers with but a vague notion of a defense in the vicinity, the twin fears of pain and danger removed. Aaron Rodgers attended Elite 11 years ago, not as a high school kid but as a future Hall of Famer. He was blown away by how well the quarterbacks threw, but wondered whether they'd experience the kind of adversity required to steel yourself for the job. As a skinny senior at Pleasant Valley High in Chico, California, Rodgers sifted through online rankings of quarterbacks, seething at the names. He received a letter from a Purdue University assistant that read, "Good luck with your attempt at a college football career." Now he can draw a straight line from that moment of being doubted to a career's worth of proving everyone wrong.

Several star NFL quarterbacks weren't invited to the Elite 11 finals when they were in high school: Rodgers, Josh Allen, Lamar Jackson, Russell Wilson, Matt Ryan, Tony Romo. Patrick Mahomes of Whitehouse High in Whitehouse, Texas—the most physically gifted quarterback in a generation—failed to qualify for the Elite 11 finals. He showed up at a regional tournament in Texas but didn't advance. His coach was pissed. His dad, Patrick Sr., was *really* pissed.

SETH WICKERSHAM

When I ask Mahomes about it, I wonder how angry he was and maybe still is over it—if it became the clichéd chip on his shoulder that helped propel future greatness, like Tom Brady's draft slide or Drew Brees's shoulder injury or Rodgers's atypical path, something that becomes lore in retrospect.

"East Texas isn't known for producing quarterbacks," he says with a shrug. "I was never really on the football circuit."

Everything that has made Mahomes great in college and the NFL—an adaptable release point, immortal processing power, a willingness to absorb hits in service of a completed pass—worked against him in this space. "That setting didn't highlight what he did well," says Adam Cook, Mahomes's quarterback coach at Whitehouse. "The way he can extend the play, the way he can get you two to three more seconds. Those things you can't see in a combine."

If Elite 11 had noticed those skills, of course, history might have been different. Powerhouse schools would have recruited him, rather than the programs that did: Texas Tech, Rice, and Houston. "There's no telling what recruiting would have been like," Cook says. But then Mahomes might not have become Mahomes, author of the impossible. Attending Texas Tech and playing somewhat under the radar in the wild Big 12 provided the quarterback version of free play. He got to throw and screw up and throw again and learn and develop. It was a gift. Brady conditioned himself at Michigan to believe that a mistake in practice meant that he would sit on game day. Mahomes essentially had permission to throw as many interceptions as he wanted. He learned to play without fear.

Each Elite 11 2023 finalist submitted a personal essay. Most wrote a paragraph or two. Colin Hurley's was five pages, with photos. He called it "Me: Who Am I, Anyway?" and described his life and his love for football, his parents and coaches—and his signature hair. He wrote that he loved that football "lets me be me. . . . I can be comfortable in my own skin." Is he performing a kind of confidence? Is it the exact kind of self-knowledge and self-belief foreign to most of us but innate in the greats? Elite 11 counselors tell Colin that his essay was the best of his class. Wired up, he hops on a bus and heads to Redondo Union High, where the first day of competition takes place. Who he is, anyway, won't be answered.

———

The legend of Caleb left Oklahoma before it became legend. When Lincoln Riley bolted for USC in 2022, Williams followed him.

In his first season, Williams accounted for at least four touchdowns in eight of the Trojans' fourteen games. Riley rarely permits his quarterbacks to call plays—he wants them to execute—but against Utah in October, he allowed Williams a measure of freedom. Williams saw that Utah was going to have unblocked rushers from the right side. He checked from a pass to a run left. If Williams could get running back Travis Dye the ball fast enough, he thought, USC would essentially render the free rushers moot and have more offensive players than defensive players—and an easy touchdown. Quarterbacks often talk about plays in terms of looking for a numerical advantage, a situational edge in which the offense has one more player in space than the defense. Dye took the ball and ran left, scoring from eight yards out. Williams raised his fist; this would be the play from 2022, his Heisman year, that he was proudest of. He felt at the height of his powers, and yet he was spreading the ball around, sharing glory, providing the same feeling to his teammates that Shack Harris did when he called their number so that they'd get their name in the paper.

Life tightened around Caleb, a mania he had envisioned but couldn't truly prepare for. Carl had first noticed it the previous year, at the Alamo Bowl against Oregon. Carl and Dayna were at the hotel bar the night before the game. Caleb pulled up a seat. Carl noticed that his son kept looking over his shoulder. "Dad," he said. "I gotta go."

A line had formed, waiting for Caleb to sign and pose and bless them with a few seconds of time. Caleb started to order room service, eating alone. Fans and TMZ soon waited for him at airports. He tried to outfox them by exiting airports at Departures rather than Arrivals. He noticed how people tried to sneak photos of him, holding their cameras vaguely in his direction. He'd pose anyway. When they'd ask him to take pictures of them, he'd flip the camera to himself and take photos of his own face. He enlisted Smith & Company, a strategy firm, to manage his business portfolios and endorsements like Beats by Dre headphones. He pitched products on *Good Morning America*. He insisted that his teammates have a role in commercials, like Tom Brady once did with his linemen. By July of 2022, he was USC's first multimillionaire quarterback. He had yet to take a snap there.

Williams didn't party at frat houses. He lived in a high rise, with views of downtown. Carl ordered condoms in bulk, knowing that the only things that could derail Caleb's career were a bad injury or a bad relationship. "If something's gonna happen," he told his son, "I'd rather you be protected and safe."

In late 2022, Caleb and Coach Riley separately attended a Rams game at SoFi Stadium, watching from different suites. Caleb wanted to visit Riley, and Riley texted him a location pin. When Caleb arrived, he had a security detail and a gaggle of fans behind him.

Riley had played quarterback at Texas Tech around the turn

of the century, and he was like thousands of quarterbacks before him: a sort of hometown hero, married to town and school. What was happening to Williams was something else altogether. "Take five million people at home, 100,000 in a stadium, watching a game and every moment, every single snap of every game, most people, unless they're the right tackle's family, are watching this one guy," Riley says. The coach tried to find small ways to take pressure off Caleb, hoping to not overwhelm him, reminding him that no matter what fans or the press think, a quarterback is only "one-eleventh of how the group's gonna perform." He read *The Inner Game of Tennis* by W. Timothy Gallwey, a book about how to quiet doubt, and gave it to the quarterbacks to read, hoping that they—especially Caleb—would see themselves in it, sharpening their skillsets and confidence so that they could feel liberated and unincumbered on game day. Caleb listened to some of it on audio. He might finish it someday.

The night of the Heisman, there was a waiting room where finalists could pose for pictures with a replica trophy. Williams watched the others huddle around it. "My trophy," he said quietly. He received 544 first-place votes for the Heisman. C. J. Stroud of Ohio State received 37. It was one of the most decisive Heisman wins ever. When he got back to LA after the ceremony, he put his Heisman on a shelf and dangled a pair of Beats from its arm.

———

When Charlie Hurley arrived at Elite 11, he glanced at the three-day schedule. Only one event was in all-caps and bolded, and it wasn't the final contest, or a throwing competition at all: **PARENT MEETING**.

Charlie attended it. The point was to help their sons and themselves navigate a jungle, but the subtext was to save parents from themselves, to let go of all the hardwired urges to control every aspect of their son's career. Charlie left the meeting with the rest of the parents, all learning on the go.

"So cool," he says.

Charlie jotted notes on his hands. "Being/Doing" is scribbled on the back of his left hand. The speakers urged the parents to try to separate who the kids are from what they do, so that their entire identity wouldn't be wrapped up in being a quarterback, all of that you-are-not-your-job stuff that any ambitious person knows is useless. The version of ego required to be a successful quarterback—required to reach Elite 11—is uniquely ill-equipped to traverse such distinctions.

The Elite 11 book *5-Star QB* is filled with firsthand accounts of its contestants, the vast majority of whom came up short of their dreams. I read them all, feeling a vague kinship to those whose dreams were crushed. Dylan McCaffrey's hit me hardest. His family is loaded with exceptional athletes. His grandfather, David Sime, won a silver medal in the 100-meter dash at the 1960 Olympics and made the cover of *Sports Illustrated* in 1956. His father, Ed McCaffrey, won three Super Bowl rings as an NFL receiver. His mom, Lisa, started at Stanford in soccer. His brother, Christian McCaffrey, became an NFL superstar running back. Until Dylan left for college, he appeared to be the most talented family member, at the most coveted position. He had earned a scholarship to Michigan, figuring that it was a layover on the way to the NFL and its spoils. Something went wrong, which he's still sorting out today. McCaffrey never started a game for the Wolverines. When he interviewed for *5-Star QB*, he had graduated from Northern Colorado, salvaging a college career with no grand designs for the next level. He spoke with the perspective of scars and knowledge: of what it was like to enter a crowded quarterback room, of what it was like to go to class, of what it was like to be benched, of what it was like to go to a therapist. The wounds felt fresh, all these years later.

The book itself is a giant premonition to Charlie Hurley, all of the ways a fragile dream can go sideways. What other elements can he control? Or try to control? He puts it on paper. Elite 11 gave parents an assignment: write a letter to their son. Charlie cries as he writes. He tells Colin that he takes "every breath" for him, that his son is "my hero," his "first thought, and final thought, of my every day." Each paragraph ends with "You are ELITE." *Being* and *doing* feel closer than ever.

Charlie arrives at the first day of Elite 11, settling into an empty row halfway up the bleachers at Redondo Union High. He likes to perch high, where Colin won't feel his presence.

"I'm not one of those dads," he says.

He's surrounded by those dads, and moms, most wearing at least one article of clothing from their son's school. Michigan. Notre Dame. Alabama. Penn State. Georgia. Charlie has LSU shorts. On the field, quarterbacks warm up. Music plays. Older alums filter in. Matt Leinart, USC's Heisman Trophy winner, with his son Cole—a high school quarterback, of course. Jordan Palmer, an NFL quarterback and now a specialist. Everyone wants to be the next Elway; some believe they already are. Charlie has noticed something over his years on the quarterback circuit that mirrors what a lot of coaches and football observers privately say: that this entire racket is a breeding ground for entitled young men who expect the world to revolve around them. Elite 11 is "basically collecting little assholes," says a veteran of the showcase.

Quarterbacking is full of them. Johnny Manziel and Ryan Leaf were abject train wrecks, though both eventually straightened out their lives. Peyton Manning was a pitiless perfectionist; he once ordered a player out of the huddle on a kneel-down because the player had jumped offside on the prior drive. Michael Vick treated everyone but the team owner with indifference. Yogi Roth of Elite 11 was once asked to define quarterbacks, and he equated them to models, ravaged by fragility and insecurity. That mindset rarely ends where the white lines do.

Reporters from across the country fly to cover it. A film crew is on hand. An old man in the stands recites the Emancipation Proclamation as he critiques throwing motions. Maybe Elite 11 prepares them well for being a quarterback. Artifice is as real a part of the job as throwing the deep out. How one deals with it is arguably more important.

Charlie leans forward as Colin steps up to take snaps.

"He goes first," Charlie says.

What does a life based on continual destinations and aspirations and development, not to mention the conditional nature of it all, do to a guy? I spent much of 2022 with an Elite 11 alum: Andrew Luck, who was once considered a generational prospect and was drafted first overall by the Colts in 2012 to replace Peyton Manning. He wasn't a little asshole, but he had it in him to be one. He learned quickly that greatness requires an undefined and unlimited selfishness. There's no punchlist or road map. You have to figure it out. Not every quarterback has the ruthlessness required to silo his life and put family to the side, in pursuit of a singular goal, of which he has only nominal control. Luck arrived in the NFL with scant awareness that the best quarterbacks are often maniacal and fragile, controlling and pouty, both the only adult in the room and a grown child. Most of them don't question what they're doing and what it's turning them into, lest the exercise itself threaten their identity and pierce the story they tell themselves. Luck had always been different: He couldn't mine himself enough. He spends more time in his own head than any quarterback I've ever met, pondering, probing, deciding, reconsidering, on decisions big and small. Early in his career, Luck chatted with Anthony Castonzo, his left tackle, about the requirements of great quarterbacks. "You have to believe that you are God's gift to the world, or else doubt will start to come in," Castonzo said.

Luck was uncomfortable making himself God's gift to the world, but he couldn't afford to doubt. Couldn't even entertain it. He was twenty-two years old and coming into a building that was used to the quarterback making organizational decisions. He had to convince himself that he had "some level of control over the outcome." He turned into someone he didn't want to be—or, more precisely, he tapped into a part of his personality that already existed. He ran offensive meetings. He was so involved in blocking and route-running techniques that players nicknamed him the assistant tight ends coach. When people visited his downtown condo and it was getting close to his 9:52 p.m. bedtime during the season, Luck would disappear to the bathroom, brush his teeth, strip to his boxers, tell the group good night—and kill the lights. He simplified his life to extremes, using a flip phone. He turned down most endorsements until he felt that he had accomplished something in the league. Trying to control every variable extended to dinners out with teammates, where he'd order for everyone without being asked. "To play quarterback, you're not allowed to worry about anything except the task at hand," Luck told me. "And that seeps into other areas of life. It's not the healthiest way to live."

Only a few people on the planet could play quarterback as well as he did. He developed his own signature snap count, a weapon—Green 80, Green 80, hut-HUT-hut!—one of those overlooked quarterbacking tools that he loved. "My baby," he often called it. He delivered in critical moments, helping to rally the Colts from a 38–10 third-quarter deficit to beat the Kansas City Chiefs in the playoffs in his second year. In his third season, the Colts reached the AFC Championship Game. A championship, and Luck joining the elite group of immortals, seemed inevitable. Those decisions, his survival mechanisms, his "design," as he calls it, worked. Then, on a third down in the second quarter of the third game of the 2015 season, Luck's fourth, a Tennessee Titans defensive end named Brian Orakpo hit Luck from behind, driving him into the ground and onto his side. Luck hopped up, but he winced. Something was wrong with his right—his passing—shoulder.

A word on pain. Its impact on football players, and quarterbacks, the fear of it, is universal and fundamental to the game and to the gig, and yet it's still often overlooked. The effects of pain go beyond what might require an injection before the game, sometimes even before practice. It affects mood and decision-making and relationships. Even now, there's no way to mask the vulnerability of a quarterback. On most plays, at least four huge men are trying to collide with him. The quarterback can't look at them—the moment you drop your eyes to the rush rather than keep them fixed downfield, it's a death spiral—but he must know where they are, just enough to open his body, planting his feet and exposing his ribs, to deliver the ball through slimming openings. If quarterbacks have been glamorized, so has the destroying of them. NFL Films used to produce VHS collections of hits.

I watched them back when I was a quarterback, and I watch them now. Those videos are the only thing that's successfully erased the individuality of the quarterback. You often couldn't tell who was being hit, couldn't decipher helmet logos and jersey numbers. Was that Steve DeBerg, trampled underfoot? Vinny Testaverde? Tommy Kramer? Neil Lomax? Who cares? What mattered was the blur and crash and noise. The pops and crunches of plastic and bone, followed by two sharp and opposing breaths—the glorious exhale of the defender and the wind getting knocked out of the system of the quarterback—were amplified and distorted and overdubbed. Gruesomeness was the point. The idea of opening your body to throw in the face of a particular kind of cruelty runs counter to every instinct—unless, of course, the urge to place a ball in an incompressible spot outweighs the urge of self-preservation.

You cannot describe what it's like to play quarterback without describing pain, and yet pain, and the threat of it, is so indescribable that even those enduring it can't find the words. I've spent time with injured quarterbacks. I watched Tom Brady nearly fall off a podium platform due to a high-ankle sprain. I listened to Kurt Warner discuss how ligament damage to his *thumb* nearly derailed his career. I nodded as David Carr told me about what it was like to be drafted first overall by the expansion Houston Texans in 2002 and absorb

249 sacks in five years. "You try to rack your brain and ask, 'Why?'" he said. "It was God's plan." He ended up as Eli Manning's backup with the Giants. One day he met Archie, who had spent most of his pro career under duress and in pain.

"I know what you went through, man," Archie told him.

"I'm glad to see you're walking," Carr responded.

There's a strange dismissiveness in the NFL when it comes to injuries, even concussions. I've noticed it in my decades covering the league. Coaches, executives, owners, even agents—all of them are conditioned to move on. If a player, even a quarterback, gets injured, they care—to a point. But there's always a replacement, a guy eager to make the most of his opportunity. Injuries are accepted consequences of this line of work, a tacit trade-off for making millions. In 2022, Tua Tagovailoa of the Miami Dolphins was sacked in a game against the Cincinnati Bengals. His head bounced off the turf. He rolled over, and his arms and fingers were in jagged positions, crossways and bent. Medical experts, and those that play them on television, immediately recognized it as what's called a "fencing response." It was like watching Tagovailoa have a stroke, unnerving and grotesque. Just as there were the familiar prayers for Tagovailoa after the game, there was the familiar outrage and questioning and reconsidering of football.

But within days, all of that talk faded. Tagovailoa returned to play within a month. The league, and owners, have long believed that if they can just get to the next weekend, to the next round of games, to all the excitement and beauty, all will be forgotten. It has served the league well during controversies ranging from Spygate to Ray Rice. Just get to the weekend. Just get to the quarterbacks. The unofficial twin mottos of the NFL.

The quarterback injury that, for me, stands out was in 2007, when I spent a few days with Alex Smith of the 49ers. One evening, he pointed to a brown leather recliner. That's where he slept for a month during the NFL season, facing the flat screen, next to his vanity shelf with trophies and plaques and framed newspaper articles. Smith knew that it was ridiculous that during the greatest physical pain of his life the only place he could find enough comfort to doze off in his 6,500-square-foot home overlooking the Northern California hills wasn't the fancy mattress upstairs, or the plush couches downstairs, or even the other, more rotund loungers sprinkled around, but instead this one.

Hell, he didn't even recline the recliner. He slept upright.

He told me that the 49ers doctors advised him to sleep in it to accelerate the recovery time, after what happened on the third play of the fourth game of that season. Smith had taken a shotgun snap and stared right, before switching left, hoping to catch a receiver on a crossing route. When he turned, Seahawks defensive tackle Rocky Bernard was *on* him. Smith collapsed underneath Bernard's 308 pounds, landing hard on his right shoulder, and felt three internal pops coupled with a relentless, unbearable spasm down his arm. On the sideline, he tried to throw, but his arm wouldn't lift. Within minutes, he was carted off the field, moments away from being diagnosed with a Grade III shoulder separation and resolving to accelerate his rehab so he could return to action sooner. That meant, in part, sleeping upright to lessen the swelling.

But as Smith and I chatted after his season of trying to be honest but then lying, trying to be courageous but then having his toughness questioned—after hours of intense and ultimately evasive attempts to make sense of the NFL's twisted injury culture—Smith was baffled that he had to serve up a recliner as proof that he had actually hurt his shoulder in the first place. Nothing in the NFL is more valued than the ability to play with pain. No one can gain the admiration of a teammate quicker than those who trade their health for a win. Gritting through pain isn't a rarity—every player, in one fashion or another, does it—but *how* they do it determines whether they become eternally revered, or branded as unreliable.

After the 49ers medical staff and reputable doctor James Andrews evaluated Smith's shoulder—a Grade III separation meant that the AC and CC ligaments attaching his shoulder blade to his collarbone, and the surrounding capsule, were torn—they gave him a murky diagnosis: Some play with a Grade III, some don't. Some have surgery, some don't. The good news was that Smith's untethered collarbone hadn't sprung free. If it had, the doctors would have recommended surgery.

Backup quarterback Trent Dilfer, a veteran of eleven separated shoulders, told Smith that his injury wouldn't get better or worse. "If you can handle the pain," Dilfer said, "you can play." Smith took that to heart. "You definitely want to be one of those guys who can get back out there quickly and play through an injury," he told me.

Despite Smith's toughness being celebrated with a game ball after the 2006 season—he was the first quarterback in team history to play every snap—he had yet to truly connect in the locker room since being drafted No. 1 overall out of Utah in 2005, so much so that before the season teammates elected the outgoing Dilfer as a captain, not the reserved Smith. Smith had the gift and curse of self-awareness. When he arrived in San Francisco, he thought he had to be Joe Montana, Steve Young, and Peyton Manning all in one. He had been a straight-A student, and this was the first time he was failing at something. "I felt like I had to be perfect. Kind of became my own worst enemy." He'll never forget how in one week, he went from sitting at the draft, in a suit that barely fit, to a plane to San Francisco, to the practice fields, with every camera aimed at him as he stretched. "It felt claustrophobic," he says now. The infrastructure to help him wasn't there; he would sit in a film room for hours, staring at footage because that's what he thought he had to do, with nobody telling him *how* to watch film—"not even knowing what I was looking at." When games rolled around, he was riddled with insecurity and anxiety. He'd *what-if*-ed himself to paralysis. "I was consumed with self-doubt," he says now. "Like, was I even deserving of the number one pick? Did they make a mistake?... All I did was worry."

Playing hurt is how you speak football. With his arm in a sling, his shoulder shaded purple and so swollen that he couldn't even see the outline of his collarbone, Smith attacked his rehab, adhering to a code. If the trainers advised him to ice the shoulder for two hours a day, Smith did six. The recommended hour of rubber-band exercises became three. When he was allowed to throw 5-yard passes, Smith moved back to 10, 11, 12, 15, and finally 20. He targeted a game against the Giants as a return, meaning he'd miss two weeks, not the usual six to eight. When teammates asked Smith how his shoulder felt, he responded as a tough guy would: "It's fine."

But to practice, Smith had to sit shirtless as the trainers taped down his collarbone—up his armpit, over his shoulder, and as hard as they could pull back down—to ensure that it wouldn't dislodge, and thus require surgery. When Smith threw, he noticed that his forearm spasmed as he wound back, affecting his grip. Smith didn't tell the trainers about it—he didn't want to slow his return—but while rushing to play he'd compressed a nerve. During practice before playing the Giants, he wound back, but his arm locked up, and the ball slipped out of his hand. Next play, a rollout pass, it happened again, leaving Smith clumsily trying to corral a bobbling ball. He walked off the field, humiliated. Then Mike Nolan, the 49ers' head coach at the time, made it worse. He told reporters that Smith wouldn't start against New York, but not because of the injury. He said that Smith was "fully healthy" but lacked confidence.

That appalled Smith. "I didn't want anyone, least of all my teammates, to ever think I could have played in the Giants game and all of a sudden I wasn't confident," he says. "The entire position is *based* on confidence."

Nolan told me that he was trying to protect his quarterback. "I was thinking, if you're going to play, don't let them know you're hurt." But it was a lie about an injury that Smith was lying to himself about the severity of, and shifting the focus to the quarterback's psyche left teammates quietly questioning him. Smith needed an adult in the room, like he would have later in his career in Kansas City. There, Smith sustained a concussion, and passed the tests to return to action. But coach Andy Reid refused to allow him back into action, and held him out the next game, too. It felt like the right thing to do. Nobody in San Francisco had that perspective in 2007.

"I don't think too many people knew he was still injured," Jeff Ulbrich, a 49ers linebacker at the time, told me. "And I'm sure that some guys thought that he was struggling because of confidence."

In the NFL, a question is all it takes. A player's toughness is as personal as his DNA, but injuries are routinely compared anyway. Very few injuries are universally acceptable for missing games, especially for quarterbacks. Broken legs or collarbones, the "unhappy knee triad"—ACL, MCL, medial meniscus—severed rotator cuffs and Achilles' heels, herniated disks, and spine or neck injuries, those don't raise questions. Concussions, high ankle sprains, pulled groins or hamstrings, broken forearms or ribs, and a torn MCL are generally permissible excuses. Shoulder separations, hip pointers, cracked ribs, stingers, turf toe, even torn ACLs—John Elway played sixteen years without one in his left knee—usually don't pass muster among peers. And don't even mention broken fingers. Or sprained fingers, even though they matter more for a quarterback than a good knee. How do players truly know if their teammates are badly injured? Is it possible to know? Guys don't discuss it. Quarterbacks definitely don't discuss it. They lie to everyone. It's typical to not know which teammates are playing with injection-inducing pain. Guys deal with team medics on their own, behind closed doors, and then seek second opinions from doctors often based in other states. With players shuffling through a season-long tunnel that runs from meetings to practice to film study to treatment and then home, it can be hard enough to get themselves ready to play, body and mind, much less worry about anyone else.

Deep down, Smith wanted his teammates to know he was sucking it up. That urge heightened after he was awful in a loss to the Saints and missed six wide-open receivers in a loss to the Falcons a week later. He was dying to publicly confess that his shoulder—not his head—was to blame; that his injury was no longer an issue of subjective pain tolerance but also objective functionality. A hit by Saints linebacker Scott Fujita popped loose his collarbone, despite the pregame tape job, and it now kicked like a pinball-machine paddle during each throw. When Smith took off his pads, he saw the bone pushing against the skin of his back. But if you play, you're *not* injured. "I never wanted my teammates to think I was using it as an excuse," he told me. "I didn't want to be like, 'Hey, this is what's really happening with my shoulder.' They don't want to hear that. They don't need to hear that. They don't want to deal with it. I didn't want to have to plead my case. So, I didn't."

Smith patched together a throwing motion—sidearm, overhand, follow-through, no follow-through. Nothing worked.

"The more I tried to adjust," he says, "the worse it got."

He told trainers that his shoulder and forearm were bothering him, under the presumption that a report would travel up the chain to Nolan. But Smith doesn't know if it did. Coach and quarterback rarely interacted, about the injury or anything else, typical in a league where coaches primarily get injury information from the medical staff, not the player. Nolan knew at the time that Smith was hurting, but considering jobs were on the line, the coach believed his player needed to perform better. In team meetings two days after a 12-for-28 passing game on Monday night against Seattle—Smith stood on the field thinking, *Am I tough or stupid? I'm not getting any points for playing hurt. What am I doing?*—Nolan repeatedly ripped him. That afternoon the media pressed Smith for the reason behind his struggles. This time, he told the truth: "It's been killing me." He announced that his season was over.

Two days later, at a team meeting, Nolan called out Smith for not being completely honest about his injury: "If it's really that bad, you've got to come tell someone. You can't just keep hiding it." Smith then left for a reevaluation by Dr. Andrews in Alabama. Something changed. Suddenly, the players respected him in a different way. "Once it was out that he was really hurt," Ulbrich told me, "everyone was back on his side."

Playing while broken didn't validate his toughness. *Surgery* did. Is there a difference between the question of pain and perception of it?

By 2018, Smith was Washington's quarterback. He dropped back against Houston, and faced an onslaught from a pair of rushers. Safety Kareem Jackson hit him from the side, and defensive end J. J. Watt hit him head-on. Smith planted his right leg. Sometimes human bones ward off extraordinary force. Other times, if torque and angle are just so, they snap. Smith's fibula and tibia broke—the most gruesome quarterback injury since Joe Theismann broke his leg in 1985. The break, and ensuing infection, were nearly fatal. Smith returned to play two years later, because of course. By then, nobody dared question his toughness.

———

Andrew Luck's injured shoulder first threatened his career, then his identity, then any hope for future happiness. Nicole Pechanec, his longtime girlfriend, was losing patience, feeling like a silo in a siloed life, tired of years of Andrew putting emotional guardrails around her.

"I didn't have a place to contribute because Andrew wouldn't communicate," she told me. She felt uniquely equipped to help. They had met at Stanford, where she was an elite gymnast until injuries derailed her career. At first, Luck wasn't in the mood to hear what she might say. *Couldn't* hear it. If he stopped to examine his life, the entire world he had constructed might start to unravel, perhaps revealing it to be fatally flawed all along.

"I understood myself best as a quarterback," Luck told me. "I felt no understanding of other parts of myself at all."

Why was that? Was it because he was a quarterback, or would that have been the obstacle regardless of profession? Is it possible to have normal relationships if you're an elite professional in this line of work? Quarterback as lifestyle had evolved since Joe Namath ushered it in. When Luck first arrived to the NFL, he saw other quarterbacks with entourages: an assistant, a publicist, a chef, a body coach, a security guy, an entire apparatus, all designed to help young men play their best for six or so seconds for each play, for about sixty plays, over the course of what's now seventeen days a year and will probably soon be eighteen—and more, if lucky. "Is that what I need to be great?" Luck wondered.

He did the opposite: The more his life expanded externally, the smaller and simpler he kept his world. Luck was trying to handle everything himself, refusing to acknowledge what he felt most: a low-grade fear, not only that his shoulder might not fully heal, but scarier, that this life—the life he told me that he "didn't have a choice" but to pursue, due to his talent and our collective *need* for it—might not be for him. Something had to change. Nicole was prepared to leave him if nothing did. "There were some things that when I looked in the mirror, I did not like about myself," he says. "I was self-absorbed, withdrawn, in pain, and feeling pressure."

Then one night, when he was in Holland rehabbing his shoulder, he broke. He cried, he cursed, he vented, he confessed, and most of all, he leveled with Nicole in a way she thought he was incapable of. Luck saw a professional therapist. And a physical therapist named Willem Kramer, who had worked with Luck for years, started to serve not only as a trainer but as a couple's counselor of sorts, trying to teach Andrew and Nicole about communication and identity, both as individuals and as a unit. One day, Kramer asked Luck, "Aren't you more than a quarterback?"

"Huh?" Luck said.

"I mean, that's fine—I guess. What you do on the field is amazing. But aren't you more than that?"

If not that, then what? Luck spent hours trying to remind himself what he loved about the game and playing quarterback, the two governors of his life. He boiled them to an essence: He liked throwing the ball to his friends. He liked gifting them with that precious thing that only a quarterback can. That got him through the next season. He returned to play in 2018 and won Comeback Player of the Year. Looking back, he wished he had retired as soon as the season ended. But he didn't, because he couldn't, not yet. In August of 2019, he developed a mysterious ankle and foot issue. No advice doctors offered worked. It felt familiar to Luck. He reverted. The anger, the feigned stoicism, the moodiness, the empty responses to Nicole, the confusion as doctors were unable to explain what was wrong, despite three MRIs. As the season neared, Luck was again away from the team, off in the training room. He was a "spoiled child," Kramer says, sulking and scared, not only because of chronic pain but because of how he acted in chronic pain, a resentment less toward his body for failing to hold up and more toward himself.

Luck didn't know whether he could fully recover, but that was almost beside the point. Nicole was pregnant with their first daughter. By the 2010s, there was an entire movement toward redefining roles in marriage and parenthood. Shared investment and responsibility were expected, regardless of breadwinning status or pressure. The movement did not penetrate NFL teams, especially not at the game's most important position. But Luck took those responsibilities seriously. One day during training camp, Luck confessed to Castonzo, his teammate, that he was once again asking himself basic questions, with no easy answers: "Who am I?"

This time, he was not just a quarterback. He had responsibilities and promises beyond himself and the Colts. He was coming close to saying out loud what he had disclosed only to Nicole and a few others: that he wasn't sure he wanted to do this anymore. Not could. *Wanted.* He had proved that he could play at a high level. He had received plenty of praise and criticism, enough to know that neither of those things mattered. "It was admirable that he was able to see the bigger picture," Castonzo says today. "For him to continue on in his life as a quarterback, he would have essentially expected it to be Andrew's World, and every relationship in his life would cater to Andrew's World, which is not the person he wanted to be."

He retired on the eve of the 2019 season, shocking the football community and beyond, becoming one of those rare American success stories whose greatest success might be in leaving what made him successful. He detached from the world he had known, spending a long vacation in Europe, growing out his hair, switching to a keto diet, wondering what he had done and if he wanted to return to football, and most of all, trying to be a present father when their first daughter, Lucy, arrived. Once he saw what that entailed, of early morning breakfasts and midnight feedings, of trips to the playground and to the pediatrician, of reading and playing and long walks in the neighborhood pushing a stroller, once he understood what it meant to be the best father and husband possible, he knew how incongruent it was with his previous life. He'd never play football again. He'd never quarterback a team again. But even so, even after everything, quarterback never left him. When events would happen, political or otherwise, and other passers would put out statements, taking a stand, using their platforms for a greater good, Luck would start to prepare his . . . before it hit him what he was, and wasn't, anymore.

———

Elite 11's biggest moment is the final day, a seven-on-seven competition. Waiting for it to begin, Charlie pulls out a piece of paper with notes from today's parent session. It's titled "Nine Skills," and it is a final sendoff from the counselors, an attempt to whittle quarterbacking to the essentials:

1) Perception Speed: How fast do you process?
2) Search Efficiency: Locate target in chaos
3) Tracking: Keeping track of where everyone is—big predictor of completion percentage
4) Visual Learning: Tool to help convert classroom to the field
5) Instinctive Learning: Stitching together stuff, can see stuff before it happens
6) Decisions/Complexity: QB knows the rules (curl/flat) but can do it with added complexities, slows down game, no hesitation, can simplify game
7) Impulse control
8) Control: Can you perform a motor task with complexities and chaos?
9) Improvisation: How well can athlete deal with stuff when it breaks down?

Can feel for the game be learned? Some argue yes—if you're lucky enough to hang on until you have enough experience and maturity that the game slows down. Rich Gannon, the MVP of the 2002 season, arrived in the NFL raw, a quick athlete but not a passer. Teams considered moving him to safety. But through the good fortune of playing for smart coaches and obsessively trying to master his craft and, most of all, managing to keep his career going, he taught himself how to play, and he taught himself the nine items Charlie had noted down without realizing it.

"The only way I can explain it to you is if you're a sixteen-year-old and you just get your driver's license, you're driving down the road for the first time and it's almost like you have blinders on," Gannon once said. "You don't see oncoming traffic, you don't see a pedestrian in the crosswalk, you don't see the three cars behind you, you don't see what's going on six, seven, eight yards up the road. You just see the car in front of you and the traffic light, that's all. Meanwhile, if you're an experienced driver, you see everything. You're able to anticipate. You're able to avoid collisions. That's really the difference. It's experience. It's being a master of your domain. It's being so prepared that the game really slows down."

As the quarterbacks warm up, a fully formed entity arrives, in sweats and an oversized T-shirt. A camera follows him. The on-field action slows to acknowledge a presence. The world of a quarterback is small. If you reach a certain status, you cross paths with others who've made it. *He's* here. *Him*, one of Elite 11's proudest alums, reigning Heisman Trophy winner, multimillionaire, expected first overall pick of the NFL Draft. A group of quarterbacks circle him. He does what one does at Elite 11: He picks up a football and throws, mostly midrange fade routes. The ball is crisp out of his hand. Kids step up to throw, aware that the bar has been raised, but nobody talks to him, except one: Colin Hurley. He's been around high-profile college and pro quarterbacks before. Hurley starts a conversation, then offers a challenge: Who can hit the crossbar first? Hurley steps up and hits it on his third try. Now it's *his* turn.

First shot, Caleb Williams nails it.

———

Charlie sits up in the stands when the seven-on-seven tournament begins. "Throwing first," the announcer says, "LSU commit Colin Hurley!"

"Here we go," Charlie says.

Colin lines up in the shotgun and starts dealing. He has a rule in seven-on-seven: Get rid of the ball fast. Other quarterbacks hold the ball too long, a bad habit that will get them into trouble in an actual game. Hurley ends up throwing four touchdowns and is named MVP of the seven-on-seven portion of Elite 11.

"Not bad," Charlie says with a smile when he sees Colin at the end of the day.

Quarterbacks and parents assemble on the field, posing for pictures and wishing one another luck. Colin takes off his wired mic. The camera crew asks him to "do what he'd normally do" after a game, so he and his dad engage in a little performance art: Charlie gives him a hug, they walk off the field together . . . and then they circle back to chat with the quarterbacks and parents and staff, after the cameras have the shot. The 2023 Elite 11 quarterbacks get on a group text thread and pledge to stay in touch. A few of them will exit the chat in the coming weeks. Charlie and Colin say goodbye to Brian Stumpf, the longtime organizer of Elite 11.

"You did a first-class job," Charlie says.

"You've got a first-class kid," Stumpf says.

I walk off the field with the Hurleys, who are chatting—then quiet, as we pass something as true about quarterbacks as the leverage with which they enter a room: the unhinged father. The dad of one of the quarterbacks is ripping into him, dressing him down in plain sight. This kid had a tough time during seven-on-seven, throwing a few interceptions. I remember when I wanted this thing because you could reach for it, an achievement and an accomplishment, and as the game has changed, as quarterback has changed, fierce expectations once reserved for the top few are now trickling down to almost anyone with a glimpse of talent. Colin and Charlie watch out of the corner of their eyes. The dad yells at his son, "What the fuck are you doing?" The dad walks away.

Colin waits until it's clear, then heads straight to the kid. A friend, a competitor, a blood brother, one of the few who know what it's like to be a top quarterback in 2023. Colin gives him a hug.

IV

CRISES

Some of the strangest and coolest moments in Steve Young's life are not during games, or even before them, but when he's around other great quarterbacks. Colleagues, peers, his kind, the most exclusive tribe within an exclusive tribe. Before Super Bowl 50 in 2016 in Santa Clara, all forty-nine of the game's previous Super Bowl MVPs are honored. Young enters Levi's Stadium with his wife, Barb, and their kids, passing a statue of himself outside. Inside, mural-sized posters of 49ers greats line the hallways. His kids stop at each shot of him, of Daddy. In a waiting room with most of the other MVPs, he looks around. Namath. Staubach. Montana. Rodgers. Young has noticed something funny about being around elite quarterbacks. A weird, suppressed, throttled competitive energy.

"It's like, do we race?" he says today.

On this afternoon, most of them seem liberated, flitting about in an earned, exclusive club. Is this how living presidents feel when they're together, bonded by a shared experience, a shared test, a shared duty, luminaries who don't need a lot of words to understand what they're talking about, what they've been through? "We were as free as we could ever have been," Young says now, of guys who had survived the ascent *and* descent. "And now you get to talk about it."

All the living MVPs are introduced on the field before the game, in order. Bart Starr waves into a live feed from his home in Alabama. Then Namath, to a rousing ovation. Len Dawson, more accurate than Namath and nearly as rebellious, with a two-touchdown upset over the Vikings in Super Bowl IV and a famous photograph of himself taking a pull off a cigarette in the locker room. Staubach, who is in his seventies but still has a hop in his step. Bradshaw, with a wide grin. Jim Plunkett, who grew up poor in the Bay Area and won a Heisman at Stanford, the first pick in the 1970 draft. Montana, the gold standard. Doug Williams, icon. Mark Rypien, the best native Canadian quarterback ever. Aikman, arguably the most accurate thrower ever. Young, and all his scars. Elway, the greatest when he walked away. Kurt Warner, proof that nobody knows anything. Brady, the ultimate winner. Peyton Manning, who is shown on the big screens in the locker room preparing for his final game, the ultimate thinker. Eli, Patriots slayer. Drew Brees, a New Orleans civic treasure. Rodgers, the game's best at the time.

All receive thunderous ovations, except Brady. He is booed.

Young is part of the first group of quarterbacks who were set apart not only as an idea but as a business. In the early nineties there was a televised event at the Pro Bowl in Hawaii called the

Quarterback Challenge. Bill Walsh would analyze it on air. The quarterbacks would throw at moving and stationary targets on golf carts short and long, both from imaginary pockets and after scampering around cones. Then there was a distance competition, where guys would just wing it as far as they could, letting it all hang. It's a miracle nobody tore an elbow tendon.

Some guys loved it. Jim Harbaugh of the Bears would practice for it. Dan Marino owns the best moment from it: In 1991, he was down 100 points and had one throw left, and required a bullseye on a moving target from 50 yards away, to beat the score of another quarterback named Steve DeBerg. He nailed it. "All the money that was going to go in his pocket just went over to mine," Marino chortled. He later wrote DeBerg a check to cover some of the lost earnings, out of empathy and respect.

Young found the event draining. It was the end of the season, his body was recovering, but who was he to say no? There was a purity and preciousness to it. The greatest arms, all together, on a level field. And then, he says, "You're like, 'What have I done? I'm being defined by this golf cart and target. This was not a smart move.'"

Quarterback was finding imaginative ways to broaden its dominance. In the late eighties, an NFL executive named Frank Vuono studied the league's jersey sales. The pattern was unmistakable. Quarterbacks constituted most of the best sellers, and the most popular ones belonged to legends like Montana, Elway, and Marino, and frontline guys like Phil Simms of the New York Giants, Jim McMahon of the Chicago Bears, and Boomer Esiason of the Cincinnati Bengals. Together they accounted for close to 80 percent of jersey sales. Vuono saw an opening. The NBA, the NFL's closest rival, was coming on strong not only because of superstars like Michael Jordan, Magic Johnson, and Larry Bird, but because it knew how to market them. Vuono tried to appeal to owners to promote individual players more. They resisted. Vuono found a winning argument. At the time, the NFL Players Association was mired in antitrust litigation against the league. The NFLPA counted on apparel revenue to pay legal fees. Vuono saw a diabolical opportunity: If the league could pick off the quarterbacks and create a separate entity just for them, it could control the revenue—and drain the union. A win-win. Owners signed off on it.

Vuono understood that such a campaign would appeal to a quarterback's vanity. They targeted Leigh Steinberg and Marvin Demoff, agents of nearly every superstar. Demoff delivered Elway and Marino; after that, every celebrity quarterback followed—except Montana. He refused not out of solidarity with the union—he had crossed the picket line during the 1987 strike—but because he felt his status, with four times more rings than the other twelve quarterbacks combined, merited a larger cut than the others. "There's no way Joe will share equally," his agent told Vuono. They moved on without him, and a new cartel was formed: Quarterback Club.

I remember the first ad I saw in the early nineties, when my dreams felt most attainable: Elway, Marino, Moon, Simms, Young, Harbaugh, Jim Kelly of the Bills, Jim Everett of the Rams, Bernie Kosar of the Browns, Randall Cunningham of the Eagles. My heroes, all in horrific, striped Zubaz pants. But it was a huge flex: Between the sportswear lines and jersey sales, the group raked in millions. Earnings that would have been put in a pot and evenly distributed among all players were now theirs. It wasn't enough that quarterbacks were the NFL's highest-paid players. Nor that they were superstars. They had to take money from teammates, too.

"It was like the Rat Pack," Vuono says.

The quarterbacks were in awe of one another. On the drive to a commercial shoot, Troy Aikman asked Vuono, "Danny Marino and John Elway are really going to be there?" They were his idols. The Quarterback Club met quarterly for photo shoots and golf outings and *to be* quarterbacks—and for an excuse to drink hard.

Moon and Young felt like outsiders. Moon didn't drink, too worried about his family's history with alcoholism. He would sit with a cranberry juice and watch how Kelly and Marino could pound beers and Elway could down Dewar's and still be the first ones at the tee the next morning, ready to hit it all over again, manic supremacy clear.

Young didn't drink either, due to his Mormonism. But his awkwardness wasn't social. It was existential. Did he belong? Sometimes, when all of the quarterbacks were together, a group of misfits and privileged alphas, heroes to millions of boys yet petty as hell in person, arguing about banal things like money and statistics, Young could feel simmering testosterone. "Being around them was always a wow, because I wasn't quite as far along as I thought I was," he says.

Young was already in the 99.8th percentile of quarterbacks. He had replaced Montana in San Francisco and had instantly become one of the league's best players. In 1991, he led the NFL in passer rating. The next year, Young was league MVP, made All-Pro, and ranked first in touchdown passes, passer rating, and completion percentage. Yet that whirring of doubt that he had contended with his entire life didn't lessen, it intensified. After a bad loss to the Raiders, where he had Jerry Rice open for a game-winning touchdown and failed to see him, Young sat in his parked car for hours.

He called friends for support, and then, at 3 a.m., having run out of people to call, he cried alone.

There's a moment in the life of each quarterback when everything he has worked for is at risk. You either find a way to scrape what's required from within you, fulfilling expectations of yourself and others, or you don't. For Young, one of those moments happened after the Raiders game. It was his day off. Young flew to Utah, just to get out of town. On the flight back, he happened to be seated next to Stephen Covey, a businessman and bestselling author of *The 7 Habits of Highly Effective People*. Covey asked him how he was doing, and Young couldn't help it. He vented, whined, bitched. His problem was this: Everything he did was viewed within the context of Montana. After the loss to the Raiders, 49ers executive Dwight Clark—the receiver who made The Catch in the 1982 NFC Championship, a game attended by both John Elway, as a college student behind the Cowboys bench, and Tom Brady, as a child up in the bleachers—told the papers that it was the type of game that Montana "wins in his sleep." It was hard to know what pissed off Young more: that Clark said it, or that he was right.

Covey listened, then asked a few questions. Joe was still on the team, right?

"Yes, he was injured," Young said.

"But you get to ask him questions, right?"

"Well, yeah."

Covey then moved on to the 49ers organization, confirming that they were the best in football, then to the coaches, also the best in football, then offered that Young was looking at his world wrong. "You are in the one place in the NFL where you can find out just how good you can get," Covey told him.

What am I doing? Young thought.

He realized that the problem wasn't Montana. It was himself.

Covey's words were a breakthrough for Young, one of many break-throughs *that week*. It's easy to lapse into isolation as a quarterback. To feel like no one else understands. Bill Walsh sensed something was off. He called Young and asked him to stop by. Young hung his head, expecting a measure of empathy. Instead, Walsh was *pissed* at him.

"All you do is take the blame!" Walsh said.

"What am I supposed to say?" Young replied. "It's *not* my fault?"

Young had a code within him that a quarterback was only as great as his willingness to assume personal responsibility for things over which he had no control, to account for the chaos of twenty-one other bodies flying around, snap after snap. To do the job the way Young wanted to do it, the way only a few men ever had to that point, was to rise above. It was breaking him. He was complaining behind the scenes. He couldn't do it before the media. Maybe he was complaining so much behind the scenes *because* he couldn't do it before the media.

Walsh introduced a new idea: "There's such a thing as being over-accountable."

That wasn't what Young wanted to hear. Walsh's words were executive-function jargon. What Young needed help with was feeling less alone. He was beaten up, and beating himself up. What was his outlet? He dealt with it not with alcohol or drugs but by strapping on his helmet again, believing that he should be able to get through it on his own and that anything else was a sign of weakness. The limits of that mindset were beginning to become clear.

———

Senior Night for Colin Hurley, even though he's technically a junior *and* a senior. Charlie and Marion stand on the sideline with their son, waiting for his name to be called. Colin is ready for kickoff. Charlie is antsy, practically vibrating. The sun is starting to set, Friday afternoon becoming a Friday night, a crowd gathered under the soft stadium glow. On the drive over Charlie pumped himself up with the *Scarface* soundtrack. Now he is a bundle of energy with no outlet. Or, rather, the only place to put it is the usual one. "Hey, hey," he says to Colin. "We need a win."

Colin nods, then shifts away, creating distance, not from his dad, exactly, but from the spectacle. He is in game mode. Or was. Now he's half in the zone, half waiting for the opening ceremony to end. The curtain isn't rising when it's supposed to. Precious momentum is leaking out. "I've always hated stuff like this," he says.

Charlie lunges to a receiver. "Hey," he says. "Catch everything tonight or I'll fuck you up."

Colin's final year at Trinity has been disappointing so far. Something is just off. Last week, Trinity lost its second game 27–14. Colin's anger, at self and team, didn't dissipate as Trinity prepared for its next opponent. He felt the need to say something. He posted a statement on social media, blasting the team and himself. In the world of Class 2A Jacksonville football, Colin's words went viral. He caught some flack, but he didn't care. Louisiana State coaches told him to bring that demanding attitude to Baton Rouge next year. Charlie marveled at the statement in the hours and days after it was posted, rereading it, viewing it as evidence of growth, the man he wants his son to become, ruthless and unwavering, the type who holds those around him to a high standard. If he comes off as an asshole, or *is* an asshole, tough.

Finally, Senior Night begins. Verlon Dorminey, Trinity's head coach, works the line and hugs Colin at midfield. The announcer's words for each player are standard: position, parents, plans for college, until Colin. "He hopes to play in the NFL one day and have a successful career."

Charlie takes his index finger and thumb to his soaking eyes, hugs Colin, and then finds his usual seat in the stands: midfield, halfway up. Charlie breathes heavy. Trinity's kickoff team takes the field. He counts out loud, pointing at each player, making sure Trinity has eleven.

"High school is so different from the NFL and college, right?" Charlie says. "It's innocent."

———

July 18, 1995, Warren and Felicia Moon got into a fight. They were arguing often at the time, two people who knew each other almost too well, and were so busy trying to raise three children and perform well on Sundays and be community leaders in a place that seemed to want them gone that there was little left for each other. This time, the argument was over money, at their home in the Houston suburbs.

By then, Moon had moved on to the Minnesota Vikings. A narrative had developed in his career. He was becoming the face of a certain kind of failure, a type that defined a team and a city and, of course, a quarterback. From 1991 to 1993, the Oilers lost three straight playoff games and blew leads of 15 points against John Elway's Broncos, 32 points against backup quarterback Frank Reich's Buffalo Bills, and 10 points against Joe Montana's Chiefs. Sitting with Moon, I remind him that he played well in each of those playoff games. After the Oilers had blown the 35–3 lead to the Bills, Moon brought Houston back to tie the game and send it into overtime, facing an energized defense and deafening Bills home crowd, a great drive destined to be forgotten.

"Should've never got to that," he says.

"You outplayed Elway in Denver," I say.

He shakes his head. "The last two minutes . . ." he says. "That's what made him great, though: how he finished games."

As the face of the franchise, Moon was the face of those losses. After one bad game in 1993, reporters followed him to his car in the stadium parking lot. Moon covered his face with a piece of paper. *Is this a way for an All-Pro quarterback to act?* a reporter asked him. Something had to change, and the Oilers decided to move on from a future Hall of Famer in his prime, a move surprising and hurtful. Moon was traded to Minnesota. He thought the pressure would be off him: The Vikings had a good running game and didn't operate a go-go gadget offense. But when a talent like Moon arrived, the coaches couldn't help themselves. He threw 601 passes in 1994, the second most of his career up to that point.

And life was closing in. Felicia and the kids stayed in Houston, providing continuity for the family, but further straining a strained marriage. Moon continued his Pro Bowl play. He enjoyed his new teammates. He started to drink with them after work, testing boundaries he previously refused to consider. A Vikings cheer-leader accused him of offering money for sex; he denied the claim and later settled. He was still considered the epitome of excellence in character and integrity, but he was often in a private hell. "I didn't want anyone to ever panic or worry about me," he says. "But it got to the point where I just felt like I was gonna burst." Felicia would call him a "coward." She was angry that he was often absent, work-ing or attending charity events—busy being Warren Moon—rather than with their kids. She thought he could be mean and cruel, and her only response was to throw things at him.

When they fought on that particular July day, over a $160,000 credit card bill, Felicia could feel herself start to lose control, she later testified. Her chest was pounding. Something awful was going to happen, so she started to pray. As Warren walked away, she threw a three-pound candle at him. Arguing ensued. The housekeeper had never heard them scream this way. Felicia was on the floor, with Warren standing over her. Felicia later said she feared for her life, that his hands were around her neck, and her vision started to blacken. The housekeeper called 911. She didn't speak English, so she handed the phone to Jeffrey, one of their sons.

"My daddy is going to hit my mommy," he told the operator. "Please hurry."

———

At the start of the 2023 college football season, Caleb Williams had dinner with Denzel Washington at Steak 48 in Beverly Hills. Williams had spent the summer training, traveling, and being Caleb Williams. He had visited his old high school, a charity event that turned into a homecoming of sorts. He had walked a runway in Miami. He had ridden in a black SUV on a spring afternoon, from a midtown Manhattan hotel to an advertising showcase called the up-fronts, where he was a guest of ESPN and chatted with Peyton Manning backstage. The Jay-Z lyric "I'm not a businessman. I'm a business, man" was pinned to his X profile, notable mostly because it made clear that he would never just be a quarterback. The draft hovered over everything, and he still had his junior football season to play. Williams was featured in *GQ* magazine, and Carl inadvertently hijacked the story, using the platform to float strategies. "The truth is, he can come back to school. . . . The funky thing about the NFL draft process is, he'd almost be better off not being drafted than being drafted first. The system is completely backward. The way the system is constructed, you go to the worst possible situation. The worst possible team, the worst organization in the league—because of their desire for parity—gets the first pick. So, it's the gift and the curse."

Those comments went viral, boomeranging on his son on the eve of the season and sending a shudder through NFL front offices. Caleb was left to explain his dad's opinions from the USC podium. Carl had become a *distraction*, football's vaguest, worst sin.

The dinner with Washington was just part of the world Caleb trafficked in. Williams showed up at Steak 48 in sweats. He was nervous that they wouldn't let him in. He called his dad, wondering if he should grab different clothes. He spoke to the host.

"I'm here to see someone," he said.

The host didn't recognize him and wouldn't let him into a private area. Williams called his dad again. Carl told him to stay put. Washington came to the entrance and waved Caleb in.

A legend sat down with a legend-in-waiting. As one of the greatest actors of his generation, Washington had a better sense of the next five years of Williams's life than he did.

Picture the kid, not the icon: What must he want to hear at this moment? What strategies, pieces of wisdom, will he remember years from now, when he's either a made guy or not?

What Washington had at the ready was the hard truth of a kind of loneliness. That the kid was in it alone.

"You're gonna have to set your own sail, son," he said.

<hr />

When I talk to Elway about his career now, it's done within a certain context: We know the story ends well, with consecutive championships. He's not Tittle. But two weeks after The Drive, Denver faced the favored New York Giants in the Super Bowl. Elway played the best football of his career to that point, helping the Broncos to a 10–9 halftime lead that should have been more. In the second half, though, the Broncos were overwhelmed and lost decisively to a better team. The next year, Elway was named league MVP and the Broncos reached the Super Bowl again. This time, Denver was favored over Washington. Elway threw a 56-yard touchdown along the right sideline on the first play and got them to a 10–0 lead midway through the first quarter. Then Denver kicked off, and Washington fumbled. The ball disappeared under a pile. Denver appeared to recover. If the Broncos had recovered and subsequently scored another touchdown, the game might have been over. Instead, officials ruled that Washington had come up with it. Something changed with Elway in the following hours. It wasn't just that Washington scored 35 points in the second quarter, a record. It wasn't just that it was journeyman Doug Williams, not Elway, who pulled off an unprecedented performance. It's that Elway wasn't himself. He didn't yell, or scream, or fight. He seemed resigned to a fate that he had defined himself against.

After the game, a reporter asked him if he needed to win a Super Bowl to be considered a great quarterback. Both parties knew the story that was about to be written into record.

"That's on my mind," he said softly. His eyes seemed watery. "I will not have a good feeling about myself until I win one."

———

Himself. Not his career: his *self*.

Elway's identity and maybe even worth were tied to becoming a certain thing. Was this the natural realization of that conversation in Jack's Impala? Elway started to speak of his career in terms of having not yet plateaued, and it sounded like a prayer as much as an aspiration. He cared, maybe too much. A lot of NFL quarterbacks don't. Maybe money takes the edge off. Or pain. Or politics. Or fatigue.

Like Elway, Jeff George was considered to have a generational arm, and like Elway, he was drafted first overall by the Colts, this time in 1990. George, though, was the greatest quarterback ever at casual indifference. He lazily drifted in his drop backs; he couldn't be bothered to lift the ball much higher than his shoulder when he threw. He produced the worst record as a regular starting quarterback in NFL history. By the time he changed, he was in his eighth year and third team. He threw 29 touchdowns and nine interceptions, a better touchdown-to-interception ratio than Joe Montana ever produced. But it was too late; the narrative was set on his career. He was out of the league shortly after. Two of his sons, Jayden and Jeff Jr., became Division I quarterbacks. When he was up for the draft in 2021, Jeff Jr. told a reporter that he was "willing to put his life on the line" for football. "I don't want to do anything else."

Jeff Jr. cared. And went undrafted.

Elway was painting on a particular canvas, making a play for history and posterity. In 1989, two years after the bad loss to Washington, Denver lost to the 49ers 55–10, the worst blowout in Super Bowl history. Elway was so despondent that teammates asked if he was okay, as reporters and photographers watched on. "Can't you let a guy sulk in peace?" he said.

Over the next few years, Elway was stuck in a strange cultural place, considered great, with a qualifier. He kept pulling off show-stoppers, like converting a fourth-and-10 with a 49-yard bomb to set up a game-winning field goal against the Chiefs on *Monday Night Football* in 1990, and The Drive II against the Oilers in 1991: 98 yards, two fourth-and-the-season conversions. But he was stuck. At times, he wanted to play until he was forty. Others, he considered asking for a trade. And so where did Elway, and all of the other great quarterbacks left alone to fend off missiles, put that stuff? What do you do? Where do you go?

Football teams are almost reverse engineered to support their most valuable players, from scheme to psychology, but at some point, quarterbacks are alone with a question: Can I do it? Can I make the throws when it matters most? You won't know until you do it, and just because you do it once, or twice, or for twelve years, it buys you nothing, it's no insurance that you'll come through the next time. All great athletes cling to a religion of sorts, some place to store anxiety. Beer, women, Instagram, avocados. Or some go straight to the top.

———

At 6:50 on a Saturday morning, Kirk Cousins passes through a Phoenix hotel lobby holding a laptop and a Bible inscribed with his name. He's in a suit. He walks into a conference room, where he's due to receive the 2023 Athletes in Action/Bart Starr Award, given annually to the player that "best exemplifies character, integrity, and leadership on and off the field."

But the award is more than that, of course. It's a faith-based award. The press release announcing that Cousins has won ends with this statement: "When we truly experience the love of God, we are moved to share it with others."

Cousins is famous for two things: being the first player in the NFL's salary cap era to sign a fully guaranteed contract, and for being emblematic of a quarterback with a very high but discernible ceiling. He's not a great quarterback, though he's proven himself capable of great quarterbacking. Consistency is his biggest problem, and so the question of Cousins's career is the question of his faith. There are at least 1,000 people in this room, wearing HE GETS US hats, here to be in his presence, in *His* presence, and in one another's presence, for a sort of salvation—and a continental breakfast.

There are two ways to enter a conversation about quarterbacks and religion. One is a discussion about the expansiveness of theology itself, the proposition that God has a rooting interest on a football field, given the state of the world, that He helps a team win or lose—a selective God. But the other is a simpler and more concise entry point, given the unknowability of quarterbacking if not of life itself: to take the quarterbacks at their word.

Look at those who have won the Bart Starr Award: Eli Manning, Russell Wilson, Kurt Warner, Drew Brees, Peyton Manning, and Trent Dilfer. Eight combined championships. Look at who has yet to win it, but no doubt will: Patrick Mahomes. It surprises people that he is an evangelist, and not just because of the frequency with which he cusses during games. Watch Mahomes make throws novel and revolutionary in the highest-leverage moments—2–3 Jet Chip Wasp in Super Bowl LIV against the 49ers, his scrambles on a high ankle sprain in a comeback win over the Eagles in Super Bowl LVII, Corn Dog in Super Bowl LVIII, his two-play, thirteen-second masterpiece against the Bills in the 2021 playoffs—and, despite his relative lack of speed, watch him always find a way to avoid pass rushers, a sense for which there is no explanation other than feel, and you know that he is gifted, and that he augments his gifts with relentless grinding and unyielding focus. He argues that he is *blessed*.

Mahomes doesn't wear his religion on his sleeve, but he does on his calf: He has a tattoo of Eutychus from Acts 20:7, reminding him that he can't be "half in and half out on God." He has used his biggest platform—Super Bowl week—to state that his commitment to Christ has increased alongside his notoriety. "My Christian faith plays a role in everything that I do. I mean, I always ask God to lead me in the right direction and let me be who I am for His name. . . . It will be on a huge stage in the Super Bowl that He's given me, and I want to make sure I'm glorifying Him while I do it. I know that I am here for a reason, to glorify Him. It means everything, not only about my football career but all the decisions that I've made. I have a faith-backing, and I know why I am here. It's not about winning football games. It's about glorifying Him. I have no pressure when I step out on that football field; I know why I am here."

Quarterbacking, of course, is all about regulating pressure. From the clock, from the crowd, from the rush, from the secondary, from yourself. A game plan is designed to immunize a quarterback from it for sixty minutes. What happens in every other hour except for those three on Sunday? Mahomes is a boon to the movement, a godsend, not only because he's the greatest quarterback today, but because he's *cool*. He counts Taylor Swift and Steph Curry as friends. He has changed the way people style their hair, buzzed on the sides and curly on top, and the way quarterbacks throw the ball, underarm and no-look and even behind the back. He's one of *TIME* magazine's most influential people and could end up as football's first billion-dollar enterprise. I once asked Mahomes if he has ever had to think about throwing. "Not a lot." But he has had to think about being Patrick Mahomes, and all the complications that attend its blessings.

In Mahomes's first eight years in the spotlight, there has been no record of him slipping up. No yelling at a pap, no sign that he's cracking under the weight of his gifts from above. That's not true for some of his family. His father, Pat Sr., and his younger brother, Jackson, had a several-year run of bringing constant drama. Only Mahomes knows what it's like to manage his position and find a focus known to a few men. There are some inside the Chiefs building who believe that the fact that Mahomes has managed to avoid trapdoors and has shown himself to be a decent guy despite constant family drama is an accomplishment up there with his championships. Maybe that's why his faith, as Mahomes says, has "grown" alongside his notoriety. "I can only handle so much. I can only control so much." The Bible, he says, "has made it where I can play a little bit more free now, and I'm not so worried."

When Mahomes's former high school quarterback coach, Adam Cook, texts him scripture each morning—Joshua 14:12: *So give me the hill country that the Lord promised me. You will remember that as scouts we found the descendants of Anak living there in great, walled towns. But if the Lord is with me, I will drive them out of the land, just as the Lord said*—he knows better than to assume there's a football answer in there. He just hopes it helps. Mahomes attends Bible study and speaks of those meetings in the language of game-planning sessions, where he and his teammates can "keep up" and "not lose track of where we're at with our faith." He prays before each game at the altar of the goalpost, and when he's interviewed after big games, he sometimes begins with, "All glory to God. Without Him, none of this is possible."

He wasn't always this way. Randi Mahomes has said her oldest son's dedication to faith arrived when he was in middle school, not long after she and Patrick Sr. divorced. He needed an infrastructure, and he found one. Isaiah 40:31: *He who walks in Him shall find great strength, shall do great things, shall rise above.* A savior helped Mahomes save himself, and belief means believing he can make any throw and handle the chaos of celebrity. He does.

———

Cousins creates his own unique fervor in this crowd. He's in a roped-off area, stage right. Tony Dungy, the Hall of Fame coach, stands behind the lectern. This morning, Dungy speaks of faith not with the scars of a parent who has lost a child to death by suicide but with the cockiness of a former jock. He tells a story from his days as an assistant coach in Kansas City in the late eighties. Back then, the league prohibited prayer on the field.

"Well, God changed that," Dungy says.

That draws laughs and scattered applause. The league's relationship with Christianity is almost as symbiotic, and symbolic, as its relationship with the military. And like the relationship with the military, which was formed after 9/11 and never left, prayer is now not only accepted but part of the integral, and normalized, game-day experience. There's been an evangelical revolution in football over the past two decades, especially at the professional level. Is it because it's the hardest sport to control? Because it's the most dangerous? If God chooses those who can do it, then they arrive justified. It's a cloak, not just a comfort.

Cousins offers a theory when he takes the stage. He tells a story from two months earlier. Against the Colts, Cousins led the Vikings to the greatest comeback in NFL history, rallying them from down 33 points to win in overtime 39–36. He threw for 460 yards and four touchdowns. After the game, he looked at his phone and saw a text from a North Carolina area code. It was from Frank Reich. He was a longtime backup to Jim Kelly in Buffalo who had led the Bills back from a 35–3 deficit in the third quarter against Houston in the playoffs in 1992—the record until Cousins. Reich is a devout Christian who attended seminary school after his playing career. That comeback defines him, and he defines that comeback as a testament to the deity of football. It was, in Reich's words, "a moment you share your relationship with the Lord." Cousins cries behind the podium as he reads Reich's text: "Kirk, for 30 years God has given me the opportunity to tell the story of the biggest comeback in NFL history. The torch has been passed. And may He give you 30 years to share the gospel."

Cousins pauses, choking up, not because of the comeback, and not because God is offered as the only possible explanation for something unlikely but that falls within the bounds of reason, especially after 28–3 in Super Bowl LI, but because Reich is telling Cousins that he has not plateaued, that there's another level of faith to be discovered, a deeper and more meaningful level, not unlike a higher space of the craft. The crowd roars.

"God's grace is sufficient," Cousins says.

"I call this the playbook for life," Cousins tells me in a hotel lobby, holding the Bible etched with his name on the bottom of the cover. He touches it as he speaks. Cousins himself is unremarkable in stature. Usually when you see modestly proportioned quarterbacks, you can tell where they got lucky, with calves like pony kegs or hands huge and soft. Cousins isn't a hulking figure. He doesn't have a thunderbolt hanging off his shoulder. He doesn't have a computer chip in his head that's faster than others'. And he doesn't have the kind of wheels that define an era, much less help him flee the pocket. What he has is a blessing.

"I believe that God gave me the ability to throw a football," he says. "I remember in third grade I had a friend. We were playing catch at recess, we were nine years old, and he said, 'You really can throw a football.' I said, 'Oh, thanks, man.' He said, 'No, you *really* can throw a football.' So I realized at that age that I didn't do anything to learn to do that. I just showed up and could do that. And so that's why I believe it's a gift that God gave me, and I want to steward that gift well and allow God to write my story and not get in the way. So that involves trusting Him, that involves obeying Him, and that means even when my path might not be how I want it, like when I broke my ankle my junior year of high school and missed most of my junior year, which affected my recruitment to college. I gotta trust Him, and I gotta believe that He has a plan. I've trusted Him for fifteen years."

Is the proper way to view that story within the argument of Christianity and football, and its inherent conflicts and contradictions? Or within the context of the stories that athletes tell themselves, to explain the inexplicable? Of Michael Jordan's high school coach cutting him from varsity, even though it occurred during his sophomore year. Of Tom Brady insisting that he was an overlooked recruit coming out of Serra High, even though he had a menu of major-college scholarship offers and chose one of college football's most iconic destinations. These are not just the stories that such figures have told many times, they are the only stories they've ever told. Where does the story stop and the legend begin? Where does a narrative stop and a *quarterback* begin?

Kirk Cousins knows where he stands. He has won big games. He's occasionally cut loose, in his own librarian way. He once yelped "You like that!" to cameras after a win, an unremarkable statement that went viral because of its author. But fans of Cousins haven't forgotten what happened in 2016, and he hasn't either. It was the last game of the regular season, a playoff berth at stake for Cousins's Washington team against the Giants. It had been a breakout season for Cousins, throwing for almost 5,000 yards and 25 touchdowns, the type of season that would move most quarterbacks into the conversation of the game's best. Washington was down 13–10, less than two minutes left. Cousins got the ball, with game and legacy at stake. He moved Washington to midfield, then dropped back in a clean pocket. Nobody was open. He pump-faked, trying to shake a receiver free. It didn't work. He felt the clock ticking in his head, like a detonator, and drifted outside the pocket. He saw something that looked available over the middle and threw, off-balance and into traffic. That's where he got himself into trouble. That's the one thing you can't do if you're Kirk Cousins, even with God's graces. The ball sailed and the Giants intercepted it, ending the game and Washington's season. Prayer cannot salve that pain. "I have fears, doubts, anxieties, insecurities," Cousins says. "I don't know where else to take that, except to God."

Cousins read another book, the same that Lincoln Riley read and gave to his quarterbacks: *The Inner Game of Tennis*. In it, Gallwey breaks himself into Self One and Self Two. The first is the conscious, the second is the subconscious. "There are always external obstacles between us and our external goals, whether we are seeking wealth, education, reputation, friendship, peace on earth, or simply something to eat for dinner. And the inner obstacles are always there; the very mind we use in obtaining our external goals is easily distracted by its tendency to worry, regret, or generally muddle the situation, thereby causing needless difficulties from within."

Inner obstacles? Needless difficulties? It was like Cousins was lost, then found. Unlike some of his peers, who believe that they are a gift to quarterbacking, Cousins still can't believe he has the stage, after all these years. When he's around other star quarterbacks, or singing with Kelly Clarkson during NFL Honors, something about it doesn't make sense. His truth is our truth. He has never asked for sympathy. He has never asked for the masses to help him slay those who doubt him. He has asked for help, from all corners, from books to brain-mapping exercises to conversations with the indisputable greats.

You don't just *arrive* at quarterback. It's an ongoing process, of both becoming and maintaining and growing. If your curiosity ends, what's left? A plateau, which is worse than throwing an interception to cost your team a playoff spot.

Cousins once approached Tom Brady after a game to ask if football ever slows down. Brady, of course, is the son of a man who nearly became a priest. But he doesn't believe in miracles, outside of those he can control. He has his own gospel, revolving around kale and avocados and hydration, promising that drinking enough water will prevent sunburn. I once sat in Brady's living room and asked him if he ever feels doubt. "Not often," he said. He was lying, of course—or at least not being entirely honest. But his tale of transformation left no room for public reflection. He once said that to succeed, quarterbacks have to believe that *they* are "the magic." Brady told Cousins that no, the game doesn't ever slow down. It humbles you. It stretches your mind to dangerous places. You need something to help get you over. The Playbook of Life might not provide Cousins, or Mahomes for that matter, the answer. But it gives *an* answer, without fail. Sometimes that's enough to get to the next day and the beauty of the next snap.

Elway prayed, too, not for strength or for wisdom, but to be in a close Super Bowl. He didn't pray for a win. Just for the game to be close in the fourth quarter, with a *chance* to win. A prayer to shape the outcome rather than to make peace with it.

With three Super Bowl blowout losses together, Elway despised coach Dan Reeves, a good man and good coach—and a stubborn one. Realizing that the Broncos were exposed as one-dimensional on the biggest stage, Reeves wanted a balanced offense, emphasizing the running game. It was a good idea but faulty execution: Denver shut down on offense, throttling Elway until two minutes were left and they were desperate to score. Making matters worse, Reeves's playbook wasn't evolving with the league. Teams caught up to them. Elway's numbers tanked. For a few years he barely averaged a touchdown pass a game, while Montana and Moon and Marino and Kelly were breaking records. At one point, Mike Shanahan, then Denver's quarterbacks coach, got Elway and Reeves in a meeting and tried to play middleman. Elway kicked it off, looking at Reeves and saying, "I hate you more than any person on this planet."

Shanahan laughs at the memory now. Maybe the meeting was a bad idea. Elway came to regret what he said—he can be breathtakingly critical but then usually feels guilty, sometimes bringing himself to apologize—but he felt trapped. Terry Bradshaw was on television with his four Super Bowl rings, ripping Elway as a spoiled and overrated choke artist. After almost a decade in Denver, press coverage hadn't let up. If anything, it intensified, making fun of Elway's California blond hair, his prodigious teeth, his pigeon-walk. One day, when the press was trying to find him, Elway ducked out of the building through a back door, where a teammate was driving his truck, to escape.

"I'm about to suffocate," he told *Sports Illustrated*'s Rick Reilly. He'd ask Broncos staffers why the city was so infatuated with him. You're blond, rich, handsome, and Californian, they'd reply. As his statistics sank and the Super Bowl losses piled up, drinking rumors started to spread—fueled by Reeves off-the-record gossiping to reporters, Elway believed. The papers reported that at a local bar Elway drank five ninety-nine-cent Bud Lights and left pennies as the tip. Elway found some levity when he read it. "I think I'm going to sue. Those were *Coors* Lights." Elway had been raised to drink as much as he had been raised to be a quarterback, two areas of his life that were not only intertwined but rarely existed without each other. Elway felt at peace in a bar, loved the Golden Bee, with its two sizes of draft beers—Half Yards and Yards—and Hondo's, where the locals wouldn't bother him. Jack made sure his kid knew that the bar was a sacred home for a football team, and that the quarterback always picks up the tab. A few beers deep, Elway's competitive streak would kick in. He wouldn't let anyone leave. He'd catch teammates trying to sneak out of the bar, hoping to get a few hours of sleep before practice the next day, and John would haul their asses back in.

Reeves suspected Elway had a drinking problem. At one point, he called Jack to discuss it.

"Did he ever get busted?" Jack asked Reeves. "Was he in rehab? Was it interfering with his ability to do his job?"

No, no, and no.

"Then what's the problem?" Jack asked.

The problem was that three losses on the biggest stage, with no place to hide, began to impact the way he saw himself and his own potential. "It's hard to look at yourself from the outside," Elway says.

In 1991, Reeves knew that Elway was miserable and so he offered him a chance to call plays. Elway did, and the Broncos came out attacking teams like they hadn't in years. They kept winning, but Reeves eventually reeled the power back. Elway heard rumors that Reeves thought Elway wasn't smart enough to call plays, and that he didn't have the work ethic to come in and game plan with the coaches on the players' off-day.

One morning, Elway showed up for a game-planning meeting too hungover to breathe. "Go under the table," Shanahan said.

Elway did, and Shanahan went on with the meeting—until Reeves walked in.

"Where's John?" Reeves asked.

"He's in the bathroom," Shanahan told Reeves.

Reeves took a seat, waiting for Elway to return. Shanahan went on with the meeting. Elway was hiding under the table, two feet from Reeves. "Longest five minutes of my life," Shanahan says.

Finally, Reeves left. Elway popped up. He and Shanahan looked at each other, too scared to laugh.

Colin Hurley begins Senior Night in his home grays, walking to the line of scrimmage and scanning the defense. First play, a handoff. Not much. Second, same. Third, a quick throw short of the sticks. In the stands, Charlie dips his head, pissed off, a rift between him and the coaching staff widening with each series. If quarterbacks sometimes have issues with coaches and play-calling, quarterback dads *always* do. Charlie rubs his face, already too irritated to mask it, and shouts, hoping the sideline hears. "RUN, RUN, SHORT PASS.

Terrible play-calling. Typical. TYPICAL! Don't even challenge for a first down! And then blame the kids!"

People in the stands look at Charlie and freeze. A noisy high school game suddenly feels quiet. Hurley has screamed so loud from the stands that during a game a year ago, Trinity was penalized 15 yards for it, one of three unsportsmanlike conduct penalties against Trinity on that play: one on Coach Dorminey, one on Colin, and one on Charlie, combined to result in a *second-and-55* for Trinity. Then Colin threw a touchdown pass. A great quarterback can bail out anything and anyone.

Charlie keeps venting tonight, loud enough for everyone to hear. A man two rows down eating fries looks up. He and the Hurleys have had longstanding issues. The man turns around, staring at Charlie.

"Fucking Pop Warner offense," Charlie yells. "Yeah, I'm gonna say it until they change."

"Pop Warner quarterback," the man says.

"What did you say? Fuck you! Talking about my son?"

They go back and forth, Charlie's voice rising with each exchange. "You wanna go? Put down your french fries and let's go."

People start to moan and hush.

"Yeah, I'm the one," Charlie yells, as if entering a ring. "I'll fight him at halftime. I'll take him to the parking lot."

Down on the field, Colin throws inside but his receiver breaks outside. A pick-six.

"This fucking place sucks," Charlie says. "I can't wait to get out of high school football."

Fixating on the notion of a lost football dream sometimes reveals Charlie to be the exact kind of quarterback dad that for two years he has insisted to me he is not. I've spent time with a lot of quarterback parents over the years, from Tom and Galynn Brady to Pat and Randi Mahomes. They seethe at real or perceived slights to their sons; when Galynn battled, and ultimately survived, breast cancer in 2016, the family wondered if the diagnosis was related to stress over Tom's Deflategate suspension. I once—once—saw entirely different behavior, on an October afternoon in 2023. The Tennessee Titans were at home against the Atlanta Falcons. Rookie Will Levis, the Titans' second-round pick, was making his first NFL start. I was in the Row N seats with his parents, Mike and Beth, his three sisters, his cousins, and his extended family, including Phil Levis, one of my dearest longtime friends. Some of the family wore Will's number 8 jerseys. Will threw a deep touchdown pass early in the game, first of his NFL career. Row N went nuts. Families can always tell when their quarterback is hot, sometimes before the quarterback can. The Levises knew it was going to be Will's day— he'd become the third quarterback ever to throw four touchdown passes in his debut, and his game jersey would end up on display at the Pro Football Hall of Fame—which meant that it would come at the expense of another quarterback . . . whose family happened to be seated in the row before us: Malik Willis, a third-round pick in 2022. Mike Vrabel, the Titans' coach at the time, had indicated before the game that Levis would start, but both quarterbacks would play. When Willis got his chance, midway through the first quarter, the shotgun snap was errant, and the Falcons recovered the ball. Not Willis's fault, but that didn't matter. When Willis saw some snaps later in the game, the crowd booed. Vrabel waved at the fans to stop; they continued. Mike noticed. He felt horrible for the Willises, all wearing Malik's number 7 jersey. He knew that both the Levises and Willises had been through a certain American wringer, and that their sons had come out better than almost everyone ever to throw a football. But that fragile last step, for which no parent can plan . . . "Let's go, Seven!" Mike yelled, clapping hard. A member of Willis's family turned and nodded.

Colin Hurley rebounds, as usual, connecting on a 39-yard fade down the right sideline, taking a shot to his already-sore ribs. He then throws a touchdown pass. Rockledge High takes away easy throws, forcing Colin to throw outside and long. Hurley takes the challenge, cutting loose a few beautiful deep passes, both of which fall incomplete, one dropped, one overthrown. Still, he is the difference. In the third quarter he escapes pressure left and hits a receiver on a crossing route in stride for a first down. Trinity wins in overtime, 19–13.

Charlie turns to me. "He's elite, man."

The San Francisco Airport Marriott was the 49ers team hotel the night before home games, and Steve Young always stayed in the same room: 9043. It faced east, toward the runway and the water, open space, where Young would watch planes come and go, late at night and early in the morning, calming his mind, wishing at times that he were leaving town. What roots did he have here? He was single. He didn't carouse. For his part, Young saw it as a positive. "Fewer distractions," he says now. At one point, Mike Shanahan suggested that he hit the bars with teammates. "And drink what— milk?" Young replied. Yes, Shanahan said.

Young did. It helped, but not as much as sitting in a nondescript room and watching airplanes and trying to not live too far inside his own head. He had done everything but what mattered most: win a Super Bowl as a starter. In 1994, the 49ers loaded up, signing future Hall of Fame cornerback Deion Sanders and a few other defensive stars. It only added to the pressure. The 49ers faced Montana's Chiefs in Kansas City early that season and lost. Three weeks later, the Eagles pummeled the 49ers. George Seifert, San Francisco's head coach, benched Young, trying to prevent injuries with the game out of hand.

Something in Young broke. San Francisco's other star players weren't benched. Only him. Only the quarterback. *It's me? Is this how this is going down?* He wanted to fight. On the sideline he unloaded on Seifert. The coach ignored him, which was good because if he'd turned around, Young would have decked him. Players held him back.

After the game, he was still hot. Young sat in the locker room, wanting to break everything he could see, but there was nothing worth breaking because Candlestick Park was such an old stadium.

In the following days, after his blow-up became national news, Young noticed that something changed. It wasn't him. It was how the team perceived him. He was now one of *them*, in a way he hadn't been before. He laughs as he tells me a critical and ridiculous lesson for quarterbacks, which guys like Unitas and Tittle had learned their own ways: Once you tell the coach to fuck off, you're not just a quarterback anymore, you're a tribesman. It's hard to describe, for guys who are so set apart, how important it is to belong. For years, Young had busted his ass in every imaginable way, trying to live up to a legend and establish his own. All it took for Young to truly belong was threatening to fight the coach. From there, the 49ers and Young were united, and unstoppable. They ripped through every opponent and won the Super Bowl against the Chargers. Young threw six touchdown passes, beating Montana's record of five. Not an accident.

———

Twice a week, on Tuesdays and Fridays, Warren Moon ducked into the back entrance of a Minneapolis building. He didn't want anyone to know where he was. He would go to a nondescript room, and there he would talk, free of judgment or consequence. This was in the mid-nineties. There was a stigma around therapy, especially for men, especially in sports, especially for this gig.

"You're the quarterback, man," Moon says. "You don't want people to think you have all these problems. Now you can have a sports psychologist, no problem. Back then, you didn't let the world know. And still today, even with that, people still look at you a little side-eyed, like, is this guy strong enough to do this?"

Moon needed help. Confidentiality was vital because the rest of his life was playing out in a courtroom and in the papers. In February 1996, he attended the *State of Texas vs. Warren Harold Moon, Jr.* Felicia testified in his defense—*against* the government. When the police had arrived at their house, Felicia told them that Moon had hit and choked her to the point of unconsciousness. Moon was arrested and charged with assault. He and Felicia held a press conference at their home four days after the incident, reaffirming their love and support for each other, their faith, their pledges to seek help. Felicia later insisted that he didn't hit her.

Local authorities pressed charges without her. If convicted, Moon faced up to a year in jail. Awaiting a trial, Moon started sixteen games in 1995 and played well: 33 touchdown passes, led the league in completions, made his eighth straight Pro Bowl. Over two days on the stand, Felicia called herself a victim of an overzealous district attorney and blamed herself for starting the fight in July. She described a troubled marriage, exasperated by the fame and demands of the job of quarterback.

"He can be mean," she said, adding, "I had learned the only way to get his attention was to get in his face."

She insisted that the marks on her neck that day were due to her own fingernails, not his. Moon looked on silently, sometimes lowering his head.

"Did he at any time swing at you?" asked Rusty Hardin, one of America's most sought after and aggressive defense attorneys.

"No," Felicia said. "One time, during all this, he drew his hand back as if he was going to hit . . . He was trying to get me to calm down, 'Felicia, calm down, calm down, you're getting out of control.'"

A jury quickly acquitted Moon, but the experience told him that on its current path, his life was unsustainable. In therapy, Moon began to examine himself, mining for answers. Why did he have a "burning need," as he put it, to succeed? Why did he value taking care of others above himself? Why had he taken on the problems of others without ever seriously examining his own? What could help him become a better person might be at odds with his job, or at least the job as he had been forcing himself to do it, as we celebrated him for it. Ever since his father died and his mother had told him that he was the man of the house, Moon had "overloaded" himself, living up to a role that defined him and that he allowed to define himself, and then coupled that with a job that defined him and that he allowed to define himself.

Progress was slow, but as Moon describes it now, sitting in his living room south of Seattle, surrounded by few relics and trappings of his past life, he learned that he couldn't allow himself to be alone. "I learned that I have to share some of my experiences with other people. I learned that I have to talk to people that I have confidence in, whether it's my wife, whether it's my therapist, whether it's my mom or people that are close to me, and let them know what I'm dealing with that particular day or that particular week or whatever it is. And not compartmentalize everything that I'm dealing with, because that's what I was doing. I was just putting things in compartments and saying, 'Okay, I'll deal with this later because this is more important now. And let's keep moving on to this next thing.' And pretty soon, that old brain just got full of stuff that needed to come out."

He retired in 2001, in the top five all-time in yards, touchdown passes, attempts, and completions. Moon was forty-four years old, and he was still standing.

At first, junior year chugged along as expected for Caleb Williams. Southern California started 6–0, scoring more than 40 points each game. Williams accounted for 28 touchdowns while throwing only one interception. His face was on national commercials for Wendy's and Dr Pepper. Then something changed. At Notre Dame on national television, he threw three interceptions and passed for only 199 yards on 37 attempts, a horrifically inefficient 5.4 yards per pass. Then the Trojans lost the next game at home to Utah, killing any hope of a national championship. Typically, Caleb's old coaching crew sent him notes after every game, on everything from reads to fundamentals. Most now concerned body language. To them, he didn't seem as locked in as he had been in 2022. He never said anything negative about a teammate—even in private, it was a quarterback code he refused to break. But he would stare off on the sideline, almost detached from the known world, pissed and sulking.

The various throwing motions he had worked on—stuff he had noticed in Aaron Rodgers and Patrick Mahomes and tried to incorporate—helped him at times and didn't at others. When he got the ball out on time and in rhythm, he tended to do well. When he was pressured, he would miss open receivers or, worse, throw to guys who were covered. As if on cue, scouts started to whisper about whether he was truly going to be the first pick, or whether it should be someone else, a different quarterback—the *other* guy.

There's almost always two. Jim Plunkett or Archie Manning? Peyton Manning or Ryan Leaf? Andrew Luck or Robert Griffin III? Bryce Young or C. J. Stroud?

In 2024, the initial foil to Williams—North Carolina's Drake Maye—was uniquely suited to be a two. A pair of his older brothers, Luke and Beau, played basketball for the Tar Heels. Another older brother, Cole, played baseball at Florida. Really, Drake had essentially grown up a five, because his father, Mark, was one of the greatest quarterbacks in North Carolina history. And Luke didn't just play for North Carolina, he carved out a legend. Against Kentucky in the 2017 Elite Eight, the game was tied 73–73 with 7.2 seconds to go. Luke got the ball, inches inside the three-point line, and in a single motion released, holding his follow-through like Michael Jordan always did for his last-second shots, accentuating fundamentals in the face of exhaustion. Splash. Ballgame.

A week later the Tar Heels claimed a seventh national championship. Drake was fifteen years old, but he remembers the power of that moment, what one person could provide, how strangers told Luke that he had changed their lives. Years later, when Drake was a highly recruited quarterback and he chose North Carolina, he knew the standard. That in itself was one of the biggest differences between Williams and Maye, the reason why I flew to Chapel Hill to visit him. He had been though something rare, and maybe predictive of future greatness. Williams was more polished and famous. Maye was taller, six-foot-four to six-foot-two. Both men were quiet stewers. Williams had spent his life preparing for the NFL; Maye had prepared for being a Maye at North Carolina. If Williams had washed out in college, few outside of his family would have cared. Maye risked being the Maye who couldn't cut it, not just around the state, city, and street, but at Thanksgiving. None of the Mayes would have rubbed it in, of course. But if you talked as much trash as Drake did as a little kid to his older brothers, staking a claim that you'd be something more than just the youngest, and then failed to deliver, the consequences would've been worse than anything his brothers could say. They would *know*.

―――――

I hear Drake Maye before I see him at the North Carolina football offices—a kind of full-gut holler. It's April 2023, before his final season at Carolina. He's not even twenty-one yet, so he's missing out on one of the primary benefits of being a college quarterback: the bars after a big win. Or on a random Tuesday.

His father, Mark, experienced that life in abundance. In 1987, Mark's senior year, Carolina was down 21–3 against Georgia Tech at halftime. Mark threw for 296 yards in the second half, including a 93-yard touchdown pass, and Carolina won 30–23, and he went out on Franklin Street. Time and alcohol blur the memories, but it was a fun night, he says.

Drake, though, is not just too young to hit the bars. He's too famous to get away with it. If he snuck in with a fake ID, it would be on social media within seconds. Maye is already confused by fame, how weird it is when other students—his peers—tell him how much they idolize him, when they try to sneak a photo of him on campus. He has trained himself to recognize the slyly angled phones and tries to pose for them, letting them know that he knows. He watched Sam Howell, the quarterback ahead of him who ended up in the NFL, deal with girls giggling as he passed. Maye has a longtime girlfriend, Ann Michael Hudson, and in the coming years they'll get engaged, so it's mostly dudes who approach and wish him luck. A few weeks before we met for the first time, rumor was that Pitt was trying to lure Maye to transfer with $5 million in NIL guarantees. Maye later said it wasn't true. But he broke one of his cardinal rules and looked on social media for what people said about him. It was "hysterical," he says. "That stuff's not good for your mental health."

He decided that he needed college—he needed the bubble, imperfect and unrecognizable as it was. Mark had wanted Maye to enroll early, like Caleb Williams did in Oklahoma. By his math, Drake would have been eligible to be drafted in 2023. Drake is glad he didn't enroll early. He understood something about himself: He wasn't ready, even if his arm was.

Drake wasn't the first of the Maye kids to dabble with quarterbacking, but he took it most seriously. He initially loved pitching, and he barely knew how to grip a football—but he sensed his dad wanted at least one of the boys to be a quarterback. The way Mark's career ended was like "going off a cliff," he says, leaving him with the scars of unfulfilled potential. Mark left Chapel Hill with nearly every meaningful school passing record and a business degree. He went undrafted in 1988 and signed with the Tampa Bay Bucs, backing up Vinny Testaverde, the prior year's first overall pick. The Bucs cut Maye in 1989. He played in the World Football League and retired in 1990. Mark's identity was wrapped up in being a quarterback. "Maybe self-worth," he says. Mark became a father. The boys had to learn about their dad's heroics from others. Drake remembers being four or five and throwing the ball in the backyard, finding something fun and empowering about it, but it wasn't until later in elementary school, when he'd play quarterback at recess, that he started to hear it: *Just like your dad!* He had no idea what that meant.

Drake played shortstop, where he dabbled with arm angles, and point guard, where he learned how to manipulate bodies to create space—exemplar of all the reasons why quarterbacks shouldn't specialize. But by middle school, Mark realized that he had a quarterback, not just in the way Drake threw, but in the way he acted. Luke sometimes felt that Mark had raised the boys to be "a little bit too humble." But Drake was rebellious. That's what his mother, Aimee, noticed when her youngest son—she'd be lying if she wasn't hoping for a girl—was at sporting events. "His little brain was gathering information. His heart beat a little faster. He was aware that all his brothers were bigger, but that didn't mean that he couldn't compete."

Drake would sit in the dugout with Luke's high school team and talk junk. *Why couldn't you hit? Why did you strike out?* It enraged his brothers.

Mark had one rule for the boys: They had to have one another's backs. But Drake talked so much that even Aimee thought the older brothers needed to put Drake in his place. During one afternoon of driveway basketball, Drake was digging into his brothers. *Aiiiirrball. Come on!* They pinned him against the car, with Aimee's tacit approval.

The unofficial family motto was Go Kick Somebody's Ass. Aimee had played softball, tennis, and basketball—the family sport, after her dad played at Cornell. She was county player of the year. "I liked that Drake had that edge," she says.

When legendary Tar Heels basketball coach Roy Williams visited the Maye home to recruit Luke, Drake told him that Nick Saban, the head coach at Alabama and arguably the greatest college football coach ever, would one day be in the same living room to pitch him. He was right. Drake played well enough at Myers Park High in Charlotte to be ranked as the fifth-best quarterback in the nation. College coaches assumed that he'd go to North Carolina. Scott Chadwick, Myers's head coach, told them they were wrong. Drake didn't want to go to a place where everyone would primarily see him as the youngest Maye. He decided to commit to Saban and Alabama, but then Saban recruited Bryce Young. Mack Brown, Carolina's head coach, saw an opening. He had coached Mark at North Carolina in the eighties. "Drake," Brown told him, "not coming here is like a Manning not going to Ole Miss."

Maye started fourteen games in 2022. Against Duke, North Carolina was down 35–31 when the Tar Heels got the ball with 2:06 left. Maye had fumbled twice against the Blue Devils and in his career had yet to complete a rite of passage for quarterbacks: the fourth-quarter game-winning drive. He hit a pass for 24 yards.

Then another for 10. Avoided a sack by scrambling for 14 yards, then completed another pass for 11 on fourth-and-five. With sixteen seconds left, Carolina had a third-and-goal from the Duke nine-yard line. Maye was pressured coming up the middle, so he moved right. Two Blue Devils shadowed him. He was nearing the sideline, with two defenders in his face, when he threw toward the pylon and hit Antoine Green inches from the sideline. Touchdown. Game-winning drive. His first. "A feeling like no other," he says.

He finished the season a third-team All-America and first-team All-ACC, ACC Player of the Year, ACC Offensive Player of the Year, and ACC Rookie of the Year, and was a finalist for the Manning Award, the Maxwell Award, the Walter Camp Player of the Year, and the Davey O'Brien Award.

Little Drake, youngest of the boys, had earned the chance to be a top-five pick: Would the first quarterback drafted be Williams or Maye?

Mack Brown is neither as dominant as Nick Saban nor as innovative as Lincoln Riley, but he knows something about the legend of college quarterbacks. He sits in his vast office, with shelves stocked with trophies, footballs, and shoes, all surrounding a desk with North Carolina's logo in lights. There's an island at the entrance with a showcase that rises from its center, filled with three rows of rings—including one for his national championship at Texas in 2006. He's seventy-one on this day, in the final run of an outstanding coaching career. Brown knows that life for Maye at North Carolina, while crazy, is nowhere near as crazy as it was for Vince Young at Texas.

It started for Young in 2004, when he led the Longhorns to

a last-second win over Kansas. Then rallied them from 10 down against Michigan in the Rose Bowl, accounting for five total touchdowns. Afterward, Young stood at midfield, the site of the coming year's national championship game. "We'll be back," he said.

Young took over Brown's team, running offseason workouts and holding players accountable as only a quarterback can do. In January 2006 against dynastic USC, which had won thirty-four straight games and was on the verge of a third straight national championship, Young produced one of the finest quarterback performances ever, with 467 total yards and three touchdowns, scoring the game-winner on a fourth-down scramble with 26 seconds left. Matthew McConaughey wanted to hang out with Young. So did Oprah Winfrey, Snoop Dogg, and Jamie Foxx. Young told Brown that he intended to return for his senior year, but weeks later, he rolled up to the football offices in a white limo and said to Brown, "We need to talk."

"We really don't," Brown said. "You're leaving."

Young had grown up in Houston fatherless and with a mother who struggled with substance abuse. Money was waiting for him in the NFL. "I need to take care of my family, Coach," Young said. "This is a life-changing opportunity for all of us." The Titans picked Young third overall, signed him to a five-year contract with $25.7 million guaranteed. He won Rookie of the Year, made two Pro Bowls, and had a 31–19 record as a starter. But Young also drank too much and argued with coaches. By 2011, he flunked out of the league, depressed. Three years later, he declared bankruptcy.

Young's career haunted Brown, shaping how he advised Maye. The last thing he told Young before he went pro was to remember that being a college quarterback was *fun*.

"The people in my life . . ." Young told Brown.

In 2011, I spent a few days with a quarterback named Jake Locker as he prepared for the draft. He had just finished a stellar career at Washington. He had won Pac-10 Freshman of the Year in 2007. When he was a junior in 2009, Southern California came to Seattle ranked third in the nation, with Pete Carroll coaching and a roster loaded with future NFL players. Washington knocked off USC with a field goal with three seconds left, and the fans flooded the field and slapped Locker's shoulders. That night, Locker and some teammates went to the Duchess, a tavern off campus. It was packed to the chin. Everyone was congratulating Locker, feeding him drinks—and turning their phones toward him. He's never forgotten how that felt, the instant invasion from all sides. Locker kept rolling, that night and that season, finishing with 21 touchdown passes. NFL teams had him pegged as the first overall draft pick, if he wanted to leave school early. It was exhilarating and scary. Nobody taught him how to handle it, so Locker had to figure it out on his own. Sometimes he loved it. Other times he didn't. What drove him to be a quarterback—that confidence and fear of having the skillset to decide a game—was beginning to freak him out.

"That's the American dream," he tells me now, years later. "But it's also so destructive. The weight and burden of that over time compounds. And you're like, 'Holy cow, I can't hold this together.'"

A few whiskies often seemed like a cure, and an escape from the world that his right arm had forced him to inhabit. He had little say over much of his life, but when and where he got drunk—that was his choice alone. "It was the way that I could control being free from all those expectations. I had all these things that I felt, those roles and those expectations. Alcohol gave me this easy scapegoat of like, well, I was drunk. So yeah, I did this, but it wasn't like who I actually am. It was because I was drunk. I could be a careless nineteen-year-old and twenty-year-old. I could be what I so badly wanted to be: free."

He returned for his senior year, turning down millions, and everyone said that being drafted first overall was his to lose. Saturday nights were his. And then eighth-ranked Nebraska came to Seattle, a sunny afternoon on national television, the type of game that could solidify Locker's legend. Instead it fell apart, in front of the nation. Locker completed four of 20 passes with two interceptions in a loss, and that number—four—came to define him.

"All of the things that I feared came true that night," he says. "And then you're questioning yourself. 'Do I deserve all of these things that people have said?' And then, the antidote to that is work. Like, you just gotta go work harder. And you're already working pretty hard and pushing yourself pretty hard."

Hear that again. This was a man a month from turning thirty-five years old, with three kids. He had been playing football since he was eleven. Everything about being a first-round pick had depended on how hard he worked, and now he'd reached a place where the only difference between making it and falling flat, being ascending and dropping out, between realizing the dream and coming up short, was to work harder?

He got drunk after the Nebraska game, and the next morning, he had no idea what had happened. *Man, I just hope I don't get a message or a call that I did something really stupid.*

Locker ended up being picked eighth overall by the Tennessee Titans. He had the typical high and low moments of any young quarterback, but generally looked like someone who was trying to play the part, tired of his NFL career before it began. His wife, Lauren, got pregnant with a daughter, their first child, and Locker started to wonder what she would think of him. "I asked myself, like, who will my daughter know her father to be? When I found my own heart struggling with what the answer to that would be, then I started freaking out."

He walked away after four years, a surprise to everyone except those closest to him. He quit alcohol and started going back to church. He eventually moved back to Ferndale, started coaching high school football.

When we spoke, I asked: When he sees one of his old college highlights, what does he see?

"A kid living out his dream."

———

Midway through the 2023 season, Caleb Williams's numbers were down and losses were up.

From his office at Gonzaga College High in DC, Randy Trivers knew his former quarterback needed help. He had promised Caleb years ago that he would only support him. Would never ask for anything. A coach, to the soul. He knew that as Williams's life and wealth expanded, the quarterback would need trustworthy people who weren't on the payroll. Trivers reached out to Williams before and after games, when a quarterback often feels loneliest.

Trivers: *Beginning of a new day . . .*
Williams: *Haha. Hell yeah.*

Trivers: *Let it be something good, let it be something great.*
Williams: *Will do.*

But USC kept losing. Williams mostly played well, but he didn't take that next step. He expected to win another Heisman, was going to "Archie it," as Trivers put it, referencing two-time winner Archie Griffin.

Trivers: *We will rise*
Williams: *Always*
Trivers: *Keep battling. I'm always with you.*
Williams: *Yes, keep doing it coach. Keep going.*

USC lost to Washington at home. No: Williams lost to Washington star quarterback Michael Penix Jr. Williams started walking off the field—until he saw his mom, Dayna, near the tunnel. With cameras on him, Williams leaped into the stands and collapsed into her, heaving and bawling and accessing a specific emotional reservoir, crying the type of cry that you can only do in your mother's arms. The moment went viral, but it wasn't a moment for the masses. It was one person falling apart, and a parent trying to catch him.

Trivers knew that cry: Caleb always cried. Cried after wins. Definitely after losses.

After the Washington game, Williams skipped meeting with the media, leaving teammates to explain what had happened. Coverage of it—that he cried—showed how the role of college quarterback had changed. Eli Manning thought that until he reached the NFL, high school and college media almost seemed on his side, rooting for him. "They'll say other people were bad to make the quarterback look good," he says. That was gone now.

━━━━━━

Twenty minutes after Trinity's win on Senior Night, Colin walks slowly out of the locker room, carrying his pads and cleats, to the front seat of his dad's pickup. Marion is in the back. Charlie eases onto the highway.

"It was very frustrating, being your father," Charlie says. "How you feeling? They banged your ass."

"Good."

"Ankle all right?"

"Yeah."

"Ribs all right?"

"Yeah."

When Colin decided that he wanted to be an NFL quarterback, Charlie made a promise to his son and to himself, the promise of many quarterback dads: that the ride home from the game would always be worse than anything delivered on the field. Charlie felt that the best way to prepare for looming pressure at higher levels— from press, fans, self—was to preemptively blunt it. If Colin made a bad throw? Shut your fucking mouth. There's nothing you can say. Move on. Tonight, though, Charlie's target for abuse is not his son, but the coaches, saying they called "a shitty game."

"It wasn't even that," Colin says.

"It was."

"No, it wasn't."

Colin explains that Rockledge dropped eight players into the middle of the field, taking away easy completions. "We couldn't hit anything underneath. There's nothing else we could do."

Charlie and Colin dissect the game. The father vents, the son analyzes, breaking down the X's and O's looking for explanations and things to do differently next time.

The attempt to break down X's and O's, to see it through the quarterback's eyes, and most of all, to assign blame, has become an in-demand component of the quarterback industry. In January 2023, ESPN analyst Dan Orlovsky broke down a play from the Cowboys' loss to the 49ers in the playoffs. Of course, he wasn't just breaking down a play. He was breaking down Cowboys quarterback Dak Prescott—what he did, and most importantly, what he failed to do on a key incompletion. On the play, the 49ers showed a blitz. Prescott missed a throw deep down the middle on the right side to star receiver CeeDee Lamb. Orlovsky broke down what he saw, drawing on what he had learned over his seven years in the NFL as a backup and over the course of his life studying the game: that Prescott misread the defense and chose poorly. Orlovsky highlighted the left side of the field, which was wide open and where receiver T. Y. Hilton ran free for what would have been a touchdown, and determined that Prescott screwed up by failing to see that 49ers linebacker Fred Warner had faked a blitz from the left side and instead fled right, to help in coverage in the exact area Prescott threw. Orlovsky posted it on social media, writing "How do you miss this??????" An argument started. Not just from fans—from quarterbacks and other former football players. Hall of Famer Kurt Warner weighed in, explaining why he thought Orlovsky was wrong. To Warner, Prescott read the defense correctly because a cornerback ended up blitzing from the right side, and Prescott threw to the correct receiver; where it went wrong was that Lamb failed to look back to Prescott quickly, as he's supposed to do against a blitz. What was a deep throw should have been a short one.

But if you ask Prescott what happened, you learn that both Orlovsky and Warner were right, and wrong. First, Prescott glanced at the protection. His job was to make sure that each blocker had a man, and that if one was unaccounted for, he knew where the free rusher was coming from. His center, left guard, and left tackle all had a 49ers rusher to block. "So you're three-for-three on the left, and then you're two-for-two on the right—unless that [cornerback] blitzes," Prescott says. When the cornerback blitzed, the right guard was supposed to pick him up. The guard didn't; instead, he helped out on the left, inadvertently creating a gaping hole for the cornerback to blitz through. Prescott recognized that he had to get rid of the ball—to go to his "hot" receiver, in football terms. That was a running back that had split wide right as a receiver and was running a slant; his second option was to Lamb, who was supposed to turn around fast rather than run deep. Problem was, the running back was well covered—and Lamb failed to look. "I realized I was going to have half a second," Prescott says. "I took a step back, bought some time, tried to make the throw over the middle. Wish I could have got back to T.Y. on the left seam."

Prescott couldn't accurately explain all of this immediately after the game; if he did, it would look like he was throwing his offensive line and Lamb under the bus. So he had to eat it, sitting quiet as fans believed that he had royally screwed up when it mattered most.

And so it went, and so it always goes. Years ago, former Colts general manager Bill Polian said that when he wanted to know why a play failed, he surveyed every player and coach for their opinion.

He had the leverage to get honest answers. And sometimes even after all of that, he couldn't get a clear picture. There was a fog-of-war chaos. The game looked different depending on where you stood, and what you did.

—————————

Winning a Super Bowl changed Steve Young, but not in the way that he expected. He won, his way. Late in the game, with cameras fixed on him, he and a teammate pretended to take a monkey off his back—an instant, symbolic, lasting image. A day later at Disneyland, Young was part of a celebratory parade. People yelled at him that he was the greatest. "I *am* the greatest!" he yelled back. He meant it, in the moment at least. He knew that no matter how often quarterbacks repeated all the maxims, to outsiders and themselves, about controlling what they can control, about not getting caught up in wins and losses but instead in *process*—while everyone, including me, complicates this job—there's a binary simplicity to it: They want to win, and they want credit for winning, and nobody gets more credit for winning than an American quarterback. "No matter how much you want to rebel, you capitulate to wins and losses," Young says. "You have to."

But Young's struggle also mattered, what he had been through and how he figured it out, what he unlocked within himself . . . and what he could do to help others. He wanted to *share*. In October 1998, Peyton Manning's 1–5 Colts visited Young's 49ers. Manning was on his way to setting the rookie quarterback interception record with 26—a record that he still held decades later. "You gotta throw three in your first game, four in your second game, and three in your third game," he joked years later, after his greatness was unquestioned. "You gotta get to ten early. That's the key." This game was billed as the present against the future, and Manning played like it. He helped the Colts to a 21–0 lead. A key sequence at the end of the first half, with the Colts up 21–3, showed the difference between a true master and an emerging one. Young threw a touchdown pass with two minutes left to make it 21–10. Manning got the ball and, under pressure, threw it into the dirt. Officials flagged him for intentional grounding, killing any chance of scoring and giving the ball back to Young.

There are usually six or so moments that decide a game. Young knew he couldn't be perfect on every play, but he knew he couldn't miss on the critical ones. Young drove the 49ers down the field and threw a touchdown pass with three seconds left in the half. Manning was in one of the hardest positions a quarterback of any age can be in: trying to find a way to regain momentum after it's lost. He did. He hit Marvin Harrison on an out route that went for a 61-yard touchdown, giving the Colts a 28–17 lead into the fourth quarter. After a Colts field goal, Young came back, scoring on a short run to close it to 31–23. Manning held the ball too long on the next drive and took a sack. Young got the ball, and magic took over. At one point, he dropped back, slipped, flailed trying to keep his feet, and threw off-balance for a big gain. That led to a 23-yard touchdown run. After a two-point conversion, it was 31–31, with about six minutes to go.

Manning had a chance he'd dreamed of since childhood. He knew better than to try to give a pep talk in the huddle; he had learned that as a freshman at Tennessee, when he tried to give a rally speech before his first drive, and an offensive lineman told him to "shut the fuck up and call the play." Manning needed to earn his stripes, needed to lead a few two-minute drills—needed to do something, a big road win or a blowout win over a good team—before he could be considered a leader. On a third-and-14, he hit a beautiful out route for 19. On third-and-11, he hit a pass for 16, setting up a 53-yard field goal with 1:13 left. The kick was short. Young took over, and what followed seemed like a formality, a man unbothered and in complete control of his craft. "It was peaceful," he says. He picked his way down the field, and with three seconds left, the 49ers kicked a field goal to win 34–31.

Young found Manning after the game. He recognized something in him, not only in skill and ambition and struggles, but in how he went about trying to fix them. Manning had tried to adjust to the speed of the NFL by speeding up his own play. Manning thought his drops had to be faster, his reads had to be faster. Young knew from experience that it was a trap. Manning later realized that he needed to respect the defense's speed, but also that he needed to use it as a tool, rather than an excuse to hurry his process, a pivotal but subtle difference.

"Does it get easier?" Manning asked Young.

"It does," Young said.

You think you're done with school forever when you get drafted and sign a contract for tens of millions of dollars to be an NFL quarterback. Turns out, you're just getting paid a lot to study. I'm with Matthew Stafford in a hotel ballroom north of Los Angeles, summer of 2021. He's signing memorabilia, part of an endorsement deal, one of the mundane but well-paying tasks of a franchise quarterback. Cooper Kupp, his best receiver, is there too. They are still getting to know each other—haven't played a game together yet—but both men know that there will be a moment when they need each other.

Stafford is learning the offense of Rams head coach Sean McVay, which Kupp knows well—better than the quarterback—while trying to erase his memory of the offenses he's operated over the years. That's one of the overlooked difficulties of quarterbacking. Stafford has to not only learn a new offensive system but also *forget* the old ones imprinted into his brain like a press plate. It's tedious, which is why many quarterbacks can't do it. Your desire to be great has to supersede energy and inhibition.

"I don't like to memorize just to memorize," Stafford tells Kupp. "I want to understand why we're doing something, and how it's gonna play out. I can't just look at a piece of paper, memorize the words on the paper, and then go, okay, I know what this point is. I want to see it and conceptualize it. In some ways that makes it a little bit more difficult. But at the same time, I don't want to be playing the game without knowing everything that's going on and how to fix it."

At best, a playbook is a physical extension of a brilliant coach's mind. At worst, it's a template for an unoriginal coach to try to teach someone else's ideas. Most of all, a playbook is a contingency plan for magic. Rigid and dogmatic. An attempt to name and manifest a quarterback's genius, postindustrial America reaching into dark football offices populated by coaches who pull all-nighters not because the game is so complicated, but maybe, just maybe, because it allows them to avoid endless bedtime routines with their kids and logistical conversations with their spouses. There are usually 150 plays on a game-day call sheet; all of them have variations depending on what the defense does, and variations off the variations.

Super Bowl–winning head coach Sean Payton often says that modern football can be boiled down to one word, and it's not *passing, catching,* or even *quarterback*: It's *confusion.* "A battle for confusion," Payton says. Minimizing it for the offense, maximizing it for the defense. Words and codes vary from playbook to playbook, but the ideas are the same. A post is one of football's most basic routes. Go roughly 12 yards and break in at 45 degrees in the direction of the goalpost. But depending on the system, it's called a 7, a Bang 8, 5-Step Post, Skinny Post, Pipe, Stalk, Fish, Weave, Seam Post, Dino Post, Influence Post, Sting Post, Wasp, or Classic Post.

Kupp is trying to help accelerate the process for Stafford, so that they can move beyond words and into concepts.

"That Lucky today that Shawn ran?" he says.

"Yeah, in eleven-on-eleven?" Stafford says.

"Sit that down."

"Yeah," Stafford says. He stops signing and stares, something new crystallizing. "The safety was ready to drive it, and if you were out there, you'd have heard it too, pre-snap, he's like—whoever that was walked out of there—he was looking back and was like, 'I got your help, don't worry about it.' So I was like, 'I feel like you.' Unless you want to take that lick?"

"No. But if he was matched up, then we'd try to navigate it."

"Right, try to figure out a way. And if you can hear them talking, try a way to get outside."

"But he was dropping back there, and his eyes went straight to you, as soon as I saw that, I'm thinking . . ."

"Yeah, especially with him jumping . . ."

"With the safety."

"Yeah, you know that's coming down, no doubt."

"I just want to make sure that you were on that."

"Yep."

The conversation takes a subtle turn here, not that I notice, not that I'm meant to notice. This is their world. During the research of this book, people asked me if I was planning to ask a team if I could take some snaps, to feel what it's really like, a modern-day *Paper Lion*. The answer was no. Never. It felt gimmicky, and worse, threatened to cheapen the craft. You must earn the right to memorize these codes and keywords. Stafford and Kupp transitioned from discussing playbook theory to operation, from fundamentals to improvisation.

The biggest misconception is that the greatest improvisational quarterbacks, from Fran Tarkenton to Elway to Young to Mahomes and Lamar Jackson and Josh Allen, are out there untethered and freelancing, making stuff up. The easiest way to dismiss improvisatory feats, from passing progressions to chord changes, is to single them out as rooted in creativity rather than tradition. These guys are using the script as a launching pad, something to counter and create from.

One year Peyton Manning and Baltimore Ravens free safety Ed Reed, two of football's greatest tacticians, faced each other. They spent the week before the game studying the other's tendencies. And there was a moment in the game when preparation met opportunity. Manning knew from film that when Reed patrolled the middle of the field alone—*single-high safety*, in football terms— he would turn away from the side that the quarterback looked after the snap. If the quarterback glanced left, Reed turned right. If the quarterback looked right, Reed turned left. Reed figured he was playing the percentages: the quarterback was taught to look off the safety, hoping the safety would bite, then come back to the open side of the field. Manning knew this, and knew that Reed knew this, so he wanted to try to beat Reed deep by staring left and, rather than coming back right, throwing left. Manning figured that he knew Reed would suspect that he'd throw right after looking left. Manning wanted to add extra mustard to the design, so he decided to pump-fake left, stare right, then throw left, hoping to get Reed to bite. This isn't the game within the game. It's the game within the game within the game within the game.

And within the game, once more. When this moment arrived on Sunday, Manning looked at Reed. He was alone deep, just what Manning wanted. Manning pump-faked left. Sure enough, Reed turned right. Manning turned his head to the right, trying to sell it just a little more. As planned, Reed was drifting right. Manning saw Reed's hips turn. Figuring he had duped Reed, Manning snapped left and threw deep to Reggie Wayne. But before Manning threw, Reed was already sprinting back left. He had baited Manning by intentionally misplaying his coverage. He started to wheel left almost from the moment that he had fooled Manning into believing he had fled right. Manning thought he knew what Reed knew. But Reed knew what Manning knew, so he knew how to toy with him. He intercepted the pass with the ease of a centerfielder catching a pop fly. Bill Belichick calls it the greatest play from a free safety that he's ever seen, but that's not the point of the story. There was a brilliant dynamic at work between two players, separated by a spiral.

Seven months after Stafford and Kupp were immersed in code in the ballroom, they were in the Super Bowl against the Bengals. Fourth quarter, Rams down 20–16, Stafford with the ball in his hands. McVay calls a high-low "cheese concept," which is Rams lingo for two receivers stacked on the same area of the field: one short, one deep. Stafford's job is to dupe the defense into bracketing one of the receivers—into taking the cheese—leaving the other one open.

Problem is, Stafford's options are limited. Everybody in the building knows that Stafford isn't reading progressions; he's *willing* a way to get the ball to Kupp. It's two-on-eleven, the math of the greats.

He drops back. Kupp is covered, of course. Stafford has one trick left, and deploys it. He turns his eyes and body to another receiver in the flat, waits for the defense to react and drift a few feet that way . . . and from that angular and unnatural stance, with his shoulders pointed outside, Stafford throws inside, hitting Kupp crossing over the middle, a quarterback's version of a point guard throwing a no-look pass. The degree of difficulty is matched only by the degree of insanity, given the stakes. If that throw had been intercepted, it would have defined Stafford forever.

A few plays later the two combined near the goal line for the decisive touchdown. On the sideline, Stafford told Kupp, "Might be the best no-looker we've had all year." As in, there were several.

In the aftermath of the Super Bowl, Stafford was asked repeatedly about the physics of the pass and the machinations of the play call. He credited Kupp, saying that all he had to do was throw it on time. If Kupp hadn't found a hole, it would have been an interception. If Stafford hadn't dared to throw it, the play might have been a sack. The play was both of them.

Daddy decided to visit Arch in January 2022. That's what all the Alabama assistants called Nick Saban. Daddy wanted this kid, and he was the only coach recruiting Arch whose mere existence and résumé were sufficient selling points. Seven national championships. Want to be ready for the NFL? Who better to prepare you than Saban, whose knowledge of defense is superior to anyone's except Bill Belichick's? Alabama under Saban was an NFL factory. He had sent or had a hand in sending several good quarterbacks to the pros, Miami's Tua Tagovailoa and Philadelphia's Jalen Hurts among them. His quarterback at the time of the Newman visit, Bryce Young, would be picked first overall in 2023. A handshake from Saban was an anointing.

Of all of Saban's quarterbacks, Hurts became the best pro—in spite of Saban. In the 2018 SEC Championship game, Alabama was down 13–0 to Georgia when Saban benched Hurts. Tagovailoa, then a freshman, came off the bench to deliver a 41-yard strike to a streaking DeVonta Smith to win the game. In the moment, Tua seemed like the kind of quarterback Jalen was not, one who could rise to the occasion and do something special.

But seven years later, Hurts had become something Tua had not: a Super Bowl champion quarterback. Not just that: a Super Bowl MVP. To get there, he had relied on something more than skillset or work ethic or even hunger to quiet other people's doubts about him, doubts that perhaps he held internally, too. He had called on a kind of remarkable imperviousness. After transferring to Oklahoma and then becoming a second-round pick of the Philadelphia Eagles, Hurts seemed to develop a compact ecosystem in which to live and work. To become a good NFL quarterback, to thrive in key situations, he wired himself to look beyond them, to devote himself completely to craft but to also detach himself, to resist the narrative that said he should define himself by outcomes. At times sounding like a Zen philosopher, he spoke again and again of the difference between what he could control and what he couldn't. "It's really a process of thrills and growth," he said. "And I don't think it's about any one result."

Willing to forego the symbolic dimensions of the role, and looking to keep the public pressures of it at a distance, Hurts dove into his mechanics, with 3DQB, trying to be more fluid with his motion and quicker from read to release. He focused on leadership techniques, saying his approach was something he had "never had a label for." He hired an all-women management team at Klutch Sports Group and completed his master's degree from Oklahoma in 2023. He is not always a great quarterback, series to series and week to week, but he has shown an ability to raise his level of play to meet the moment in a way that once seemed to elude him. And in the process, he's helped make the case, and maybe remind us, that quarterbacks, not coaches—not even legendary coaches—have the last word on what it takes to do the job.

Saban arrived on a Saturday. Newman had a basketball game that afternoon, in its tiny gym near the football field. Arch was a forward. Nelson Stewart waited in his office. Alabama defensive coordinator Pete Golding popped in.

"Daddy wants to meet you," he said.

Stewart was nervous. He had never met Saban, whose default expression is dour. His sideline tirades were legendary. Saban entered Stewart's rusty old office, in a crimson blazer.

"Hello, Nelson."

Golding nudged the conversation into a good place, then left. It was just Stewart and Saban. Stewart's heart pounded. Daddy looked around the office, at some of the Odell Beckham Jr. photos and jerseys. He was still salty about losing Beckham to LSU. He switched topics.

"Tell me about the tight end," Saban said.

That curveball caught Stewart by surprise. Tight end Will Randle—Arch's favorite target, six-foot-three, 230 pounds—was a top prospect in his own right, worth discussing and dissecting, which they did, until tip-off neared. They walked across campus.

"Coach, it's a real tight arena," Stewart said.

"I don't want to get swarmed," Saban said.

Stewart had set up chairs in the rafters, away from the masses. When they entered, Saban signed a few autographs. When they arrived, Texas assistant coaches A. J. Milwee and Terry Joseph were in Saban's area, leaning over the rails.

Stewart gave them a look. "Seriously?" he whispered.

They deferred to Daddy, moving to the front row. No coaches could interact with Arch or his family, per NCAA rules. All were there to be seen. Saban was seen. Photos of him at the game went viral. When the game ended, Golding turned to Stewart.

"Daddy's gonna make it quick," he said.

Saban approached Stewart.

"Thanks," he said. And then he was gone.

In December 2023, I'm with Colin and Charlie Hurley in Frisco, Texas, for the US Army Bowl, a showcase for top high school players. Hours before the game, at a roadside barbeque joint, the players and parents huddle around a group of men holding a helmet, manufacturers testifying to the safety of their product for the game—an exhibition game in full pads, with scholarships and NIL money at stake. Most players stare at their phones. Parents seem disinterested. Today, the *Washington Post* published a story detailing the bleak state of tackle football in America. Only two states—Mississippi and Alabama—saw rises in participation. Politics and socioeconomics were massive factors. Football's existential danger is unmistakable. Quarterback has never been more potent in the zeitgeist, in a game that's both more popular than ever and unsustainable.

Standing in this barbeque joint, alongside future stars, having finished a plateful of brisket, I can't shake the weird dichotomy of it all. What happens if the game goes away? What's better? What's worse? Or what if football, and thus quarterback, is reinvented? The *Post* data showed that flag football was almost universally on the rise.

Flag's greatest player—greatest quarterback—is Vanita Krouch, nicknamed the Tom Brady of Flag Football. She and I had a long conversation one night, about her game and her rise. Krouch happened into quarterback, a throwback to when circuitous routes were allowed. She found this life not through the production line but because she was an excellent all-around athlete—a point guard at Southern Methodist and a semipro basketball player after—who happened to excel at throwing a football. Her family had escaped genocide in Cambodia and settled in Texas. Sports gave her something to do to keep her from other options, selling drugs and whatever else. After college, she wanted a way to stay in shape, and so she started to show up for a co-ed flag football league in Dallas. She played receiver. When she was around twenty-six, she was warming up before a game, catching passes and throwing them back as hard as she could. A teammate said, "V, you should quarterback." She said no, but teammates pushed, telling her that she was a natural, like her two brothers who had played it in high school. She acquiesced. Something about quarterback was fun and addictive, and she played in nine leagues weekly, throwing every day, trying to reach the semi-clichéd 10,000-hour rule. She made the US National Team in 2016 and earned a nickname: AIM—Art in Motion. That year, she was inducted into both the United States Flag and Touch Football Halls of Fame. She earned three International Federation of American Football gold medals and a silver medal at the women's flag football World Games in 2022. Life changed. She starred in a Super Bowl commercial. She coached the Pro Bowl with Eli Manning. Her record as Team USA's starting quarterback was 19–0.

In July 2022, the USA lost to Mexico. *She* lost. Something had changed as the years passed. All the little girls who had asked for an autograph and photo at previous tournaments—those she'd inspired to play quarterback, those to whom she'd showed it was possible—were in their twenties now and had her in their crosshairs. Her friends told her to stop freaking out, that she was 19–1 as a starter, but for the first time, she doubted herself. She built a wall between herself and the job. No social media. No film study. No practice. "I needed to find ways to fall back in love with it," she says. She eventually realized what all quarterbacks seem to face: At times you hate the job, but there's nothing else like it.

In October 2023, she was in Phoenix for a tournament. She woke up to thirty-some texts, all congratulating her. She was sleepy and confused. Then she saw the news: The Olympics had added flag football for 2028 in Los Angeles. She'd have a chance to represent her country, on that stage, just as she was about to age out of the sport. She lay in bed and thought about how her dreams have kept piling up, and if she could just keep going into her forties, like Brady, if she could just work until 2028 . . .

The night I was at the barbeque joint, Colin Hurley threw five touchdowns in the US Army Bowl. He won the player of the year award. Past winners include two first overall draft picks: Trevor Lawrence and Bryce Young. Hurley was loose as he held the trophy, nothing but an unwritten future before him.

What will football look like in fifty years? Our collective fantasy and collective fascination with quarterbacks fuel what's nearing a $25 billion annual professional enterprise and a $20 billion quote-unquote amateur collegiate one. Quarterbacks now suffer fewer hits and throw into larger windows and produce passing statistics once considered unthinkable, thanks to rule changes and to enterprising coaches who have created playbooks that attempt to automate the game. If that continues, and it will, and flag football continues its rise, and it will, and quarterbacking becomes more accessible but less mythical, less magical, and less seductively dangerous, what will happen? Will Colin Hurley's kids want to be quarterbacks? Will Arch Manning's? Will Caleb Williams's? Will the next Caitlin Clark be a quarterback?

You can argue that these guys have arrived at the right time, in terms of compensation and the chance to throw, who knows, 75 touchdown passes in a single season and to walk away with better knees and clearer heads. And if they have arrived at the right time, and if that is the game they end up playing, will it feel as vital and epic as it once did?

How much will it matter?

January 2024. Move-in day at LSU. Colin's fourteenth trip to Baton Rouge, and the first time he won't return home. Charlie pulls up his white pickup to Riverbend Hall, across the street from Tiger Stadium. He parks illegally, but no one cares. He's brought the quarterback.

Cameras for LSU's in-house media team film Colin as he stacks boxes. Everything is content. A massive WELCOME HOME sign made from balloons greets them in the foyer. It feels like a pep rally. Charlie has cried often this week. For months, he's been reading articles on parent separation. At first, Colin was less nostalgic. He prepared for the transition by cutting his trademark hair short and changing his cell number.

"Too many girls. And a fresh start."

But the day before he left for Baton Rouge, Colin said goodbye to Will Hewlett and Tom Gormely. They showed him two photos: one of him arriving as a twelve-year-old with a dream, and another of him leaving four years later as one of the country's best. Charlie straight-up lost it, bawling as if on command. Colin kept it in, like he has been trained to do. They started to drive away. He breathed heavy, wiped his face. Move-in day had been circled on their calendars for a long time, but Colin felt that it still snuck up on them.

"I'm going to miss you, Dad."

Colin's cheeks were wet. They finished loading up the truck. Colin went to the garage and grabbed a few photos and the gray-and-red blanket that he was swaddled in when he left the hospital as a newborn. They rolled down their street in silence, then Colin cried again.

"I'm ready to go, but I don't want to say goodbye."

He inhaled deep. "The plan worked," Colin said. "We shouldn't be sad. We'd be sad if it *didn't* work. I'm going to LSU."

He repeated it again, affirmation and reaffirmation. "I'm going to LSU. I'm going to LSU. I'm going . . ."

Late afternoon, Hurley enters his dorm for the first time. His roommates are all football players. There's a queen bed and small desk and bathroom, which he has to himself. Colin peers through his window blinds to see the view. "Not bad," he says. Colin then fiddles with his computer; his parents deal with his clothes, Charlie full of nervous energy.

"Your undies are in the top drawer," he says.

Charlie and Marion make a late-night Walmart run for a few missing items, including a phone charger for Colin. He had packed the wrong one. At the store, Charlie FaceTimes Colin to make sure he buys the correct one. After Charlie peppers him with questions, Colin says, "Dad, I'm in college now!" and hangs up. Charlie laughs, and repeats it the rest of the night. "I'm in COLLEGE now. . . ."

Ninety minutes later, most of the unpacking is done. Marion sits on her son's bed, flipping through old photos. "My baby," she says.

"No girls until you graduate or go to the NFL," Charlie says.

"Whoa, whoa, whoa," Colin says.

Charlie stares at him. "I can't believe you're leaving, dude," he says.

Charlie picks up a matted photo from a table. It's black-and-white, a shot of the two of them from Colin's signing day, when he announced that he'd attend LSU. They're in the lobby of the football offices, the sunlight cutting through at a perfect angle. Colin is talking; Charlie is listening. He hangs it on the wall, backing up to make sure it's straight. He takes his thumb and index finger to his eyes, as usual, wiping them dry.

Colin walks his parents to the truck, which is still illegally parked. Charlie asks Colin if he has his room keys, prompting a dull glare. *I'm in COLLEGE now.* Charlie watches Colin walk away, flash his key card at the building entrance, then hop into an elevator, disappearing behind narrowing doors. Charlie stares at the empty lobby, then turns toward his truck.

"He's ready," he says.

One day in a suite at Coors Field, in the middle of a Rockies game, Elway asked Woody Paige, a *Denver Post* columnist and Hall of Fame voter, a startlingly honest and vulnerable question: What were his chances of making it to Canton?

Paige shrugged. In the early nineties, Elway's highs were so fleeting as to be almost nonexistent. The Broncos fired Reeves in 1992. Elway produced his best statistical season in 1993, under new coach Wade Phillips—25 touchdowns, 10 interceptions, 4,030 yards—but the Broncos lost in the first round of the playoffs. Mike Shanahan replaced Phillips a year later. It was 1995. Elway was in his fifteenth year, straining to find hope—and even though he counted himself among the quarterbacks who never wanted to admit anything, he couldn't help it. Years later, Elway didn't remember this precise exchange. But he remembers the feeling of staring at a kind of abject emptiness, without a ring.

"Win a Super Bowl," Paige told him. "And don't retire the same year as Dan Marino."

Elway was a better quarterback than most if not all who had won a Super Bowl. But until he did what Bradshaw did, what Staubach did, what Montana did—hell, what Plunkett, Theismann, McMahon, Simms, and Doug Williams did—he was going to keep hearing the question. When Shanahan arrived, he had a different solution. He told Elway, "You're gonna get a little mad at me, but you don't have a good running game. We're gonna take some pressure off you."

"I don't give a shit," Elway said. "I just want to win."

America had changed since Elway had entered the league—and he had changed, too. Authenticity, or perceived authenticity, was in. The NFL was now governed by a salary cap, leveling the playing field for all markets and teams. Clubs could no longer outspend one another. Everyone had a limit. This became problematic with quarterbacks, whose salaries continued to skyrocket. The more cap space a quarterback consumed, the less there was to build the rest of a team. Elway was the first quarterback to take less money—to defer salary, which Tom Brady made famous a decade later—so that his team could bring in other expensive players. The country had come full circle on him. He was no longer widely viewed as a blond brat; he was an old man who still had his fastball, summoning his tricks and wisdom and will, with only one thing missing on his résumé. He told the press and himself that if he retired without winning a Super Bowl, he'd be content knowing that he'd given it his all. It was a lie. He knew it.

But then he got lucky: The Broncos won the lottery with a sixth-round-draft-pick running back named Terrell Davis, who became one of the league's most dominant players and a Hall of Famer himself. In 1998, the Broncos were back in the Super Bowl, 13-point underdogs to the defending champion Green Bay Packers.

Elway received more than 200 well-wishing packages and messages before the game, too many to open. Tied 17–17 midway through the third quarter, Shanahan called a play inside the Packers 20-yard line called Point Slice. The moment Elway heard the call, he knew he was going to have to improvise. Point Slice was a third-down pass play designed for man coverage. Shanahan and the staff had watched all of the Packers film from 1997, and every time this situation came up, Green Bay played man. In practice, Elway was skeptical.

"If they don't play man, we don't have a play," Elway told Shanahan during the week.

"You're right," Shanahan said. "We don't have a play. But you take a drop and run it like a draw." But Shanahan was convinced that it wouldn't matter: The Packers would play man. "It's one hundred percent," he told Elway.

No matter how many years you play, if by any measure you're one of the best ever, there are four or so moments, if you're lucky, that define you.

Elway came to the line, and of course, the Packers were in zone. He got the ball, scooted up in the pocket, found a crease to the left, and then sprinted to the sticks. Three Packers closed in. Elway glanced to the sideline, to see how far he needed for a first down. He needed about five yards; he couldn't risk stopping short. He lunged forward—despite being one of the best athletes of his generation, Elway couldn't jump; "White man's disease," he said—and collided with two Packers, one from each side. He spun in the air, a yard above the ground, and was hit one more time. He landed, and when he did, he knew he had done more than get a first down. He felt a surge of energy through his body unlike anything before. The sideline exploded. He still gets shivers when he discusses it.

To Broncos fans it was Kirk Gibson's home run in the World Series against the A's, or Michael Jordan's switch-handed layup in the NBA Finals against the Lakers, or Adam Vinatieri's kick to beat the St. Louis Rams in the Super Bowl. It was a statement, from which there's a definitive before and after. Elway now belonged in an elite club. A perception of a quarterback, and a city, and a fanbase, was altered forever.

The Broncos later scored a touchdown. In the fourth quarter, Elway trotted onto the field with just over three minutes left, score tied 24–24. Before the game, he had prayed, not for a win, but for a chance.

This is my career, Elway thought.

The drive featured Davis more than Elway, but he hit a 23-yard completion to put the Broncos into the red zone. Davis sealed it from there, and the Broncos defense staved off a charge from Brett Favre to win 31–24. Onstage after the game, owner Pat Bowlen handed the Lombardi Trophy to Elway, who held it against his cheek. "Relieved a lot of doubt in my mind." He was so used to losing Super Bowls that he had no idea how to handle a win. He looked around for his championship hat; someone had to tell him that it was in his hand. He held the trophy with a sense of wonder. It was real, it existed, it wasn't something that he just saw in photos.

After the game, Elway's eight-year-old son ran up to him. "Dad, where's your ring?" he said, expecting that it arrived immediately.

Elway retired a little more than a year later, walking off as the Most Valuable Player of a back-to-back Super Bowl champion. He spent the night of the second straight Super Bowl watching a tape of the game with buddies from high school and Stanford. Around 3 a.m., they laughed when Elway scored a touchdown on a quarterback draw to ice the game. He was supposed to take a three-step drop and then fight up the middle; they told Elway that he took a "half step" because he was scared of getting hit.

That was a sign. Elway considered returning for another year because he didn't want Mike Shanahan to win a Super Bowl without him, but he knew it was over. "I was out of gas," he later said.

The first person he told was his father. It was April 1999. John and Jack sat in a basement bar. It had been 148 NFL wins since the Impala, the most in history to that point. He'd done it. They'd done it.

John told Janet next. Now all he had to do was sort out what it took to become himself, and what the next version of himself looked like.

"The pressure's all gone," he said.

———

For years, I have listened as quarterbacks all but tell me that they were born control freaks, or at least possessed control-freak tendencies, and then had those urges fertilized, praised, and indulged. They know latitude and freedom. What shape does that hardwiring take next, on a new platform, in a new phase of life—and specifically *without* the one they know best?

———

Is Colin Hurley truly ready for college? In football, he performs beyond his years from the start, a continuation of expectations and trajectory. His release, already clean and high, becomes cleaner and higher. His confidence, already substantial, grows. His build, already sculpted, firms even more. He competes for the second-string quarterback job, and wins it, at age seventeen, five years younger than the starter, Garrett Nussmeier. During one particularly intense practice, when trash-talking is rampant, Hurley lofts a deep pass down the sideline that is caught—and when it is, Colin turns to the defensive coaches and players and flips them off. He later posts it on Instagram. Charlie watches it on repeat, marveling at his son's bloodthirstiness, pleased with what he's becoming—on the field, at least.

But Colin is still young, still growing, still developing in critical ways, still naïve. One day, Tom Gormely tells Hurley that he's asking for trouble by going to bars. *Don't risk your reputation*, he said. *Don't make yourself an easy target*. Hurley insists to Gormely that LSU students never take photos of athletes when they're out on the town. Sure enough, a photo of Hurley at a bar is posted on social media.

Colin wants distance from Charlie, which the father understands but still struggles with. As planned, Charlie sees his therapist twice weekly in the months after Colin leaves. Colin goes long stretches without calling. He takes trips without him. Charlie had wanted Colin to struggle in college, but from the outside, from his Instagram account, where Charlie often learns about Colin's day, life is almost too easy. After a semester in the dorm, Colin wants to move off campus. He moves into a house, against Charlie's wishes. Finally, Colin wants a car.

"No car," Charlie tells Colin. "First-year freshman, on campus. Focus. Learn college life. What do you need a car for?"

"I want it," Colin says. He wins, of course, and gets a red Dodge Charger, powerful and fast—powerfully fast.

After LSU's 2024 season ends with a New Year's Eve win over Baylor in the Texas Bowl, Colin goes home to Jacksonville for a few weeks. Something about their relationship is off. Charlie has a strong premonition that something bad will happen. He has a sit-down with Colin, but it does little to ease him. Hours before Colin goes back to college, Charlie writes a note with his name and number, writing down that he is a former police officer, and asking anyone who finds it to call him in the event of an emergency. Charlie places it in Colin's glove box. He knows where cops look.

Colin drives back to Baton Rouge.

Five days later, at 4 a.m. on Thursday, January 16, Charlie's cell rings.

V

ECHOES

Johnny U would've loved this. All his trinkets, statues, photos, jerseys, T-shirts, pants—clutter to him, memorabilia to us—are for sale. When he was alive he'd tried to offload all this stuff, giving away items worth tens of thousands. "What the hell do we need it for?" he'd tell Sandy. She hid the important stuff where he'd never look, a preemptive measure. The last known pair of his iconic black high-tops was behind the basement freezer. His two NFL Championship, Super Bowl, and Hall of Fame rings were in a porcelain goose statue in the attic. Problem was, she forgot where she'd put them. Nobody could find anything. Years passed. Then one day at dinner, Johnny sat at his usual spot—head of the table, quarterback of the family—and seemed to be flaunting his hand. Odd, but the kids—Joe, Chad, and Paige—thought little of it. His hands were weak and arthritic, the wears of his career. Finally, Chad realized:

Dad was wearing his Super Bowl ring. Sandy had gone to the attic looking for something else, and when she saw the flowerpot and it hit her where she had stashed it. . . .

Sandy and Joey are here now: January 2024, Saturday before Super Bowl LVIII in Las Vegas, a football expo in a giant and generic box of a convention center on the south end of the Strip, packed to the chinstrap with grown men in football jerseys. A smorgasbord of excess and a kind of addiction, it's officially called the NFL Experience. You can throw, catch, run. In one small square, between a Wilson football exhibit and some sort of dance party, there's an auction of hundreds of football relics from NFL royalty: an autographed photo of Joe Namath with Mickey Mantle, and signed jerseys from Dan Marino and Patrick Mahomes. The Unitases are unloading several glass cases of his items, the Johnny Unitas Collection Parts I and II, which might fetch half a million dollars today if all goes well.

"If your dad were here," Sandy tells Joe, "he'd say, 'Are they out of their fucking mind?'"

A memorabilia auction is a test of the value of memory, an accounting of what's left after an icon is gone. With great quarterbacks, we want artifacts and highlights and mementos because they remind us of something that we witnessed, that we lived, in our own way. Sandy and Joey window-gaze, a trip down their life, an American life. An autographed giclée portrait by Malcolm Farley; game-worn pants and helmet, with the old-school single gray bar; a photo of John and Sandy at the White House, with Bush 41; signed footballs and photos; plaques and trophies and handwritten notes; checks Unitas wrote, for cash, for his *Sports Illustrated* subscription, for his mortgage payment. His Delta SkyMiles card. A photo of Unitas, Montana, Elway, and Marino from a Walmart tour they did in retirement, four apex predators. They went out to dinner one night. The check arrived. Montana smiled and decided to remind everyone of who was king. He announced that whoever had the fewest rings would have to pick up the bill. He *went there*—knowing that he had taken a knife to Marino's soul in 1984, the only time Dan had reached the Super Bowl, just like he had to Jim Kelly before the 1993 AFC Championship Game, when he told him that the Bills "should just let us go. You know you're gonna go there and lose." And indeed, that marked the fourth straight year the Bills would lose the Super Bowl.

"All quarterbacks are smartasses," Elway told me. "That's the fun part: You know it hurts."

Marino cursed and grabbed the check.

Marino is a favorite of the Unitases, a mensch of the highest order. During Super Bowl LII week in Minneapolis in 2018, Paige and Chad partied for three straight nights, raising a glass with Marino more than a few times. On the flight home, Paige and Dan happened to be seated across the aisle from each other. The attendant asked for drink orders. "Keep it rolling, Paige!" Marino said. They drank wine. Marino teared up describing how much Johnny meant to him, how lucky he was that someone like her dad existed when he was a kid, an idol and inspiration and aspiration from the same streets. After the flight, Paige's suitcase didn't show up. She told Marino that she needed to go to customer service and started to say goodbye. Marino gave her a look that any Dolphins receiver would recognize. "Are you kidding me? You think I'm gonna leave you here by yourself? Your father would strike me down." He stayed with her until she had her bag and was safely in a cab home.

In another glass case is a Grand Sterling cup, almost two feet tall, the kind of trophy handed out on the eighteenth green: the 1959 Joseph A. Carr professional football player of the year award, for $5,000, a cup that holds a special place with the kids. Once, when John and Sandy were out of town, the teenagers threw a small party that quickly became a legendary one. Some of Paige's friends stood outside Johnny's office, fiddling with the giant brass handles until they unlocked it.

"Just don't be idiots," she told them.

It was a valiant attempt. The boys wore Johnny's old helmet, sat at his desk and pretended to make calls, stripped naked and filled the trophy with beer and took turns chugging—and *documented* the entire thing, taking pictures on a disposable camera. Out of Catholic guilt, Paige later showed the photos to her dad, expecting him to go nuclear. Johnny Unitas suffered nothing and nobody, but he also understood something: If you're a star quarterback, when your career ends you must kill the person that you were for the legend to float free. He ripped a laugh reserved for his family, a high-pitched cackle, augmented with tears, grateful the trophy was used for *something*.

The auctioneer reaches number 319, the first Unitas item, an autographed Colts throwback jersey, in the style of the late fifties.

Opening bid: $1,500.

Joey and Sandy look up.

━━━━━━━

The house is gone. All you can see if you park outside of 14888 Round Valley Drive in Sherman Oaks, Bob and Jane's old address, is a tall fence, a security camera, and a warning to trespassers. A place that used to welcome luminaries and regulars—a place the Waterfields designed with large and inviting windows—is off-limits now. There's still a curving driveway somewhere back there, but the house, once a sign of status, is long bulldozed and erased.

When I told Buck and Etta that I'd driven by the old property, neither feigned sentimentality. What the house meant shifted in the years after Waterfield retired from the Rams. Robert worked in film, through their RussField production company, but "he never left football," Buck says. He worked with the Rams as head coach and as a scout, part of the group that drafted future Hall of Fame defensive end Merlin Olsen in 1962. Playbooks lay around the house, each page a memory: Tight Left Fake 29 O Pass-28. But he was home. He was present. That's the main difference between coaching pro football then and football now. What you lacked in compensation you gained in lifestyle. Robert and Jane had coffee in the morning. He would drive the kids down the hill to school. At 6 p.m., Robert unplugged the phone and cooked for the family—partly because he loved to be the chef, partly because "my mom couldn't boil water," Buck says. Sacred time. After dinner, all the kids piled into their parents' bed and watched television. Sometimes Buck would stare at his dad, in awe of him, this wonder who walked around the house on his hands. Cops would pull him over and wave off speeding tickets when they realized who was behind the wheel. Buck never worried when he was with his dad.

In September 1965, the family flew to Canton, Ohio, where Waterfield was part of the third class of the Pro Football Hall of Fame, along with Sid Luckman and Otto Graham. Buck wore a suit and tie. There was a parade through downtown, starting at 10:30 a.m., an estimated 125,000 lining the streets, with floats and signs that read HOF FESTIVAL. Jane was grand marshal. Buck sat in the back seat with the mayor as the car eased south on Market Avenue from Sixth Street, then west on Second Street, south on Cleveland Avenue, a few more turns, before it hit Fulton Road Northwest, leading to the Hall of Fame building. There was a street named Waterfield.

The Hall of Fame staff treated Buck like a prince. He fished on a little lake near the hotel, stocked with trout, until the ceremony started. Bob Waterfield: two-time champion, unanimous Most Valuable Player, 97 passing touchdowns, 573 career points scored, 20 passes intercepted. There was a bronze bust of his face, strong and determined. Pat O'Brien, the star of *Knute Rockne, All-American*, introduced him. Then Waterfield stepped up—this was before Hall of Fame speeches lasted close to an hour—and read a short statement. The family posed by his bust, and that night, there was a gala for all the honorees and 1,000 others. Steak was served. An orchestra played. His bust revolved on a pedestal, draped in gold velvet.

On August 12, 2000, in Fort Lauderdale, the Class of '83 quarterbacks got together. The fact of the gathering was amazing in and of itself. Before then, not at the draft, or even at an offseason golf tournament, had all of them—Elway, Marino, Jim Kelly, Tony Eason, Todd Blackledge, Ken O'Brien—hung out. On this night, Café Martorano shut down after they arrived together, as a group, a class: six quarterbacks and their significant others. Owner Steve Martorano had hosted celebrities before, but there was something different about this crew, beyond star power. It was like they were all college buddies, bound by time and circumstance, ambition and luck. Marino was the last of them to retire, and the Dolphins were throwing him a ceremony the next night at the stadium. But Danny wanted it to be about *them*, not him, and their shared life. Marino entered carrying two bottles of wine from 1983. He poured glasses before dinner arrived.

"To the Class of '83," he said.

When Elway reminisces about it now, he notes that it felt like old times, even though it was the first time. They discussed life and each other, but not football. "Nobody ever wanted to give up secrets," Elway says. "Even though we were done." The conversation flowed away from that time Eason's Patriots beat Marino's Dolphins to go to the Super Bowl, or when O'Brien and Marino combined for 10 touchdown passes in an '86 game, or any of those epic Kelly–Marino matchups in the nineties. They didn't even discuss how infrequently Elway and Marino met—only three times in sixteen years—thanks to the league's scheduling quirks. So far, retirement had been a blast for Elway. The constant negativity that attended playing football was gone. It was funny: People seemed to remember only great throws and Super Bowls, not the years he struggled. One day he flew to Southern California for a charity event. Buck Waterfield also attended, and he spoke to Elway about Robert. Elway told them about the jersey number, how he picked 7. A pass from Elway was the event's main prize. The winner was an older woman. Elway cocked the ball, a few drinks deep. Janet seemed to know what her husband was going to do. On their first date at Stanford, they had a catch. She dared him to "show me the heat," and he broke her finger.

"Don't throw hard," Janet told him.

He eased up, but the ball left a welt on the woman's chest. "I don't know how to throw any other way," he told Janet.

Marino's body had crumbled at the end, but he hung on for one more season in 1999, hoping that it was his year, that he finally had a team around him that could win it all, his chance for an Elwaylike ending. His last game was the opposite: a 63–7 playoff loss to the Jacksonville Jaguars.

The Dolphins were done with him but hoped he would retire rather than sign elsewhere. The Steelers, Vikings, and Seahawks all courted him. But before he decided, he went to Disney World with his family. His legs killed him after walking around all day. That was a sign. Marino left the NFL with every cherished passing record, and having experienced every feeling possible, except one. He tried to rationalize it. Maybe not winning a Super Bowl was God's way of telling him that it was for his own good. Marino would tell the story of a safety named Tommy Flynn, his roommate at Pitt. Flynn won a Super Bowl, as a special teams player for the Giants in 1986. Marino would tell people that he was happy for Tommy. No, really, he was— but he wouldn't trade *his* career for *that* ring, a story that he might have needed to tell to himself as much as to us.

As they sat with each other and drank red wine, Elway liked where he'd landed out of the group. The world defined him as he defined himself: as the ultimate winner. Probably the richest of the crew, too. Still, as he watched Danny, it felt unfair. As great as Elway was, Marino threw some routes better. As accomplished as Joe Montana and Elway were, Marino put up numbers neither touched. Time erodes records. Championships last forever. They laughed and drank and argued and laughed again that night. Elway toasted Marino, not as a roast but out of deep respect, remarking how Danny's early success had made life tough on all of them but helped in the long run. "Danny set that bar so high that he made us better players."

Darius Rucker sang through speakers. All the quarterbacks danced. Kelly dropped out first. "My knees," he said.

Elway grabbed the mic, crooning Sinatra songs. "I was terrible," he says. "But you have enough drinks . . ."

———

A night later, 52,000 showed up at the stadium for Dan Marino. Speakers blared Eurythmics, Culture Club, Donna Summer, Billy Joel, and the Police—all hits from 1983. The Dolphins went overboard, as if compensating for the hole in his résumé. An announcer called each Class of '83 quarterback onstage, in the order they were drafted. They sat in director's chairs, trading memories, honoring Marino—and ribbing him. His former teammates gave him a prosthetic right lower leg, after all his injuries, and a tiny jock strap, a joke that required no explanation. The Class of '83 soon exited the stage.

Marino's idols—Terry Bradshaw and Joe Namath—were due up next. Bradshaw entered the stage and grabbed the mic like the country singer he aspired to be and became later in life, a honky-tonker who had battled depression during his playing days, suffering from a profound dislike of who he was and the things he did, married and divorced three times. He would sit at home after games and cry for no reason, and like many in his profession, he had few tools to manage it, except the redemption of the next game. He relied on those dark depths, always performing best when he was at his most miserable. With antidepressants and therapy, he would find a measure of happiness in life, as an Emmy-winning broadcaster and recording artist and, most of all, a man who could feel proud of himself. But in 2000, his third marriage had just ended. He couldn't sleep and had lost weight and "wasn't sure if I was going to drink myself to death," he later said. Bradshaw made it onstage for Marino. He was up there alone, and he exited alone. An announcer told the crowd that Namath had run into "transportation problems." But he was at the stadium, down in the VIP room, drink in hand, slouched in a chair.

You don't have to be alone to feel it. Namath felt isolated most often with strangers, in the glow of something fleeting and situational and based on persona, giving people what they want—*guaranteeing* it. He once said that "depression has a way of sneaking up on you." Sometimes an event serves as a trigger—deaths of friends and family or, in the story Namath has always told, a divorce—but maybe it's an unintended effect of this thing, the quarterback thing, *our* thing, either inborn or nurtured or both.

Namath was long retired when the blues hit him, or when he realized that they had, the energy from a well-thrown ball threading a needle long gone, its memory often a kind of weight more than a kind of lift. He had the perfect storm of a wrecked body, a practiced escape hatch in alcohol, a public persona that didn't allow for sadness, and a deep fatalistic streak. He always believed he had two guardian angels, one over each shoulder, but also knew they might run out of patience. Namath honored a life he earned and that we awarded him by stretching it to the daily limit; there was no telling what pain and hurt tomorrow might bring. He had been on nearly every type of painkiller, beginning in 1965 with Percocet and Butazolidin, which was typically used on horses. When he settled down in 1984 and married Deborah Mays, he prioritized stability, like many children of divorce. He left Broadway Joe behind. By all accounts, he was a loyal husband and engaged father to his two girls, Olivia and Jessica. Sure, he'd turn on Broadway, like a switch. He hosted his own talk show. He provided color during football games. He dabbled in acting. He reportedly was offered Sam Malone on *Cheers*—safe to say that series wouldn't have lasted as long—but he wanted to be a family guy. "I went to the best parties in the world," he told a friend. "I want to be with my daughters."

Life was quiet. Boring, even. Maybe too much. What had helped drive him to legendary status was stuck, with nowhere to go. He'd polish off a bottle of wine and drive home. He once flipped a car and, after it landed on its hood, he tried to escape. The window went *up* when he rolled it *down*. He was too loaded to understand why. Sometimes he'd stay inside and drink all day. In the late eighties, Mays told him that he had a problem. He disagreed, classic quarterback stubbornness. The very idea of help, much less asking for it, frightened him. He tried to quit the way he knew best: by doing it all himself. Starting in 1987, he made a diary entry of each day when he refrained from a drink. It lasted until 1998, when Mays wanted more out of life, and she left him. Namath returned to what felt familiar.

What's real, for a retired legend? What's fake? You forget wins and losses. What comes flooding in isn't only memories of triumph, but of mundane things. Bullshitting with friends in the locker room. Tackles and guards moving in concert. Backs hitting the A-gap. Receivers weaving simultaneous routes in the second-ary. Nights at the bar. They're part of a collective. When it's gone, it never returns.

One day, while in New York for a Super Bowl III reunion event, Namath made his appearance and told his weathered stories, lines he had recited before, that the audience had heard before, but sum-moned the energy to make them feel somehow new, still a helluva entertainer, the icon he created still vibrant. Namath left in disguise: head in hat, body in a topcoat, face behind sunglasses. He entered a hotel elevator and went straight to the corner. Another man was in the elevator with his kid, and as he always did, saw through it all.

"Joseph?" he said.

Namath looked up. It was Unitas. Johnny U.

"Oh—hey, John. How you doing?"

———

By 2003, Namath was on the verge of losing—destroying—all that he had built. That December, he offered to kiss ESPN reporter Suzy Kolber as she interviewed him during a Jets game, an instant classic train wreck. He had humiliated himself and embarrassed his family. He stopped drinking and entered rehab on January 12, 2004—the thirty-fifth anniversary of Super Bowl III. For one of the first times as an adult, he was no longer Broadway Joe, or Joe Willie, but just *Joe*, average, as powerless as the others in the room. His friends nicknamed him Diaper Joe. He babysat his six grandkids. He spent his days swimming in his backyard pool and taking cold showers—"There's something to the cold. I *believe* in the cold."—and boating and lying in a hyperbaric oxygen therapy chamber to stave off memory loss.

Years before, Namath was at a Jets game against Miami. A Dolphins fan named Charlie Hurley had flown to the Meadowlands for the game. As he was leaving, Charlie saw Namath. He introduced himself. Namath seemed wobbly. He was wearing his Super Bowl ring, and he took it off and tossed it into the air. It fell to the ground. Hurley picked it up and handed it back to him, and for a moment, was seduced by the legend, the guarantee, the mink coats, the dates, that life. Charlie wasn't yet a father. He didn't yet have a quarterback for a son.

———

He looks like a little boy.

Colin Hurley lies sedated in room 5021 of Our Lady of the Lake Regional Medical Center in Baton Rouge. Machines are hooked up to his arms. His eyes are closed. He has a brace around his neck, a tube entering his mouth, a face guard holding his cheekbones in place, chipped teeth, a deep slash under his nose and across the right side of his face. His right leg is in a brace. But he breathes deep and exhales, aided by a ventilator, as if in a relaxing dream. It's quiet, except for the muted and rhythmic sounds of an intensive care unit: whirring, pumps, drains, beeps, small talk from staffers behind the desk, popular music, eerie and turned low . . . and then blaring every so often from overhead speakers: "ADULT TRAUMA ALERT!"

Charlie and Marion sit bedside. Charlie's eyes shift between his son and his phone. Text messages from friends and family and colleagues and people that he barely knows, pop up.

"I'm devastated," Charlie says. He takes his thumb and index finger to his eyes, both swatting away tears and squeezing out more of them.

People ask Charlie what happened. He says he doesn't know, except for what the officer who opened the glove box told him. At around 2:47 a.m., Colin was driving home, wearing a seatbelt, entering the curvy intersection of Highland Road and South Quad Drive, near the gates of campus, not far from where he'd toured in the golf cart a year and a half earlier. Something happened, and he lost control. He slammed the brakes. The front right side of his Charger smacked into an oak tree so large that, upon impact, it lost only a layer of bark. The car, however, was smashed high and wide, glass all over, plastic shards landing as far as forty feet away. Police found Hurley lodged in the front seat, eyes rolled back, unresponsive but breathing, with a deep gash on the right side of his face.

In the ambulance, Colin mumbled a few words. He said he thought he was at football practice.

Police called Charlie an hour later, and he packed up. He was in the airport on the way to Baton Rouge when websites broke the news of Colin's crash. "LSU Freshman QB Hospitalized." It was the second-highest-placed story on ESPN.com that afternoon. Police said that intoxication wasn't suspected, but speculation online ran wild, with some wondering why a seventeen-year-old was driving such a fast car in the middle of the night. Charlie privately wondered the same thing. He scrolled through X in the airport, searching for any information. Media was calling LSU and Hurley. All of the reporters Charlie had handed his phone number to over the years, at games and quarterback showcases, so that they'd have it when Colin inevitably *arrived*, were texting and calling. He was crying, ignoring most calls, but he needed to say something, and the school couldn't release information on Colin's health because he was a minor, so Charlie wrote a statement, before he visited the hospital. He thanked the school, the football program, and first responders and added, "We are confident that Colin will make a full recovery from this terrible accident."

Charlie now looks at the bed.

"My son," he says.

———

Nobody knew where Arch Manning wanted to go to school. Some in the family preferred Georgia, where head coach Kirby Smart would coach him hard. Others, Alabama. The problem for Alabama was that Daddy was getting up there in years, and nobody knew how long he'd be there. Texas kept lingering. Competition was so fierce that everything was fair game. It was public record that Steve Sarkisian had battled alcoholism, a disease that nearly cost him his career. Sark had rebuilt his life and work in recovery. But during one Zoom with Arch, Golding was discussing Alabama's schematics and culture, and then he went *there*. "I love Sark," Golding said. "He's my best friend." He paused. "I hope he can stay sober."

After the Zoom ended, Stewart called Golding. "Pete, that's fucked up!"

Golding knew. He had no choice.

"Daddy's on me."

———

Before Steve Young walked away in 2000, he crossed paths with Roger Staubach. That was always a magical occurrence for Young.

A Staubach poster hung in his childhood bedroom, greeting him in the morning and night. Like Elway and Favre, Young studied the way Staubach gripped the ball, ring finger and pinkie touching laces, index and middle finger above them; he studied the way Staubach spoke, ran, lead, the way he *quarterbacked*. Before the 1992 NFC Championship Game against the Cowboys, Young walked to midfield for the coin flip. Staubach was across from him, an honorary captain. The officials were about to flip the coin, and Young was about to play in the biggest game of his life, but in that moment, he was a kid again.

"Roger! You're my hero! I had your poster up—"

"Relax," Staubach said. "We'll talk later."

Whenever they crossed paths in subsequent years, then decades, the dynamic remained. Something about being around your hero puts you back in the mind of your childhood self, only with added appreciation, scars and price tags and all, a person in totality. When retirement was on the horizon for Young, he asked his idol for advice. Like with everything he did, Staubach seemed to transition away from football into business with ease and health, building a real estate empire in Dallas and beyond. Young wanted to know if there was a secret to being able to move on. It was and wasn't as simple as losing what you love, of what Joe Montana speaks when he says that he wishes that everyone—you and me— could experience a Sunday doing the job, just once, because then maybe we'd understand. It was the lie that quarterbacks tell themselves that it can be your entire life, that it can be a life. Attacking the job with a religious type of intensity works, but only to a point. Then it turns on itself.

Staubach looked Young in the eye, as if in the huddle. What he said next was unsentimental. He'd made no truce with football.

"Run. Just run away. It'll never leave you. You need to run away from it."

―――――――――

Young ran, becoming a venture capitalist, but he also stayed close to the game, working as an analyst. He wanted to show that it could be taught, learned, honed, perfected, wanted to show that you didn't have to be born with this thing to do it at the highest level. He worked at ESPN for two decades, but he was always a little out of place. Most analysts veered into technical jargon to explain quarterbacks; Young spoke in romantic terms, mystical ones, of virtues and powers rather than reads and throws. Other analysts could make the job seem so difficult as to be impossible. But Young knew that it could be . . . *easy,* but only after you had the courage to commit yourself to it, surrender yourself to it, in a borderline unhealthy but ultimately rewarding way. "There's power in the vulnerability," he says. "But you've gotta be careful. . . . Vulnerability helps you learn and grow, but it's not a place you want to hang out."

Young tried to help the next generation, but he was up against more than fifty years of culture and nostalgia and myth and ego. He noticed other quarterbacks struggling in ways only a trained eye could see and wanted to help. One year at the Pro Bowl, Young chatted with Randall Cunningham, who was drafted after Young and won an MVP award before him and collected his spoils by dating Whitney Houston, transcending the job but not completely living up to it. Young saw untapped potential. Cunningham was running too much, short-circuiting the West Coast Offense. Announcers would praise Cunningham for turning broken plays into success-ful ones, but Young knew from experience that the plays weren't broken; they'd never had a chance to develop. He approached Cunningham and told him how the 49ers had tied up his legs, literally tied them, to force him to process from the pocket. Young tried to explain it: Cunningham would be either in front of the data or behind it. If you're in front of it, it's reflexive. "The only way to get there, you gotta go to school," he told Cunningham. "I'm telling you, it's worthwhile."

"Screw that," Cunningham said. "I'm the future."

The list of Hall of Famers, and those who will be on it one day, is built on doing the work. Sammy Baugh did it. Sid Luckman did it. Waterfield did. Van Brocklin did. Layne did. Unitas did. Tittle did. Len Dawson did. Bob Griese did. Ken Stabler did. Fran Tarkenton did. Fouts did. Sonny Jurgensen did. Bradshaw did. Staubach did. Montana did. Marino did. Moon did. Elway did. Favre did. Kurt Warner did. Aikman did. Peyton and Eli Manning did. Brady did. Mahomes and Lamar Jackson and Josh Allen do. And Young: He did.

Cunningham eventually did, too, after enduring so many injuries that he was benched, then cut—exactly what Young saw coming. He was considered so damaged that he spent a year out of the NFL. In 1997, he signed with the Vikings. Using his mind more than his legs, he led Minnesota to the playoffs before losing to Young's 49ers. In 1998, Cunningham won his second MVP award, throwing 34 touchdowns and leading the Vikings to a 15–1 record. If he could have done that starting in the early nineties, we're talking one of the greatest ever. As it was, he never started more than six games in a season the rest of his career, forever one of the many very good ones who never became universally accepted as great.

"Big graveyard there," Young says.

Children always notice the cracks in a marriage earlier than parents think, and Buck Waterfield was no different. He was ten when Jane arrived at their house—their Sherman Oaks house—and grabbed him by the arm.

"You're coming with me," she said.

"No," Buck said.

This was home. Dad lived there. By that point, Mom was staying in another of their houses, down on the beach. It was 1967. His parents were together, they were apart, they were traveling—that was life. Buck liked it when it was just him and his dad at the house, staying up late. Now Mom wanted his bags packed. Buck had inherited his father's stubbornness. He started to run around the house, avoiding her. He found a way to a phone and called Dad's office. "I'll be right there," Bob said.

When Buck told me this story, he wanted me to know something vital, because it had to do with both the idea of quarterbacks and maybe of what made his parents great professionally: There was an inherent cruelty in the way the family interacted.

"They liked to turn the knife, get a reaction, and then step back and watch it unfold," Buck says.

Alcohol added fuel to those hardwired instincts. The 1960s hit the household hard, as the cold realities of two glamorous professions arrived. Los Angeles loves to gift success and then snatch it away. Jane was into her forties and studios called less frequently, having moved on to the next girl. Waterfield resigned as Rams coach after nine wins in a little more than two years.

Quarterbacks are isolationists at heart, and Waterfield started to manufacture distance. He opened a bar a few minutes from their house called the Pump Room. He'd meet buddies at 5 p.m. for happy hours that sometimes lasted until the middle of the night. Jane and Robert's interactions were staid and perfunctory. She wanted something different for her youngest son. She showed up to grab him. Buck ended up staying with Dad. One day, Jane's mom told Bob, "If you care about your wife, you'd better start paying more attention to her."

He chose the bar.

———

In June of 2022, Nelson Stewart served as a counselor at the Manning Passing Academy in Thibodaux, Louisiana, the annual camp in the sticks that's as much of a tour stop on the high school quarterback junket as Elite 11, thirty-some years strong. Peyton was the Manning who came up with the idea, decades ago. He would read the box scores of Southern Louisiana high school games. Few teams passed; most ran. He wanted to help local quarterbacks, receivers, and coaches. The camp was launched. Archie personally recruited college quarterbacks to work with high school kids. Some of the campers could barely throw. Archie, Cooper, and Peyton used to joke about it. Then, around 2000, the camp started to draw more Texas kids. Offenses changed; quarterbacks changed; the Mannings' stature changed; we changed. The camp grew from a Southern thing to a national thing. Around 1,500 kids show up each year, 900 quarterbacks. Forty or so college quarterbacks serve as counselors every summer. Archie puts all of them in his phone, as a way to stay in touch. Daniel Jones is Duke Quarterback #4. Carson Beck is Georgia Quarterback 24. Kirk Cousins is Michigan State Quarterback.

The academy gives the participants something Archie lacked at Ole Miss: a chance to be around others with the same wiring, to talk shop, to get to know one another, to trade stories about craft and life. When Archie was in college, he rarely visited with his peers. In 1970, *Sport* magazine flew him, Jim Plunkett of Stanford, Joe Theismann of Notre Dame, and Rex Kern of Ohio State to Chicago for a roundtable interview. They were on the cover, under the banner YEAR OF THE COLLEGE QUARTERBACK.

"I knew who they were," Archie says. "I'd seen 'em play. That was cool." He pauses. "That was cool."

That interview was the beginning of a lifetime bond. All four of them were finalists for the Heisman. When Plunkett won, Archie, who had broken his arm during the season and was proud to have finished third, sent him a telegram, congratulating him. They remained friends, as Plunkett went on to struggle with injuries as the Patriots' first overall draft pick, then excel as a Raider, winning two Super Bowls. In retirement, both became exemplars of a particular Hall of Fame debate: Plunkett, why two rings doesn't guarantee entry. Manning, why mostly stellar play on losing teams can count against a quarterback. When Peyton, as a high-schooler, attended Bill Walsh's football camp at Stanford, Archie wanted him to stay with someone he knew. He could have called dozens of people, but he called Plunkett, one of his biggest rivals and enduring friends.

Years later, Archie and Plunkett had dinner with a few others. Archie mentioned the Heisman note from 1970. "I don't know if you remember it," he said.

"Remember it?" Plunkett said. "It's framed on my desk."

The Mannings have such stature in this space that if a college quarterback pulls out at the last minute, like Ohio State's C. J. Stroud in 2023, or screws up and gets thrown out, like Johnny

Manziel in 2013, it becomes national news. For years, college quarterbacks who served as counselors were put through a test more rigorous than the high school kids: a night out with Peyton and Eli at a local dive bar. Before his final year at Georgia, Matthew Stafford was a counselor. The Mannings got him dead drunk. He showed up the next morning, in the Louisiana sun and air thick and wet, nursing a skull-crushing hangover and "sweating your you-know-whats off," he told me. After a few throws, Stafford took a seat. Peyton remarked that he'd never seen an arm like Stafford's before—a compliment made sweeter in the context of Stafford's misery.

The Mannings are the draw, especially Peyton. Until recently, if a kid asked him to throw him a pass, Peyton always obliged. It was part of the deal. You pay, you want a pass, you get it. But he never wanted to be that guy, in retirement, who had to slay the younger guys, throwing like he still had it. By 2022, he had been retired for seven football seasons. "I can't," he says now. "Too embarrassing."

Arch has been at the camp since he was in middle school and is the most tenured attendee in the camp's history. Stewart was overseeing a drill at another camp, due to arrive to Thibodaux late, when he looked at his phone and saw that he had missed five calls from Arch. He wondered if something was wrong. He called back. Cooper answered.

"Someone wants to talk to you," Cooper said.

"Coach," Arch said, "I just want to thank you for everything you've done for me and how you've handled it. I just want to let you know that I've decided to formally commit and play at Texas."

He liked Sark. He especially liked that Sark was the head coach and the play-caller, increasing the odds that he'd be there for the duration of Arch's time. He liked that Texas was joining the Southeastern Conference. Texas had just finished an 8–5 season when he committed; he wanted to be part of an upswing, of bringing something back.

Holy shit! Stewart thought. "I'm proud of you," he said. He started to well up. Arch told him he needed to call more people before news broke. "Coach, I've got a lot of people to thank."

"You're good," Stewart said.

"Do me a favor," Arch said. "Don't tell anybody. It's a secret."

Within minutes, A. J. Milwee, Texas's quarterbacks coach, called.

"What's up?" Stewart said, knowing exactly what was up. They danced around the obvious.

"I can't talk," Milwee said. "But I can't believe this, we did it."

"Yeah, man. I'm so happy for you."

News broke. Texts flooded in from coaches who had been a part of Stewart's life for the past few years. Alabama's Pete Golding called Stewart. Daddy wanted an explanation.

"Why Texas?" Golding asked.

Stewart listed all the reasons, including that Arch had once said that he felt Austin was big enough that he wouldn't be recognized.

"Stop," Golding said. "No motherfucking way."

———

On a warm September evening at the Paramount Theatre in downtown Denver, a billboard reads A CONVERSATION WITH LARRY DAVID WITH GUEST MODERATOR PEYTON MANNING. Unlike many quarterbacks, Peyton is funny. He took his craft seriously, and at times himself seriously, but he has always been able to find irony within himself and his work—and deliver it well, sticking the landing. The most memorable skit of Manning's *Saturday Night Live* appearance was a United Way spoof, where he trotted onto a football field with underprivileged kids and promised to use a touch football game to teach them clichéd lessons about life. He started doing his shtick, his audibles, and then drilled one kid in the back. "You suck!" he yelled. "Get your head out of your ass!" He banished another kid to an outhouse. He threw one ball into a kid's family jewels, another into a kid's head. "I'm sorry, do you *want* to lose? I throw, you catch. It's not that hard. Okay? Get the fuck out of here." He pulled off the comedy, and then later when I chatted with him about it, pulled off comedy about comedy. "These kids were child actors," he said, "so a lot of the parents were surrounding us on the outside. I heard one of the parents yelling at the director: 'No, I want him to hit *my* kid in the face!'"

Manning's humor helped soften his image as a micromanaging know-it-all, always dry and working. And so when Manning joins a comedy legend, cocreator of *Seinfeld* and creator, producer, and star of *Curb Your Enthusiasm,* he is not only onstage with a cultural peer. He knows how to tee up good material—and maybe provide it, too. I sit in the audience and imagine, *The audibles, Peyton. Really? You gotta do all that? The waving, the shouting, the kvetching? Call the play already.*

Manning takes the stage first, introduced as a Hall of Famer who brought a Super Bowl championship to Denver. He tells the audience that he spent quite a bit of time writing a glowing introduction for David—turns out, too glowing for David's taste. After threatening to not come out onstage if Manning read it, he says, David replaced it with his own: "This theater has seen so many amazing shows and incredible performances. Unfortunately, tonight will not be one of them."

David enters stage right, in that slanted, angular strut of his, in his usual attire of a blue blazer, crewneck sweater, tan pants, high at the ankles, and white sneakers. He takes over the room, as he always did on his show, regardless of how famous the special guest was, boxing out everything and everyone, from Michael J. Fox to Bruce Springsteen. David is a huge football fan, but if anyone thinks the conversation will be a breezy back-and-forth between two charming and witty improvisational legends in their respective fields, one of whom defined himself by hard work and the other who proudly tries to avoid it, it's dispelled early. Manning asks questions. David answers them, with a side of monologues and trademark rants. David squeezes in a few football thoughts. He thinks the goalposts are useless and should be eliminated. But it's a night about craft and loathing of self and humanity and, as always, sex. At one point, David tells a story about how in his early twenties he was a chauffeur to a blind woman. Good work if you can get it, having a blind boss, he says. He went to a bar and a girl asked him what he did for a living, and he had no good answer. It hit him that he needed to find a job that provided an outside shot of him waking up next to someone other than himself.

"I needed a way to impress women," he says.

"Sure," Manning says with a nod, which David picks up on and wants to play off of.

"What do you do?" to impress women, David asks rhetorically. "I needed a good answer."

Manning nods again.

David splays his arms, in that classic way, and shouts in that screeching, cringey, iconic wail:

"YOU DIDN'T NEED THAT!"

The audience starts to laugh. Manning does too, knowing where David is headed.

"YOU'RE A FUCKING QUARTERBACK!"

———

In 2016, Young published a book: *QB: My Life Behind the Spiral*. What started as a diary intended for his kids, so that they could understand how the life they were born into came to be, ended up as a universal primer for greatness.

I loved it.

His scars made his life—that life—feel attainable. This wasn't the Elway video from the eighties, the bare basics. This was real stuff. In explaining himself, Young helped me understand myself. We'd discuss this, Young and me. It felt silly. Young was Steve Young, and I was, well, me. And yet, Young could explain what it was like to be a quarterback at all walks of life, from high school to the Hall of Fame, even for those—especially those—who didn't play at a high level. Many quarterbacks, from Aaron Rodgers to Michael Vick to Tony Romo, would call him for help. Another of them was Zach Wilson. Young loved Wilson, a fellow star at BYU. "A baby-faced assassin," Young says. He made impressive throws on air at his Pro Day, and the Jets picked him second overall in 2021. By the end of his second season, Wilson essentially had a football version of the yips—the disease that undid Chuck Knoblauch and Rick Ankiel in baseball and Ian Baker-Finch in golf.

Young wanted to help, but wasn't sure how. He wanted Wilson to get back to reacting, rather than overthinking. He almost hoped that Wilson could view every play like it was fourth down, with nothing to lose, so instincts would take over . . . but then something almost worse happened. As if being an NFL quarterback who forgot how to throw isn't bad enough, Wilson couldn't own it. After a loss to the New England Patriots in 2022, in which the Jets scored three points and had *two yards* of total offense in the second half, the press asked Wilson whether he thought he let his team down. This was a layup, as quarterback moments go. But Wilson couldn't do it. "No," he said. He had doubled down. An unforced error.

In retirement, Young would listen to postgame press conferences of losing quarterbacks, wondering who could own the moment. I ask Young: Why can't some quarterbacks just say something performative and move on? Can't they fake it, for a greater good?

He tilts in his chair, trying to find the words for an ability and willingness for what blue-collar workers everywhere, not to mention spouses, know as eating shit. "I'm going to be held accountable for way more than I actually can do. I need a lot of help to do it, but I'm also gonna get blamed for everything. And I know for a fact every time I step out there that eighty percent of it's not about me. So there has to be a sophistication of personality that can deal with that creative tension."

Tom Brady can eat shit with the best of them. Over the course of his Patriots career, he ate shit from the media, and he ate shit on behalf of *and* from Bill Belichick in his Monday morning squad meetings, where he would famously rip Brady in front of the team to prove that no player was above criticism. At Michigan, Brady was a self-described "whiner." Nothing was *ever* his fault. Something in him changed, to the point that he stretched the boundaries of what a quarterback could control, amassing authority over the course of his career. We once discussed how he became expert at faking it, at eating shit. "You learn to compartmentalize your emotions," he said. "I've certainly learned to do that in winning and losing and answering questions. You're always suppressing your emotions. I mean, I lose a game and then I've gotta go talk about it ten minutes later. And really, how I feel inside is not the message I feel I always convey, because you need time to reflect on those things. I think I do a relatively decent job of compartmentalizing how I may feel and how I truly feel versus what I express. I don't think I'm really a whiner or complainer. You grow out of that stage at some point. But, I've been in two environments. Whether it was in college, where I really learned to compete, and I really learned to grow up. And then I came to an organization where that's really what's asked of you."

Brady never broke in public, even during the years when Belichick surrounded him with good—but not superstar—players. And the times when he lost his cool with the press are so few as to count on one hand. But within the walls, it got on his nerves toward the end of his career. After one loss, to the Chiefs, Belichick was reviewing film in the squad meeting, cussing out the team in the dark, and after a poor throw by Brady, he said, "We're supposed to have the best fucking quarterback in the league, and he plays like this." Brady broke. He stared forward. He looked to the left. He looked to the right. And he walked straight out of the meeting. He went to his locker, sat down, took out his phone, banged out something, put his phone down, then sat back in his chair and exhaled. Running back Brandon Bolden saw it all, wondering who Brady had texted and what was said, and worried. Maybe this was it.

"Twelve, you straight?" Bolden asked.

"Yeah," Brady said, leaning back and exhaling, as if meditating. "I'm good."

———

No great quarterback in NFL history had a longer runway to retirement than Tom Brady. He played until his stated goal of age forty-five, giving him plenty of time to ponder what life might be like with a gaping hole, and he played well, a continuance of the iron law of his career: His performance *always* outpaced his notoriety, rather than the other way around. A full year before he decided to walk away, he had hatched multiple ways to keep himself busy. His TB12 lifestyle business. His performance apparel line, called Brady. Two production companies: Religion of Sports and 199 Productions, named after the pick number in which he was drafted. Endorsement deals with Under Armour, Hertz, Subway, and many more to choose from. Finally, he had his projected main job: serving not only as a broadcaster but also an "ambassador" for Fox, which paid him around $37.5 million annually for ten years, beginning in 2024, after an anticipated year off. He was retiring from football into football, an icon with ultimate leverage, a man who after twenty-three years in the NFL answered to nobody but himself.

Most quarterbacks are not as famous as they claim to be—or, specifically, as they feel. Brady, of course, is that famous, and he's also that *tall*: a long six-foot-four. Most quarterbacks can blend in. Brady cannot, which wasn't fun for him at times, but if you happened to be with him, in his crew, talking to him at a party, he would not only live vicariously through you—his buddies could get away with behavior that for him would end up in the gossip pages—but you'd have a chance to live vicariously through him. Brady once told David Letterman that he had a hard time getting dates, until he "started playing quarterback." The joke covered for a truth: He became a quarterback to be one for life. He grew to love the work so much that his wife of thirteen years, Gisele Bündchen, often called football "his first love."

Brady earned his status alongside American luminaries, and, by any standard, he has managed fame well. No rehab. No charges. No bankruptcies. His last-minute drive in 2001 to upset the heavily favored St. Louis Rams in Super Bowl XXXVI—nine plays, 53 yards, one minute fifty-four seconds—was a dividing line in his life. *People* put him on the cover under the headline "Those Lips, That Chin— That Super Bowl Win!" A week after the game he told his parents, "Our life has changed. You're gonna change, I'm gonna change."

Brady's performance and fame changed, each skyrocketing. He dated actress Bridget Moynahan; they had a son. Later, after three years together, Bündchen and Brady married in 2009 and had two children. As celebrity couples go, they were relatively transparent about their struggles with photographers and privacy and how they were both denizens of a world that they could neither control nor stop. In 2007, with paparazzi hounding him in unprecedented volumes for a quarterback—there was no TMZ or internet at peak nighttiming Namath—Brady had the finest-ever season for a quarterback, at the time: 50 touchdown passes, eight interceptions, and an 18–0 record entering Super Bowl XLII against the Giants. If New England won, it would have been the NFL's first undefeated season since the 1972 Dolphins, unheard of in the salary-cap and free-agency era, and he later said he would have retired earlier, having accomplished everything imaginable. But the Giants beat them, and in many ways, the more consequential year in his quarterback life was in 2008. Brady injured his knee in Week 1, ending his season. He rehabbed in Los Angeles, away from the team, and watched football go on without him. He never wanted to experience that feeling again.

He started to speak of playing until age forty. Then moved it to forty-five. Bündchen retired from modeling and moved to Boston to raise the kids, with an end in sight. Brady had told her early in their relationship that he planned to retire in his mid-thirties. He blew past that. Brady *couldn't* stop. He fell in love with many feelings, beyond winning football games and throwing touchdown passes, all of which he did at unprecedented clips. He loved to over-deliver for his team, loved to do more than what even those closest to him believed he was capable of. He might have taken his cultural status for granted, but not his job as a quarterback. He wanted to prove himself daily. "And I believed that if I got the respect of my teammates, through my work ethic and through my commitment to the team, they would respect me," he later said. "When they respect you and they trust you, then they're going to play hard for you. When they play hard for you, you can have the ability to create competitive advantages on the field."

That commitment took time, away from family. His football career breezed past fifteen seasons, then twenty, and four, then five Super Bowl championships, some of history's greatest games and greatest quarterback moments. Before Super Bowl LIII in 2019, his final one with New England, he opened his blue game-plan binder and wrote himself affirmations, in all-caps like an architect, which he repeated out loud, until committed to belief:

YOU ARE THE TOP DOG!
YOU DON'T NEED LUCK!
NO FEAR!

WATER THEIR SEEDS OF DOUBT!

YOU'RE MOTHERFUCKING TOM BRADY 5x SUPER BOWL CHAMP

HAVE FUN

THIS IS A LIFETIME MEMORY

THIS IS YOUR TIME!

YOU LOVE THE BIGGEST MOMENTS!

And the biggest moments loved him back. He won a sixth Super Bowl that night, then a seventh two years later in Tampa.

"What more do you have to prove?" Gisele asked him.

But it was the wrong question. Super Bowls, for Brady anyway, had become the byproduct of an obsession. If we knew then what we know now, the real question would have been: Why is quarterback worth risking everything for?

Her patience was wearing thin. She wrote him a letter, all but begging him to be more present in her life. He tried, adding more ruthless efficiency to what was already a ruthlessly efficient existence, and he kept going, now talking about, who knows, playing beyond age forty-five. Yes, he'd tear up wondering if he was as good of a father to his three kids as his father was to him . . . but he suited up, and kept suiting up. Brady made quarterbacking look easy, which it isn't, and winning look easy, which it isn't, and navigating fame look easy, which it isn't, but toward the end, he let those close to him in on a secret: He enjoyed practices more than games, his own private playground, where he could take chances and nobody cared if he threw four interceptions.

The craft *has* to be its own reward. That's the journey—and the secret to finding joy on the other side. Brady, however, was a man alone out there, in cultural and professional thin air. Who could he relate to? Who knew what his life was truly like? He retired in

2021, telling us that it was time to prioritize family, then un-retired a month later, telling us that he had learned that his true place was on the field. Before his twenty-third and final season, word broke that Bündchen was divorcing him. "I've done my part," she said.

Brady asked for privacy. "I'm forty-five years old, man. There's a lot of shit going on." But by then, he knew the deal. He lost twenty pounds due to stress that final season. But he also still had it, that last-second magic, the impeccable ambition, that surreal competitive stamina. He got almost everything he wanted out of football. He redefined so much of what was possible from a quarterback, out of a football player, out of a professional athlete—and for a while, out of a celebrity in a celebrity marriage—that he became his own singular definition of them all.

When Brady retired for good on February 1, 2023, he was single, and for the first time since age fourteen, he was not a quarterback. He soon compared it to being in a washing machine, bouncing around directionlessly. "I feel like, naturally as a quarterback, I was in control. I loved flying the plane, being the operator. I think what you realize in life is that you're not in control that much. . . . I need to be better with less control. I need to be better operating in that gray area. I can't be so anxious when things aren't going exactly the way that I want." He posted videos of himself running sprints, as if preparing for training camp. At high-society parties, newly single, friends had to implore him to speak with women. His confidence seemed lower than usual, those friends noticed. But when he started to date again, when all logic and sanity would ask for him to go with someone anonymous, he linked up with supermodel Irina Shayk, who had previously been in relationships with soccer star Cristiano Ronaldo and actor Bradley Cooper. Photographers followed him again, shooting her as she entered his New York apartment building at night and left in the morning. Not ideal, but not unfamiliar, either.

Thomas Edward Brady Jr. had decided to play football at age fourteen because he enjoyed having teammates and being part of something larger. In the end, it was all on him. Brady and I had a conversation years ago about the night before his first game as a quarterback. In 1992, he was the sophomore junior-varsity starter at Serra High. I was the sophomore junior-varsity starter at Service High that same year. He was nervous before his first game. In a near-panic, he told his dad, "I forgot how to throw."

"What do you mean? Of course you know how to throw."

"No, Dad, I've lost it. I just don't know how to throw a football."

If Tom Sr. had patted his son on the back and told him not to worry, where would his son have ended up? Maybe in finance. Tom Sr. took his son to a local quarterback coach named Tom Martinez. They threw—first ten passes, then twenty, however many it took. Tom Brady threw until he was ready, until he was at ease, in his place, until he was a quarterback again.

A few hours after Brady posted his retirement video on that February morning, Caleb Williams texted his dad, "I need eight."

Eight what? Carl asked, but then it hit him. Eight Super Bowls. Brady won seven.

By the time Caleb and Drake Maye started to prepare for the 2024 NFL Draft, they were two of five top quarterbacks: Washington's

Michael Penix, Heisman trophy winner Jayden Daniels out of LSU, national champion J. J. McCarthy out of Michigan, and Oregon's Bo Nix.

The NFL Draft has become so popular, and so intertwined with the hope of a young superstar quarterback, that the media machine does as much granular evaluation of skillsets as teams do. Mock drafts and television scouts discuss who is rising and falling on various teams' draft boards, ranking every player by need and talent. While making media rounds at the 2024 Super Bowl, Broncos coach Sean Payton—it was no secret that he was in the market for a quarterback—admitted that he hadn't even started scouting the prospects in earnest yet. The draft was four months away.

The 2024 quarterback class *seemed* special, but college football had evolved into a game that often failed to prepare quarterbacks for the next level. Many factors were at work, but one of them was so basic as to be overlooked: the geometry of the field. The college fields are spaced with hashmarks forty feet apart—in the NFL they're eighteen feet, six inches apart—giving college offenses more room to operate and leaving college defenses with more space to defend. The wide side of the field is vast, making it easier for offenses to open windows for the passing game, and harder for defenses to disguise coverages and blitzes. The NFL is played in the middle of the field; in college, it's almost all outside.

The result is a football version of what happened in the seventies and eighties for Major League Baseball's Milwaukee Brewers. For years, the Brewers struggled to determine the quality of prospects that came out of its Denver Zephyrs farm team. The mile-high altitude skewed their numbers, giving hitters more power and pitchers less efficiency. The same thing is now playing out every year in evaluating quarterbacks. College offenses, many of which are jazzed-up issuings of the famous Hal Mumme Air Raid, exploit the extra space with schemes simple and potent. For years at the turn of the century, quarterbacks who played for the late Mike Leach at Texas Tech put up staggering statistics, even though few were top prospects out of high school and even fewer caught on in the NFL. Evaluators couldn't trust throws or statistics. Can any college offense prepare a quarterback for the NFL—or is it all extrapolation, luck, circumstances, talent, and mentality?

"It's tough," J. T. O'Sullivan, a nine-year NFL quarterback, tells me one morning. He runs a business called the QB School, where he breaks down film and tries to explain the job to both participants and the masses. "There are certainly things that translate," he says. "But it's not college's job to create transferrable offensive experiences for the quarterback. There's a natural disconnect."

Kurt Warner watched film of the top 2024 prospects and was underwhelmed. The qualities that Warner, who famously went from stocking grocery store shelves to winning league and Super Bowl MVP, possessed that nobody saw except himself—an ability to react and anticipate and throw accurately regardless of danger— he didn't notice in the current guys. He believes that something has been lost as the pressure and adulation on quarterbacks has increased: a basic idea of how to play the position. Of how to read defenses. Of understanding football. Too many college teams rely on superior talent and what he calls "pure progression passing," where quarterbacks sift from reads one to five, as the playbook dictates, regardless of coverage.

Warner watched college quarterbacks who seldom threw on time, much less with anticipation. They were so worried about executing those reads and getting their feet in place and doing it all on time that they weren't considering the defense, its weaknesses and opportunities—elemental stuff for greats. In the NFL, a quarterback needs answers to different kinds of questions, questions college offenses weren't asking. "The game is so skewed," Warner says. "It allows guys who aren't great quarterbacks to look great because the nature of the college game and the rules play to their favor. Completion percentage doesn't mean what it used to mean. Records are going to get skewed and not mean anything anymore. Who can play? Who can see it? Some of these guys have decent stats and have no idea what they're doing. They've never had to play under *constraints* before."

If everyone can do it, I ask, what will make it exceptional?

"You gotta know what you're looking at," Warner says. "But if you know, you know."

Archie Manning took pride in the way he ran huddles back in the day. In some ways, he felt more like a quarterback in a huddle than when he threw passes. It was his pulpit, in control and in command. Arch once asked for quarterback advice, and Archie—Red to his kids and grandkids—told Arch about the thrill and duty of having ten men looking at you for guidance.

He couldn't tell how it landed; Arch needed to clarify something: "We don't ever huddle."

It's not just the huddle that's been stripped from quarterbacks. For a while, college coaches have eroded what was once also an essential piece of the job and the idea of quarterbacks: calling plays. Not *choosing* plays, but saying in the huddle, *Zero Out Slot Right 335 Max Base Throwback Chip Flare*, or *13Z, Devry Henderson, Chris*

Ivory, Green Right Nasty, Z Peel, Fake Slash, 37 Buster Bluff, Naked Right, X Post, Y Bite. College coaches replaced words by holding posters on the sideline to signal the play to the entire offense. During predraft meetings, general managers would ask quarterbacks if they'd ever called a play in the huddle. The number dropped every year, a receding of Johnny Unitas's life's work.

In the absence of experience, NFL teams have turned to cognitive tests. Football is too messy, too interconnected, too human to completely give itself over to the quantitative revolution known as advanced analytics. But the holy grail would be a methodology to measure a quarterback's processing and reacting speed—to chart how quickly guys now do what Tittle, Montana, Moon, Brady, Mahomes have done as a matter of habit: reduce the game to two-on-eleven. The latest attempt is called S2. In 2023, the Carolina Panthers traded two first-round picks and a receiver to the Chicago Bears to move up from the ninth pick. The Panthers wanted a quarterback. That year, the two best were Alabama's Bryce Young and Ohio State's C. J. Stroud. Young scored 98 out of 100 on the S2; Stroud scored 18. Both results were leaked to veteran NFL writer Bob McGinn. Stroud's score, an anonymous executive told McGinn, was a "red alert. You can't take a guy like that. That is why I have Stroud as a bust."

Carolina picked Young. Stroud went to Houston, with the second overall pick. By the season's midway point, it looked like Carolina's decision would be one of the biggest debacles in history. Young was frozen; Stroud processed quickly. Young was inaccurate; Stroud joined Tom Brady and Joe Montana as the only quarterbacks to ever lead the league in passing yards per game and touchdown-to-interception ratio. Stroud led the Texans to the playoffs and tied the rookie record for passing touchdowns in a postseason game with three. His passer rating in their first postseason game was 157.2, nearly perfect.

The Panthers not only lacked a talented surrounding cast, but they also put too much on Young's shoulders, especially with pre-snap decisions—the stuff college quarterbacks rarely learn.

The NFL play clock is forty seconds. Under the most efficient circumstances, it takes most coaches a few seconds to process the previous play and initiate the next one from their headset to a speaker in the quarterback's helmet. The call typically comes in with thirty-three seconds left on the clock, maybe five or so seconds later. It took about eight seconds to relay that call to Bryce Young. New personnel jogged onto the field. Young would digest the play for one to two seconds, then repeat the call in the huddle. When Young walked to the line of scrimmage, he needed to get the players lined up correctly. *Seventeen, 16, 15, 14* . . . He was responsible for adjusting the protection based on the defensive front, so he'd yell out codes like Black 57; offensive players knew that a dark color meant that the play wasn't about to start. *Thirteen, 12, 11* . . . Young needed to decide to kill or keep the play. But smart defenses would stay in a basic formation, trying not to give anything away. Young would scan the defense again, with no clues. *Ten, nine, eight* . . . He would send a player in motion, as an attempt to gather information . . . but by then, the play clock was winding down. Players would get antsy, like in basketball when a team clears out and waits for someone to take the last shot. Offensive linemen would look back at him, wondering who to block. Everyone needed direction.

Stroud was luckier. His coach, Bobby Slowik, Houston's offensive coordinator, had come from the 49ers and ran a version of Kyle

Shanahan's revolutionary offense. Most offensive coordinators try to call the perfect play for a given situation. What made Shanahan's offense prolific was that it had redundancies. The answers were built in. Each play had passing options for man coverage and zone coverage, and a run option. The point was that not all of them needed to be used—only one did. The center on the offensive line called the protection. The quarterback's pre-snap options were reduced. The process was streamlined. Stroud only had to call a pass or run. If it was zone, he threw to the side that had zone beaters. If man, he threw to the man side. There were variations within those concepts, but the principles remained constant. Before the draft, the Panthers interviewed Stroud twice, six weeks apart. The second time, they asked him to recite and draw plays that they had gone over in the first meeting. Stroud got most of the plays right.

Young played twenty games—for three different coaches, two different general managers, and an impulsive owner, the definitions of organizational instability—and was benched. He regained his job later during the 2024 season, after some time to recalibrate, and showed promise. But by then, he was trying to prove that he wasn't a bust. Carl Williams couldn't allow his son to be next.

Over the course of my career writing about football, the NFL Combine has transformed from something essential in the inexact science of scouting into the weirdest week in sports. Three hundred or so of the best college players are invited to Indianapolis. Coaches, general managers, scouts, doctors, trainers, and executives from all thirty-two teams attend. Most agents do, too. More than 1,600 media credentials are issued. When the Combine started in 1982, it was small. The idea was to invite players to a central location to increase exposure and save teams money and time spent having to travel to each school. Teams would run prospects through an array of tests, from the 40-yard dash to the bench press to the three-cone drill. None of those tests had any predictive value. But the process, at least, was earnest.

In 2003, the Combine changed forever. NFL Network decided to broadcast the tests live. A massive audience wanted to watch young men run and jump in tights for useless drills, often more than they wanted to watch some NBA or NHL games. The Combine's cultural relevance skyrocketed as its practical relevance decreased. Teams started to judge prospects less on how well they did in useless drills and more on how seriously they prepared for useless drills. It was optics and artifice, as scouts paused from feverishly jotting down notes and spitting dip to take a pull from a Smoothie King cup. By 2019, teams began to question the value in sending dozens of coaches and scouts to Indianapolis. Fewer coaches showed up to the Combine in the following years. The week essentially became a media convention, with real futures at stake.

———

Caleb Williams and Drake Maye arrived at the Combine in 2024 with different strategies to handle the most vulnerable part of their young professional lives. Maye went by the book: He signed with Creative Artists Agency. He met with the press. Unlike with Williams, there was no question whether he would play for the team that drafted him. Not only was there doubt over whether

Williams would sign with the Bears, there was a question whether he would show up in Indianapolis. Since USC's season ended, he had come off as anything but eager for his NFL career. Specifically, a Bears career. He waited until the day before the deadline to announce that he would forgo his senior season and enter the draft. He declined to sign with an agent, a first for the slated first pick of the draft, opting for his contract to be handled by a team of lawyers and marketers and public relations specialists.

And, of course, his dad.

Carl was serving as his unofficial representative, regardless of whether Caleb was aware of it, regardless of whether Caleb wanted it, regardless of whether or not Caleb's paid representatives wanted it. Members of Williams's inner circle wanted Carl sidelined. Carl later told me that there was some distance between himself and his son during this time. Not that he cared. Carl had waited years for this moment. He would chat with agents, telling many, "I don't want my son playing for the Bears." Chicago's head coach, Matt Eberflus, had spent his entire twenty-two-year coaching career on the defensive side of the ball. He had won ten games in two years, and the Bears, under his direction and in an offense-friendly era, had scored forty points in a game only once.

What were Williams's options?

Carl left it to the agents with whom he spoke to tell him if there was a loophole or an idea to assert some agency, anything Carl hadn't thought of or heard already. Could Caleb play for the upstart United Football League and then re-enter the draft in 2025? Or sign for the league minimum and then try to be cut after a year? Any ideas? He told agents that the Dolphins, 49ers, Rams, Raiders, and Jets were interested in trading up for Williams. Agents would call those teams, and each front office would repeat the same refrain: *You're the tenth agent who's told me this. It's not true.* Many agents felt used by Carl, but he didn't care.

"Don't try to be Superman," Carl told Caleb. "We can make something change."

Caleb insisted publicly that he was honored at the prospect of being a Chicago Bear. That he played neither for fame nor money but for immortality. He complimented Chicago's roster and said that it was "pretty exciting to be going to a situation like that." He shrugged at the problems the Bears had at developing quarterbacks for the past seventy or so years. "I don't compare myself to other guys. I think I'm my own player. I tend to create history and rewrite history."

Another question hovering over both Williams and Maye was whether they'd throw at the Combine. It's a televised event. Most agents of top quarterbacks dissuade them from throwing, viewing it as an event that can only hurt your stock. Both Williams and Maye elected against throwing. Williams, though, did throw at the Combine in a private room—trying to keep his routine while on the road. After a session, he liked the way the ball came out of his hands and wished he'd done it for the cameras.

"Should've fucking thrown," he said.

Williams met with a handful of teams in Indianapolis. His meeting with the Bears was at 10:40 p.m. on Wednesday. How it went depended on which side of the table you were on. The Bears saw a fine young quarterback who could handle the media market. Caleb was polite and affable, but felt like the team was testing him, peppering him with questions rather than trying to form a bond. It was an awkward setting, speed-dating in a stadium suite. Caleb later told associates that he didn't vibe with anyone—not like he did, for instance, with the Minnesota Vikings. Williams appreciated how Kevin O'Connell, the Vikings head coach, thought about quarterbacks, how he spoke of them, his scars from having tried to be one.

O'Connell was an excellent quarterback at San Diego State, a four-year captain, addicted to the wave of momentum he felt spread across the team when he did his job well. The Patriots drafted him in the third round in 2008. He figured he would watch Tom Brady up close for a few years, then take that knowledge to another team. O'Connell threw six passes as a rookie in New England, completing four for 23 yards. He had no idea at the time that those would be the final regular season passes of his career. He was cut in 2009. The Lions signed him, then traded him five days later. He auditioned for teams; it never went well. He always wanted to create "the wow factor," he says, an exceptional throw that would make a team believe. "I learned that's the *last* possible thing you should do," he says now.

Good NFL quarterbacking, O'Connell learned, is often about embracing the mundane: checking down to a running back or throwing it away to avoid a sack. He watched Brady and Joe Montana execute game-winning drives in the Super Bowl. What stood out was how unspectacular they were when the stakes were the highest. "If they called the same play in the middle of spring practice, they would have executed it the same way," he says. "They weren't trying to do anything other than just play the position consistently at a high level." As a coach, he would demand a lot out of his quarterbacks, but he vowed to forgive them in a way that he could never forgive himself.

In 2024, O'Connell was in the market for a quarterback. He got on with Williams well enough for the quarterback to fantasize about blowing up the draft and forcing a trade.

"I *need* to go to the Vikings," Caleb told his father.

"Let's do it," Carl replied.

A few times each hour, Colin thrashes in his hospital bed, kicking his legs and reconfiguring himself until he's lying diagonally. Charlie laughs. It reminds him of a memory. When Colin was seven or so, he says, he and Charlie had an autumn routine: They'd watch *Monday Night Football* in Charlie and Marion's bed. Charlie let Colin sleep there, a weekly treat. They'd dissect plays, the son showing an eagerness to learn and the dad more than willing to teach. By halftime, Colin would doze off. Charlie would finish the game as his son slept, calling it a night when it ended, and then, a few hours later, he'd be wide awake from Colin's kicking and flopping, until he was crossways on the bed, at his most comfortable.

Doctors say it's a good sign that Colin is tossing around. Charlie sits bedside, in layers of disbelief. He dips his head, then looks me in the eye.

"The last ten years of my life . . ." he says. "He had a God-given skill. This wasn't part of the plan."

When Elway retired, he felt behind the rest of the world.

He had always been the precocious one. But businesspeople had been working while he played sixteen years of pro football. Little was transferrable, aside from his name. Everyone with the luxury of myopically pursuing their dreams, and then succeeding, faces a transition into a less-selfish version of adulthood. More than anything, they chase a feeling, as fleeting as it is rejuvenating, of coming close to perfection, of realizing potential, of having not plateaued, of what they had in abundance as a young man—power and beauty, and all that attended it. Elway got into the Arena Football League, running the Colorado Crush, which he considered to be graduate school. He won a championship when everyone thought he was just a quarterback. He tried to engineer an NFL franchise in Los Angeles. That went nowhere. Some investments tanked. He twice served as a frontman for an investment group to buy the Colorado Avalanche, the Denver Nuggets, and a downtown arena, and twice the bid was too low.

Even though he played golf so well that he competed in pro-am events, and played it so often that his kids complained that they saw him more when he was a quarterback, that didn't compare to the rush of football. He started to miss the torture of chasing something. He thought about becoming a scout. On the surface, it was an odd fit: Scouts slave on the road. Low pay, long hours. But he always loved and wondered about that aspect of football, the inexact science of it all, and it was a way to spend time with Jack, who was working in the Broncos personnel department. John stopped by the Broncos draft room one day in April 2001. The room was discussing quarterbacks. Jack loved Purdue's Drew Brees. He was undersized at six feet but possessed those mysterious and rare qualities: accuracy, anticipation, decisiveness, leadership, motivation, stuff that would lead him to winning a Super Bowl in New Orleans and walking away with most major passing records.

John didn't see it. He liked tall quarterbacks. "Do you see the heart and passion he plays with?" Jack told John. "Do you see how much he loves the game?"

John loved those moments with his dad, sitting around and talking ball, the language of their lives. Sometimes John wished they'd moved beyond football into life: marriage, parenthood, what it meant to be born and bred to compete. Elway figured there was still time. Days after that Brees conversation, Jack and Jan decided to get out of Denver to Palm Springs for a long mid-April weekend before the draft. On the morning of April 16, Jan called her son.

"Dad died last night," she said.

A heart attack, at age sixty-nine. Elway's mind spun so fast that he couldn't process. Something deep inside told him he needed *out*. Now. He put on shorts and tennis shoes and walked through the front door. He started to run down the street, deep into his Cherry Creek neighborhood. Picture him out there, alone, without a destination or plan. He ran to burn his lungs. He pounded the ground on worn knees—"Make something *else* hurt," he says now—punishing his body because he couldn't punish the world.

Waterfield lay in bed one day when Jane blew in, screaming.

"You rotten, lying bastard! . . . Tell me her name! Say it! Say it, you son of a bitch!"

On their wedding night she had tacitly given him permission to stray, as if she knew that his life—their life—was uniquely ill-suited for classic guardrails. She had vowed to Robert that she would be faithful and told him that if he needed to have an affair, he could, but only if the woman was "really important" to him. She had suspected over the years that he had taken her up on it, but he swore it wasn't true. Now a friend had tipped her off.

Bob took a pillow to his face and started to wail. . . .

Quarterback is often zero-sum. Its rise comes at someone else's expense, often those closest to them. None of that is new—athletes say that the infidelity rate among the greatest ever is 100 percent—but outside of Dan Pastorini, a star quarterback for the Houston Oilers in the seventies, few discuss what happened and why. Pastorini was drafted third overall in 1971, after Jim Plunkett and Archie Manning, the first time quarterbacks went one-two-three. He was something out of a quarterback romcom, strong-armed and tough and handsome and ready to roll. Over the coming years, he starred in a movie called *Weed*, posed for *Playgirl*, married a *Playboy* model, divorced her, reached a Pro Bowl, won some big games, lost consecutive AFC Championships to the Steel Curtain–era Pittsburgh Steelers, and only missed five career games as an Oiler despite a host of injuries, including a punctured lung. He suffered drug problems, money problems, anger problems, *thrill* problems. He drag-raced cars and once launched a boat at 100 miles an hour into a crowd, resulting in two deaths, for which a jury later found he had no criminal responsibility. Most of all, he indulged. He had juggled girlfriends since his days at Santa Clara University. One morning as an Oiler, he was about to leave his apartment to go to work. His fiancée, Pat, showed up at the door—as his girlfriend, Sandy, exited the bedroom in a robe.

He looked at both women, knowing that he was in trouble. Worse for a quarterback, he was also late to work.

"Sandy, meet Pat. Pat, that's Sandy. I'll talk to y'all later. I've got to practice."

When Pastorini returned hours later, both women *were still there*, laughing, surrounded by empty bottles and trading stories. Both ended up dumping him. Pastorini once told the *New York Times,* "I try to enjoy life, and I've never made a secret of it. The only difference between me and a lot of guys is I'm honest about it—and I get caught."

We usually learn about accusations of affairs in divorce filings, like we did with Johnny Unitas, or in paternity matters, like we did with Dan Marino, or when one decides to send an unsolicited photo to a team employee, as Brett Favre did, or when it accelerates and solidifies a devotion to Christ, like with Jim Kelly in 2004. If you're a mere college or NFL star, you get accused on TikTok. Rumors and realities are constant. Covering the NFL means seeing the room tilt a quarterback's way at parties and wondering what you do with what you see—"You workin'?" a married Hall of Fame quarterback once asked me when we crossed paths in a VIP room— and it means people are telling you that they've heard something, or that *everyone* knows. Part of this dynamic is simply the wages of choice, of the pursuit. Janet Elway has talked about what it was like to share her husband with the rest of the world, how there were "a lot of temptations lurking all around," how she didn't blame John, not exactly, because it was just what came with his status.

"I wanted him to just be *mine*," she said. "And I couldn't ever ask for that."

———

If Bob Waterfield was the first quarterback to get *the* girl, and become the envy of many men, then he was also the first to learn it was not enough. When you look at quarterbacks up close, you see a deep and urgent imperative to dominate. Interactions with old friends, with accountants and business partners, with girlfriends and wives, are every bit as geared toward filling some bottomless hole in their personality as is calling a play at the line or threading a needle in between defenders.

Jane Russell wanted to leave Bob, but she had a problem: She had strayed too, years earlier. Bob wrote her a letter, hoping to convince her to stay. "I'm writing this on the loneliest night of my life. . . . I love you. It's really hard for me to even write what I feel." That moment kicked off some good years, maybe their best years. They attended church. He was not America's quarterback, she was not America's sex symbol, they were Robert and Jane . . . and then she was blindsided by something she never saw coming: not another woman, not work, not football, but *pool*. Bob had played it for years, and now he had put a table in the Pump Room. Urges that landed him in Canton were now confined to a San Fernando Valley saloon and deposited into the corner pocket.

"It became his life," Jane said.

Robert stopped going to church. Jane hired surveillance on him. It confirmed what she suspected. She told her therapist.

"Notches in his belt," the counselor replied. "Like a gunfighter."

━━━━━━━━

The night before Jack Elway's funeral, fifty or so coaches and football men who had worked with and loved him gathered at a hotel bar, drinking vodka martinis in his honor. At the memorial the next day, John told the assembled that he had lost his best friend. But he had lost something greater. A foundation, a hero, a drinking buddy, a life guide, an ear who always understood, a voice that always helped set John at ease. When Elway took the most important snap of his career—the victory kneel to end Super Bowl XXXII—NBC panned to Jack, looking down from a box. And when the final seconds ticked off, Jack raised his arms to the sky, then hunched over, burying his head, a relief as profound as John's, maybe more. John lost *that*. What Elway needed now was space to grieve, cry, scream, curse, process, breathe, but the life Jack had built for his son didn't allow for it. "There's nothing you can do about it," Elway says. "The only thing that cures it is time. And it's never really totally cured."

Shortly after Jack died, John took a walk in the neighborhood. He stopped at a bench and cried. A boy, out walking with his dad, recognized him and asked for an autograph. Elway looked up, face soaked. Elway saw the boy's father standing a few feet away behind him. He decided to sign, but made the boy promise that every day, no matter what, he would hug his dad.

Jack's death was the beginning. Shortly before he passed, Jana, John's twin sister, was diagnosed with a rare and advanced form of blood cancer. Jack had blamed himself, thinking that her cancer was related to his smoking. John later believed that his dad had died of a broken heart more than from cardiac arrest. John leveraged his status, muscling Jana into clinical trials at Stanford and buying her a new home in Palo Alto. He did all the quarterback things, telling her to take cancer head-on. But cancer doesn't work that way. He was filming an Arena League commercial when word arrived that she didn't have much time. John arrived just in time to say goodbye. As she was being wheeled into a CT scan, she kept trying to wrestle off her oxygen mask. Elway yelled at her to keep it on. Finally, she said, "I'll be back," put on the mask, and slid her fingers up as if to run them through her hair. Then she stopped, with her middle finger pressed against her forehead—an Elway until the end. John was the last person to see her alive. It took him ten years to visit her grave. In the middle of it all, John and Janet separated after eighteen years of marriage, two people who had drifted apart. Each confided separately in the same few friends, who in turn implored them to confide not in them but in each other. During the year that Jana was sick, Elway and Janet tried to reconcile. They attended counseling. She wanted to move out of the Denver fishbowl and experience something new. Elway was accustomed to belonging to the world. They eventually split for good, lonely within their own marriage.

For years, John had told himself this story: He was a family man who had overcome the pain of three Super Bowl losses and walked away a winner. He was in control, with the ball in his hands, able to overcome every situation and circumstance. "I could always *play* my way out of pain," Elway tells me. He doesn't mean a high ankle sprain, although he could do that. He means the pain of being John Elway. His family was mostly healthy and happy during his career. But now familiar tools no longer worked. His four kids had a broken family. He lived with a friend for a while. He needed purpose, but a specific type. The kind that governed the rhythms and questions of his entire life. One of the hardest aspects of retirement was that he suddenly didn't have a schedule. Ever since he was fourteen, it had been set. "Now you have to start organizing," he says, "And doing that is a helluva lot harder than I thought it was."

He met with Mike Shanahan, who was then the Broncos' head coach and who oversaw all football operations, in a private room at Del Frisco's steakhouse. He asked—all but begged—to be part of the personnel department. Elway offered to start as an area scout, traveling the road, working his way up. He needed work. He needed purpose. Shanahan felt for his friend. But even if Elway would truly start at the bottom, he was still John Elway. He was too big. It wouldn't work. Elway kept him there, well past closing, but in the end, Shanahan said no.

Y. A. Tittle had the misfortune of retiring in the sixties in the Bay Area. A Texas child of the Depression entered the confusing first few years without the game down the coast from Haight-Ashbury— and with a daughter *of* that scene. He was part of the first generation of men who could expect to live into their eighties. Tittle had half his life to go, without the freedom, power, joy of what he cherished most. Now he was an insurance man, and a dad. He worried about Dianne because no one ever asked her for a date, only his autograph. He was horrified that she was a poet rather than a cheerleader. If he made a crash landing from his glory days of football, he tried his best to hide it from his kids. He woke up at 5 a.m., yelling to them about early birds and worms, and made a power breakfast, practically killing them with oatmeal, eggs, bacon, sausage, toast, pancakes, muffins, and milk. Dianne knew from mythology and legend that heroes took power from funny things. Breakfast was the new game day.

Dianne's mother, Minnette, often told her that there was "no such thing as a hero up close." Now that Y.A.'s career was over, Minnette wanted to travel the world, hunting for artifacts and primitive art. They visited New Guinea, China, Tibet, and Mexico, and were in Berlin when the Wall crumbled—and grabbed a piece of it as a souvenir. It isn't always easy for quarterbacks to follow others around, but Tittle did it so seamlessly that *Sports Illustrated* wrote about it. No other quarterback was helping his wife launch a folk-art museum. Tittle joked that he put the "folk" in folk art, and that he accompanied her and wrote checks, which was just enough to convince people that he was content.

But Y.A. missed football. He missed the camaraderie, missed raising a vodka. The game was, as Dianne says, his "emotional home," and in retirement, he "was homesick for it." Y.A. and Minnette fought a lot during those early empty years, struggling to adapt to a new reality; Dianne once screamed at them so loud to stop arguing that she lost her voice. Y.A. developed real estate in the Bay Area and made a lot of money and bought houses around the country. He threw a party every year at his home in Caddo Lake in East Texas, a half hour from his high school. One year a friend named Keats Mullikin was sitting on the porch. Mullikin's ten-year-old grandson was chatting up Y.A. "Son, I want to tell you something, and don't you forget this," Tittle said. "Nothing in life worthwhile is ever going to be easy." He handed the kid a photo. It was the Blood Picture. "I want to give it to you," Y.A. said.

Whenever Tittle flew back to New York for autograph signings or speeches—he would use Dianne's eyeliner to make notes on his hand—he knew how to turn it on: He would stand a little straighter, ask fans questions, making them feel the spotlight. When a stranger would tell him what a difference he made in their lives, it made him want to live up to it and make a difference. He could have made a home in New York after he retired and felt the adulation daily, that dopamine hit that so enriches and tortures the lives of the famous. But he wanted to live in the Bay Area. "He wanted family more than anything," says Steve de Laet, his son-in-law. "Those were forces greater than the roar of the crowd."

Tittle never sought to punish those who loved him most. Maybe that was his greatest accomplishment. When his kids had kids of their own, ten in all, they told him the names—Ayla, Taj, Huck, Lauren, Arrianna, Laura, Mera, Luke, Kelly, Jack—and he heard them all through his own floppy ears, funneled them through his own dreams, repeating each name out loud to hear how it sounded with . . . *drops back to pass.*

Warren Moon was driving through snow when his phone lit up. He pulled over. He recognized the number—John McClain, longtime Houston sportswriter and a Hall of Fame voter. He had presented Moon's case. On this day, February 2006, the inductees were announced. Moon wanted to hear from McClain, win or lose, in or out.

Moon was in Detroit to broadcast the Super Bowl, Seahawks against the Steelers. There was one honor left. Moon knew he would get into the Hall. The question—once again—was when. Throughout his life, he never got what he had earned when he had earned it, from a college scholarship as a quarterback to a starting job in the NFL. The waiting angered him, as did the fact that he knew why. He expected it to be no different with Canton. "I'd wonder, what will be the excuse?" he says. Moon now sat on the side of the highway, windshield wipers batting away the snow, hanging on the high Texas-accented words of a sportswriter.

"Congratulations," McClain said.

He was a Hall of Famer. A *first-ballot* Hall of Famer. Snowflakes fell on the windshield. He thought of Shack Harris, of Marlin Briscoe, of Doug Williams. . . . "All of the things they went through, all this stuff just came pouring out of me."

Later that day, Moon entered a Super Bowl party, hosted by agent Leigh Steinberg. Troy Aikman, a fellow inductee, was there too. Steinberg had set and reset the market for quarterbacks, representing a record eight quarterbacks who were drafted first overall, and then destroyed nearly everything he'd built, due to drinking and ego and pain, eventually entering detox centers and, after they kicked him out, moving into his parents' house. Many clients left him. Moon stayed, just as Steinberg stayed after Moon's trial. The moment Steinberg saw Moon at the party, he started to cry. They hugged and cried, not just as quarterback and agent, not just as friends, but as two parts of a whole.

—————

Thirty hours after Colin's accident, he has stabilized. He's going to live; that much the doctors know. Everything else is unclear. Charlie hovers over Colin, who is still sedated, and holds his hand. He squeezes Colin's hand. Colin faintly squeezes back.

"Love you, bubba," Charlie says, crying. He kisses his forehead, then says to me, "I want him to wake up, man."

Visitors have been in and out, including LSU head coach Brian Kelly. There's a core group that stays long hours: offensive coordinator Joe Sloan, senior associate athletic trainer Owen Stanley, and a lawyer who has advised the Hurleys in NIL matters named Brian Davis. In some ways, everyone is here for Charlie more than Colin. People keep telling Charlie that a normal person would have died, a mere mortal, reminding him that his son is special, gifted, blessed, a quarterback . . . but now the Hurleys are regular folks to whom regular things happen. Colin is a teenager. Charlie, a dad.

Doctors say that what Colin needs most now is rest and quiet. But Charlie can't help it. "Colin, can you hear me? Can you hear me? Colin?"

Charlie backs away from the bed. "He's not saying a word. He still hasn't said a word."

Charlie's exhausted. He leaves his son and catches a ride to a nearby hotel. He's had the room booked since he landed in town, but is just checking in now. He showers and unpacks, his mind racing and in triage mode. He wants a plan. He makes lists. First thing, Charlie wants to discuss Colin's recklessness with him—at the appropriate time. Second, what resources are available to Colin? What will his life look like? LSU has helped the family since the crash, but this isn't a football injury. Colin has embarrassed the program. And other quarterbacks on the roster will be competing and improving while Colin is in rehab. What will happen if he ends up not in the Tigers' plans?

There are other questions, of course: What will happen to Colin if he can't play football again, or doesn't want to, or if he's not the same guy anymore, not *the* guy, not in demand, not getting flirtatious Instagram direct messages, not signing NIL deals, not competing, not throwing, no longer part of an exclusive world?

Charlie doesn't want to go there. Not yet.

―――――――――――

A few hours later, Charlie is back in the ICU, hovering over Colin. "You feeling better?" he asks.

This time, Colin moves his head. Is it a nod? It's a nod. A nod! Charlie stands up and leans over the bed, holding Colin's hand, wanting and hoping for more.

"You want your phone?" he jokes. "You want Instagram?"

He sees a hint of a smile. Or thinks he sees. It doesn't matter. "I love you," Charlie says.

"I love you, too," Colin says, a whispered mumble clear enough for the room to hear.

"He said 'I love you, too!'" Charlie says. "That's a first down in my book. You're my best friend. I love you, buddy."

"We're drafting you, no matter what," Bears general manager Ryan Poles told Caleb Williams.

That didn't go over well with Carl. But by now—late March 2024—the Bears were both working hard to make Williams comfortable and drawing a nonnegotiable line in the sand. The night before his Pro Day in Los Angeles, Caleb met Poles, Eberflus, newly hired offensive coordinator Shane Waldron, and a few others in a private dining room at the Bird Streets Club in West Hollywood. The Bears invited some of Williams's USC teammates, to see how Caleb interacted with them. It was a fun night, further solidifying Williams as their pick—Poles loved how Williams didn't look at his cell phone the entire evening, which Caleb had learned from Carl— but it left Williams unsure.

"Do I want to go there?" Williams told his confidants. "I don't think I can do it with Waldron."

Carl had made it known to the Bears through third parties that he hated the hiring of Waldron, a Phillips Academy graduate who had briefly served as tight ends coach for both the Patriots during their dynastic reign and for the Los Angeles Rams. Waldron had a good reputation around the league, but Carl wanted the Bears to hire someone who was *the* brains behind the league's most dynamic offenses, not someone who had learned how to carry over a playbook. Caleb was wary, too. He asked those close to him, "What do you think about the Bears? What do *you* think, not what does my dad think?"

Bad organizations are usually bad for a reason, most replied.

———

The main question on Caleb's Pro Day isn't how Caleb will perform. It's whether Carl will show up. For a minute, it appears that the answer is no. Caleb is well into his stretching routine, and there is a small gaggle of family and friends in the stands. But not *him* . . . until Caleb starts to warm up, and heads in the stands turn.

He's here.

Carl's presence carries a whole new element, creates its own force in open air. Caleb is on the other side of the field, talking with USC teammates and preparing to throw. Carl is not trying to draw attention to himself. He's wearing a red USC shirt. He chats with friends as he walks across the stands. Reporters introduce themselves. He's polite, but he doesn't want to chat. He leans over a railing separating the stands from field and extends his hand to chat with the men who will be his son's bosses, despite his best efforts. Eberflus introduces himself. Their conversation is friendly. Poles comes over next. They look each other in the eye, two men whose reputations precede themselves.

A half hour later, Williams walks to midfield. He goofs around, throwing with his left hand. After a few minutes, Will Hewlett asks him if he wants more easy throws to warm his arm. "No," Caleb says.

Carl walks alone to another side of the stands, to get a better view. "Been waiting a long time," he says.

Will Hewlett looks at his script, fifty throws deep. Twenty-seven to the left, twenty-three to the right: Whip (sell over), Swirl @ 16, Slant, Flat Right, Scout (spray release out), Post Curl, Slant, Flat . . . A USC receiver tweaks his hamstring. Another isn't running full speed. They scrap seven routes from the script and run what's possible. "Give 'em a chance to catch their breath," Hewlett tells Williams.

Carl stands alone, shuffling in place, hands in pockets, then out, rubbing them together. His heart is at the top of his throat, visions he had for his son's future playing out in real time. *Stem (18 back down stem), 9 Stop, 18yd Over (climb op #), Glance spray release, Through Nod . . .* After twenty or so minutes, Williams throws a 65-yard deep ball—Big Post—to cap the workout.

"Not bad," Carl says. "Had better days."

Williams hugs Lincoln Riley. He waves to the stands. "Thanks to everybody coming out!" He shakes hands with Adam Peters, Washington's general manager and holder of the second overall pick. Both Williams men wouldn't mind it if he fell to them. "We'll go for it before we let you punt, all right?" Peters says.

Hewlett and Tom Gormely find Carl, on the edge of the stands.

"Well," Hewlett tells Carl. "We got through it."

Williams returned to Jacksonville to train with Hewlett and Gormely. One day on the football field, they had visitors. A white pickup had rolled up. A father and son got out. The son approached Williams and reintroduced himself. Williams remembered him—the kid from Elite 11, with the big hair, the LSU quarterback, the one who challenged him to the crossbar competition.

"Beat your ass," Williams said.

"You got me," Colin Hurley replied. "You got me."

The auctioneer pauses in the middle of the Unitas Collection, not to catch his breath but to wake up the audience, the way rock stars do a dead crowd. Do they realize who Johnny Unitas was? What he did and what he meant? Sandy and Joe sit among strangers who are bidding on their possessions. Being the family of Unitas, or Staubach, or Waterfield, or Graham, or Luckman, or Bradshaw, or Starr, means watching that quarterback fade a little more each year, their legends receding, and listening to people rank the greatest ever and seeing those names slide a little more, first behind Montana, then Marino, then Elway, then Brady and Manning and Mahomes. . . .

"Look at the age group here," Sandy says.

Johnny's brown leather briefcase is up next, item number 157 for $400. Inside are seemingly unremarkable things: his reading glasses, a calculator, business cards, binoculars, a writing pad, and his cell phone, which he seldom answered, much to the irritation of his children. Joe looks up.

"That was in the car when he died," he says.

September 11, 2002. The year *after*. John was running errands. Next on his list was the cleaner, to pick up rugs. Sandy called his cell. For once, he answered. She told him to skip it. Grab a workout instead. That was vital for Unitas, not only because of the arthritis that landed him on the cover of *Sports Illustrated* as an exemplar of the damaged football afterlife, but because of his heart. He was sixty-nine. He had nearly died in 1993 from cardiac arrest. John drove to his usual gym, parked at his usual spot. As he aged, Johnny had a funny habit of leaving his keys in the car. If someone wanted to steal his car, he'd tell his kids, "Why make it hard? Let 'em just take it."

Inside the gym was John's longtime friend, a physical therapist named Bill Neill. As John went from machine to machine, they told jokes. Unitas had grown to love filthy jokes, like only a devout Catholic could. That was new. For a while, as a player, he only listened to them. At the leg machine, John had a dirty one ready. But first, he made Neill promise to take it to the grave. Johnny Unitas, that holier-than-thou bastard, couldn't be on record with this one. Neill gave his word. Unitas let fly. It was suitably filthy. Laughing, Neill said, "Get out of here. . . ."

Just then, Unitas lost consciousness and fell over. Doctors later guessed that he died before he hit the ground.

Sandy was at a beauty parlor, and almost at that exact moment, she wanted to talk to John. She assumed his cell was off, as usual, so she called Neill.

"I need to tell him something," Sandy said.

"Sandy, I think you better call your doctor."

"What in the world for?"

Sandy had so many scares with John over the years that she had conditioned herself to not worry. John Steadman, the legendary *Baltimore Sun* sportswriter, once called her with news that Unitas had died in an airplane crash. But this sounded different. She was crying when she got the doctor on the phone.

"I'm very sorry to tell you that your husband's gone."

His funeral was a week later at the Cathedral of Mary Our Queen in North Baltimore, with 2,000 people in attendance. Church bells and bagpipes began at 9:10 a.m. as his casket arrived, covered in flowers. Speakers told stories of a man who helped them to be the best version of themselves. All six of his children spoke. So did Frank Gitschier, who recruited him to Louisville after seeing the empty coal bag. So did Raymond Berry. Local politicians sat in the pews, along with NFL Commissioner Paul Tagliabue, baseball legend Brooks Robinson, and lots of Baltimore football heroes, from Ray Lewis to Art Donovan. Cardinal William E. Keeler told a story of visiting a monastery as a young priest and praying for Unitas's knees in that weekend's game. Peyton Manning asked the league to break its uniform policy and allow him to wear black high-tops. The league told him no. He considered wearing them anyway and eating the $25,000 fine, but he didn't want controversy to overshadow Unitas's legend. He later wished he'd just worn them.

As the Unitas family put one step before another in the days and months and years after his death, Sandy always wondered: What were his final words? She decided to ask Neill.

"A joke," he said. "A dirty one."

Which was?

"Nope," Neill said. "I'm taking that to the grave."

Years later, at Neill's funeral, Sandy and Paige shook their heads.

"Yep," Sandy told Paige. "He took it to the grave."

In a gold jacket, at a lectern, with 330 friends and family among those in the audience, Warren Moon stood on the cusp of two generations. He knew that many Black folks believed that America hadn't come far enough; others believed it had come a long way. His lot in life, Moon straddled those mindsets on a sunny August day in Canton. The Hall, the press, and the NFL celebrated. It was a theatrical moment, a chance for the narrative to shift. Moon's profound ambivalence was internal, collective, and institutional. For years he saw race as an "extra burden." People always said, *Warren, we're watching you. Warren, you gotta do this for us.* He often imagined his career without it, what he might have accomplished, how much *fun* he might have had. Football wasn't fun—at least not after he was good enough at throwing a football to make men *believe.*

Moon held a piece of paper with eight bullet points, themes to hit. He was three months shy of his fiftieth birthday. He toured through a career that had started forty-four years earlier, beginning at Baldwin Hills Community Park in Pop Warner, playing with a receiver named James Lofton, who would reach the Hall of Fame. Then to Hamilton, to Washington, Canada, Houston, Minneapolis, Seattle, Kansas City, thanking coaches and teammates and his mom and his family—even his ex.

Finally, there was only one thing left to address.

He could have steered clear of it. But his mom was in the audience. Shack Harris was in the audience. Thing was, if Moon leaned into it, if he went there, how far would he go? Never presume that what a Black quarterback says in public in front of a largely white crowd and institution is what he thinks and feels. Every moment he speaks as a representative of the role, he knows he's talking to white people, and he's aware that he's speaking for a bunch of guys who never had the chance.

"A lot has been said about me being the first African American quarterback into the Pro Football Hall of Fame," he said. "It's a subject that I'm very uncomfortable about, sometimes only because I've always wanted to be judged as just a quarterback. . . ."

Fans started to cheer, like the build-up in a campaign speech, ready to stomp the floor. But Moon didn't want it. He talked through and over. "But because I am the first, and because significance does come with that, I accept that. I *accept* the fact that I am the first. . . ."

You could feel his journey. You could also feel his ambivalence. He didn't say he was *proud* to be the first. But before he left the stage, he leaned down and kissed his bust on the head, as if to reassure his younger self that it would turn out all right, as if to lay down a burden. When I ask Moon about that moment, I wonder if his Hall of Fame speech was yet another thing that he didn't have agency over. Did he want to go there, or did he feel like he had no choice? His presence is a breakthrough and an accomplishment, but it's also an indictment. The standard he carries, the reason it's the very particular kind of burden that it is, isn't because he's the first. It's because whoever was first was going to damn all that had come before, was going to, by virtue of his presence, deliver a blow to the heart of the game he loved. Moon had revealed something about the position, and the nature of the position had revealed something about us.

"All of it was from the heart," he says.

———

Auction item number 161 comes up: Johnny Unitas's black high-tops. Size ten. Number 19 written inside. RIDDELL 89T 10 D punched into the tongue. Right toe busted at the seam. The last pair the family owns.

"One of one," Joe says.

Starting price: $17,500.

Being the family of a legend, being born into the world as the child of a superstar quarterback, brings blessings and drama beyond belief. For Joey, it means daring to play quarterback in high school, with that last name and set of expectations, moving to Hollywood to be an actor, getting a cameo in *Any Given Sunday* alongside his old man, and later writing a script about the 1958 NFL Championship Game. For Chad, it means putting down the credit card at the local bar, because the quarterback always pays. Being a Unitas also means unending drama with Johnny's first set of kids, all of it playing out in the papers, watching their father declare bankruptcy, watching him learn to navigate the world in a damaged body. He lives in each of them in ways beyond a pair of shoes. Joe has written a parenting book about his dad, *Unitas to Unitas*. Chad wears his father's belt buckle on most days. Paige has a shrine to her father in her new home, outside of Charlotte—the house is Colts blue, number 19 on the street, and closed on his ninetieth birthday—and she hangs on to stuff nobody else would think exists, like a brown paper bag; he would pack her lunch and scribble a cartoon of her. Sandy remembers when each kid was born and he got them the custom-made black leather high-top baby shoes. The family still tears up when discussing him, a loss still fresh, robbed of a massive presence. "Lots of shit I had to figure out on my own," Chad says through tears one evening. Paige sometimes plays interviews with him on YouTube over her house's sound system when she's doing chores, just to hear his voice, that voice, from above, as intended.

The auctioneer takes bids so fast that it's one constant and indecipherable mumble over a microphone. The bidding increases to $23,500 . . .

Once.

Twice.

Sold.

——————

"Do you promise with every shred of your integrity that you won't discuss this with anyone?" Sean Payton asks me on a March 2024 afternoon.

"Yes," I say.

Payton is sixty years old and in his eighteenth year as an NFL head coach and twenty-seventh season working in the NFL, one of the greatest offensive minds in history. He's in the market to draft a quarterback. I want to know what's possible.

Payton wants more than just a quarterback. He wants a *franchise* guy. A year earlier, a Broncos scout had given him an analysis of a particular quarterback, slotted to be drafted high, and said that the quarterback would need everyone in the building supporting him to succeed. Payton shook his head. If you're going to pick a quarterback in the first round, he said, "it needs to be a guy who *builds* the building, like Elway." If Air Raid statistics and the Combine and a Pro Day and a fifteen-minute interview and pee tests and interviews with coaches, secretaries, trainers, and teammates don't help answer the single most important question in sports, it's worth looking at something wholly different. Nobody knows what that is. But Payton has a theory. A series of metrics. It's inside a folder he holds one morning, with the logo from the Denver Broncos on the top and QUARTERBACKS on the side. It's filled with the names of prospects—Caleb Williams, Drake Maye, J. J. McCarthy, Bo Nix—and numbers.

In 2017, when Payton was with the Saints, he thought he had found his future replacement for Drew Brees in Texas Tech's Patrick Mahomes, who was raw and quirky, with a low but fluid release. New Orleans held the eleventh pick in the first round. Payton was sure that Mahomes would fall to him. Golfers Ryan Palmer and Jordan Spieth were visiting the Saints facility on April 27, Draft Day. This Mahomes kid, Payton told them, "is the steal of the draft."

With Mahomes, Payton wanted to develop a formula to evaluate processing speed. He tried to do it not by researching a quarterback's successes but by analyzing his failures. Quarterbacks with high rates of sacks and turnovers either freeze or panic, he felt. "If a quarterback is sacked quite a bit in college, per drop back, you can improve that some," Payton says now. "But it generally means the processing is a little delayed." He was unconcerned with arm strength. Brees had a B-level arm. What he did at a Hall of Fame level was multitask—making adjustments at the line of scrimmage and recognizing problems and solutions, all in seconds. Payton valued this skillset because he knew it was what he lacked as a quarterback at Eastern Illinois in the early eighties. He could throw well enough to play in the Arena Football League and as a replacement player during the 1987 NFL players strike. But he wasn't a multitasker. That command, that magic—that was the difference between making it and not. Payton says it's like if he's driving a new Mercedes-Benz, with dozens of cutting-edge features. Payton would get in and be overwhelmed by all but four of the dials and keys. Drew Brees would ease onto the road and select music and adjust the temperature in the front and back, all while seeing traffic from all sides.

Payton looked at the rate of negative plays against the quarterback's total drop backs: percentage of sacks, fumbles, interceptions, then added them together for the average. Like golf, a low score was best.

MAHOMES
Attempts: 1,349
Sacks: 68 (5%)
Fumbles: 14 (1%)
Interceptions: 29 (2.1%)
Completion percentage: 63.5
Average: 8.1

Payton liked that score. It meant that on average, something negative happened only 8.1 percent of the time. But he had little context for it. He was starting from scratch; he didn't have a database built over decades. The score was augmented by his meeting with Mahomes. Payton typically gives a prospect a seventeen-page packet of offensive designs the night before a meeting, stuff for the quarterback to study. Payton would test recall the next day. Mahomes was the gold standard: He knew everything. Payton was floored and asked him how he did it. "I'm pretty good with tests like that," Mahomes said. On Draft Day in 2017, everything was going Payton's way. The tenth pick arrived. It belonged to Buffalo. The Bills didn't need a quarterback. Mahomes was still available. Payton was ten minutes from his guy. What happened next, of course, is lore only in retrospect. The Chiefs traded with Buffalo. As soon as it happened, Payton knew. He respected Andy Reid. Mahomes changed Reid's life and legacy, turning him from a good but under-performing playoff coach into a first-ballot Hall of Famer. Payton is now on his second team, trying to re-create old magic.

———

In 2024, the Broncos hold the twelfth pick in the first round. Payton has met with Caleb Williams and Drake Maye, out of dili-gence. He knows both will be gone when the Broncos pick. Payton sees in Caleb all the elements of a prodigy, including the vibe of being a legend in his own mind. That amuses Payton; most greats appear detached and above it all. He loves Williams's arm; he's wor-ried a little about his processing speed. Like Bill Belichick, Payton sees too many easy completions left on the field, open receivers that Williams fails to spot quickly. But his primary concerns with Williams are existential. Williams has yet to be broken in his life. Payton remembers when the Saints signed Brees. Most of the league thought his shoulder was shot. It propelled him to greatness. You'd watch Brees during a game and he seemed angrier after settling for a field goal than after a punt. What would happen when the NFL would gut Williams, as it does to every quarterback? Could he relate to his teammates, when he lived in a downtown high rise? Were the USC coaches a little too lenient with him? Tom Brady always said that the first thing he does is watch how, or if, a quarterback endears himself to his teammates. If he doesn't endear himself to them, he's not playing two decades and certainly not rewriting the record book. Quarterbacks need the best out of their teammates. Payton knows it when he sees it: Elway, Montana, Young, Brees, those guys had it. Some of Southern California's football staffers privately seem relieved that the Legend of Caleb is over. Payton plugs Williams into his processing formula.

Attempts: 735
Sacks: 83 (11.2%)
Fumbles: 32 (4.4%)
Interceptions: 14 (1.9%)
Completion percentage: 66.9
Average: 17.5

The average is high for Payton's taste, but it doesn't matter. Williams has the potential to be great, and to be a bust. No, a special kind of bust, a generational one that haunts a city for a century, with crying, fits, fights, complaining about coaches, with the dad hovering over it all. Regardless, it'll be in Chicago, not Denver.

Payton doesn't even run Jayden Daniels through his formula. He knows he'll be gone, too. With Maye, Payton likes his size and arm and competitive upbringing. Like with Williams and Daniels, he won't be an option at pick 12. But he looks at Maye's data:

Attempts: 942
Sacks: 69 (7.3%)
Fumbles: 14 (1.5%)
Interceptions: 16 (1.7%)
Completion percentage: 64.5
Average: 10.5

J. J. McCarthy of Michigan has a better average than either Williams or Maye: 7.8. And the Broncos theoretically have a chance at him. But the guy Payton loves, the quarterback who he has a shot to pick, is at the top of the sheet that the coach pulls out of the file and hands to me.

"I want this kid," Payton says.

Bo Nix, from Oregon. He had a strange college career, starting sixty-one games—an NCAA record. He was twenty-four years old, compared with Maye, who was twenty-one. He began his career at Auburn and transferred to Oregon. Payton visited him, and Nix had memorized the entire seventeen-page packet that the Broncos share with prospects, writing formations and plays neatly on the white boards in an office. Payton likes that he led the NCAA in completion percentage—and he likes the type of completions. At one point, Payton asked him what he had in his backpack, curious if he'd see anything suspicious or revealing, like dip or pain pills or candy. "Everything," Nix said. He pulled out cleats, a backup pair of socks, and a lacrosse ball, which he rolled on his back and shoulders to loosen up.

Attempts: 878
Sacks: 10 (1.1%)
Fumbles: 0 (0%)
Interceptions: 10 (1.1%)
Completion percentage: 74.8
Average: 2.3

Nix's data is the best in the draft—and is better than Mahomes's was. Payton doesn't think Nix is the best prospect since Mahomes, of course. But he believes in his potential right now, for what Payton needs and where he's drafting. And he believes that together, they can be special. He has a plan for his quarterback. And he knows that sets him—them—ahead of so many rookies. This is rare. In any sector of American business, half the people are incompetent compared with the other half. You know the type. Nobody knows how they got there, but they're there. Owners are as bad at picking coaches as coaches are at picking quarterbacks. In 2022, ESPN reported that over a five-year span, owners spent $800 million paying coaches, executives, and staffs that they had fired before the end of their contracts. When that data was shared with owners in a private meeting, their response was not to vow to hire better, but to pay them less. Most years, at least half a dozen coaches are fired. When that happens, the quarterback is affected most. It means he must work with new staff, new systems, new personalities. Payton knows why Carl Williams is worried about his son going to Chicago. A quarterback needs coaching and infrastructure. Nix will end up as one of the best quarterbacks of the 2024 class because he has a head coach who knows offense, knows quarterbacks, isn't afraid of being fired, and is more invested in him than in covering his own ass.

"I'll get criticized for taking him at twelve," Payton tells me of Nix. "I don't give a fuck. Three years from now is what I'm worried about."

———

Matt Ryan knew about Steve Young's book. They had discussed it. More than that, he knew about Young's transition, from good to great, the final step in quarterbacking, an impossible increment to quantify but that changes lives and legacies. Ryan had checked almost all quarterback boxes. He was drafted third overall in 2008.

He helped resuscitate a franchise reeling from the Michael Vick dogfighting fallout. Like Young, he was consistently one of the best quarterbacks in the league, and like Young, he was known for what he could not do. Aaron Rodgers was Ryan's Montana, an impossible shadow. Like Young, what seemed to gall Ryan was that the outside narrative mirrored his own internal voice. Everything seemed to change in 2016, like it did for Young in 1994. Ryan won league MVP and earned first-team All-Pro honors. During the Falcons' playoff run, he threw nine touchdowns and zero interceptions. He outplayed Rodgers in the NFC Championship Game, and in Super Bowl LI against dynastic New England outplayed Tom Brady—for fifty-two minutes. But then Brady cobbled together nine unanswered points, cutting a 28–3 score to 28–12. The ball was in Ryan's hands, with a few mandates: He needed to put together a drive, spend some clock, hopefully score, but most of all, he needed to reignite momentum. Only a quarterback can do it. Great ones do it on the game's biggest stage. Ryan dropped back to pass and looked left. He didn't see a Patriots linebacker named Dont'a Hightower rushing from the far-right edge—a Wide 9 alignment, in football terms. It shouldn't have mattered: The Falcons had dialed up a good play. A receiver was streaking downfield against single coverage. This was Ryan's *moment*. He got the ball. Running back Devonta Freeman was supposed to block Hightower, but whiffed on him, leaving the linebacker with a clear path. Ryan saw his receiver open, and rather than just throw, he did something coaches call "hitching": He hesitated for a split second, resetting himself before rearing back. It's an imperceptible error and yet, in cases like this, everything. There's a reason Bill Belichick later said that it was a "fraction of a second away from being a bad play" for the Patriots. Instead, Hightower got him, knocking the ball loose, a pivotable play in what became a historic meltdown.

Was it shitty luck? Karma, somehow? Or maybe, a massive difference masquerading as a tiny one? Ryan himself saw a difference, between himself and an all-timer, but not the one fans or even the coaches saw. It wasn't a goddamn hitch. He performed close to his best in the Super Bowl—but he missed one play. *One*. And that one is all a legend needed that day, all what every legend needs. It's not a debate over who's elite. It's crueler. It's the devastating reality that you can be a potential Hall of Famer and yet be a footnote of sorts to another quarterback's dynasty—like Buffalo's Josh Allen has been to Patrick Mahomes.

"Frankly," Ryan says, "it sucks."

———

Young does this thing when I suggest that some guys got it, some don't, that it's innate, not taught: He gets bashful. He knows he was a great quarterback, but he also pushes back. He's proud of the fact that his journey was difficult, impossible at times. It's not false humility. It's what led to his greatness, that he was the kind of quarterback who willed himself to become an immortal one. That's what he misses most now, in retirement, when he studies other guys. "That pouring of yourself into something, knowing you're going to get kicked in the groin, every week. When I say it takes all you've got, I mean all parts of yourself." Like Warren Moon, like so many of them, he misses the pain, because he proved something to himself and to all of us. The effort and achievement are impossible to separate. "All of this is elite stuff," Young says.

That word: elite. It was one of those terms that few seemed to use when discussing quarterbacks until Matt Ryan. It was a talk-show debate: Was he *elite*? Ryan and I conversed many times over the years, and the subtext, overt or unspoken, was that we both knew he was trying to take a last step in his career and that indeed, it could be done, that there was something out there for the taking, a theory, a new argument, even if neither of us knew precisely what.

"If you figure it out," Ryan told me once, "call me."

"I wish it were that simple," I said.

"You and me both."

Something about that little exchange stayed with me. Remember when John Elway said that the greats never admit anything? Ryan had admitted something that made him more human and less a quarterback all at once. Moments after being hit by Hightower—moments after the hitch, the gap between the greats and the immortals—he found a higher level within himself. Less than five minutes remained. New England had cut the score to 28–20. He got the ball. The pocket collapsed. He ran right, and saw receiver Julio Jones angling toward the sideline. Jones was covered, but as we know, there is no defense for the perfect pass. Ryan threw a perfect pass: There was no hesitation, no bullshit hitching, just the reaction exclusive to the gifted. He placed the ball in an impossible slot, on Jones's fingertips and just beyond the defender's, putting the Falcons in range to kick the game-icing field goal. It's one of the five best throws in Super Bowl history, a throw worth celebrating and honoring . . . and yet, you can't. Instead, it was a prelude to disaster. A combination of bad play-calling, a horrific sack taken by Ryan, and a holding penalty knocked the Falcons out of field goal range. You know what happened next: a debacle with a world championship on the line, that even now is still hard to fathom. But more than that, the type of horrific loss that would define Ryan. Not just in our eyes; to an extent, his own.

Young believes that maybe ten worthy arms come out of college each year, and other factors are differentiators: hand-eye coordination, or fierce determination, or organizational fluidity, or if somehow there were a test that quantified what happened to concentration and heart rate as adrenaline and pressure and pain hit unfathomable levels . . . He can go on, and does. He wants to be what he calls "my full self."

But what if there *aren't* ten arms that can make those throws? Not the throws in a Pro Day. Or a preseason game. Or a regular season game. Or even a playoff game. What if in the tightest moments of the Super Bowl, when you're tired, aching, when you've got Bill Belichick scheming against you, the moments for which nothing can prepare you, when a quarterback is naked out there, because it either happens or it doesn't . . . what if the gap between guys like Matt Ryan and, say, Tom Brady—or Unitas, or Elway, or Mahomes, or either Manning—seems small when you look at statistics and anecdotal evidence and game theory, but is actually a chasm?

As a way of answering, Young tells me a story. It's about his father and hero, LeGrande—everyone calls him Grit—but it's really a story about Young himself, and a glimpse into his exceptionalism, and how even people who know quarterbacks don't know quarterbacks. Admiring his son's will and struggle, Grit once told him, "You love third-and-ten."

"I don't like third-and-ten. I *hate* third-and-ten."

"The way you live, you like third-and-ten."

"I like the game over at halftime."

———

Elway had felt alone in his life before. Quarterback alone, celebrity alone, the type of alone that nobody except the person inside a mania can understand. But the years after the deaths of his father, twin sister, and marriage—and of his life as a quarterback—were different. His house was empty; the kids went with Janet. All of the release valves that he had conditioned himself to use during his career—calling his dad, the telepathy of having a twin sister, redemption in the Broncos building—were unavailable. He was in his early forties, that dangerous time for men. Elway had defined himself by work and by results. Without them, he felt adrift. Who is he? What's he doing? There was only so much golf to play—even though he damn near played it daily, weekly, monthly, with Wayne Gretzky, with Donald Trump, with Michael Jordan, sometimes with whoever was around, sometimes alone. "I get bored really fast," he tells me. He spent more time in Los Angeles and dated a model named Carrie Stewart. She had been in the company of rock stars and actors, and she was stunned—"naïve," she said—at the levels of adulation directed at Elway in the Hollywood scene, a celebrity status that was "off the charts." But Elway's identity, maybe self-esteem, had been tied to the game. Without it, he almost judged himself harsher than anyone else, held it against himself, more than the public did.

He wasn't always his best self during those years, but he told friends that he wanted to try to live like a normal person after two decades of being a flawless role model. He sometimes struggled to empathize with others, drawing on how he was trained, to bury and move on at all costs, and he wondered why. "Is that just because of what I'd gone through in my life, that negative things I'm able to just pound down and not sit there and let 'em affect you?"

Elway, a guy who many of us thought had all the answers, is asking a question that the legends before him must have wrestled with. And the young ones coming up can't imagine. Did what make him great limit him in other areas of life?

In the years after he retired, John coached his son Jack's team at Cherry Creek High. Jack played quarterback, like his dad and grandfather, but preferred linebacker. Elway tried to do what his dad had done for him, but he later wished he'd just kept him at linebacker, rather than being an Elway, in Denver, at quarterback, wearing number 7, with his old man coaching. Cameras were at his first game. It was too much for a kid. "I didn't know the pressure he was under," Elway says now. "I didn't have enough compassion. I didn't care. I'd tell him to just go compete and let the chips fall where they may." That was why when Nate and Nick Montana decided to play quarterback, they used their mother's maiden name on their jerseys. Montana himself tried to close the distance. He called coaches on behalf of his kids and, at one point, urged the 49ers to sign Nate as a quarterback. He wanted for his kids what he had wanted for himself: a chance. Only he had to create it for himself. He didn't have a Joe Montana. Jack Elway was good enough to earn a scholarship to Arizona State, but he walked away after a year. He knew, Montana knew, Elway knew, we know: This life isn't a hereditary monarchy—and it isn't for everybody.

John and Jack didn't discuss his walking away from quarterback for more than a year, until June 2010, at Elway's fiftieth birthday. Jack told his old man that he felt he'd let him down.

You didn't, Elway said.

Then Jack told his father something unsurprising to anyone who's ever taken a snap: He missed it.

It's funny to see your childhood hero at a waffle maker. I was at the breakfast buffet in January of 2011, the Hampton Inn downtown in Mobile, Alabama, when Elway walked in. It was Senior Bowl week, when scouts evaluate college players. Elway arrived just after 6 a.m., grabbing breakfast before heading out to practice for player weigh-ins—the grunt work, the stuff nobody wants to do. Elway was less than three weeks into his new job, as general manager of the Denver Broncos, a job Pat Bowlen offered him to restore the franchise. He wore a black leather jacket. Desk clerks stared. Other scouts stared. I stared at my childhood hero, even though by then I knew him. Elway poured the batter into the waffle maker and clamped it closed. It didn't work. He fiddled with it. Still nothing. He was the only person in Mobile who didn't have to be there. And yet of course he had to be there. He was in all the way, and wasn't getting out until he had a ring.

The only thing more dangerous than being a figment of people's imagination is being a figment of your own. Elway was not the same man who had walked off as the winningest quarterback ever. He was starting over, after he tried to forgive the world and himself. He had gotten remarried, to Paige Green, who grew up a block away from his high school in Granada Hills. On their first date, he took her to Roy's, a Hawaiian joint in the Valley. They moved slowly. Elway would visit her in LA and rather than try to impress her with his jet—tail number 777MX—he veered far in the other direction, almost going out of his way to not mention money or lifestyle. Elway was wary of getting remarried, but they both understood the value of a partnership. The losses of Jana and Jack were not only something Elway lived with, they were something he used to keep living. He cycled one hundred miles at the Elephant Rock bike festival. He'd ride from home to his downtown steakhouse, Elway's, and sit at the stool at the corner of the bar, the single gold one among red ones—a tribute to Jack. It crushed him that he never got to sit next to his dad and have a drink at the restaurant with their name on it. . . .

But Elway kept his promises, to himself and the city. He made his home in Denver, as did some of his kids, who had their own kids. He slowly rebuilt his support system; it came to resemble the one from his playing days. And in 2012, Elway lured Peyton Manning, who after a brilliant run with the Colts had undergone so many neck operations that it left him temporarily unable to throw, to the Broncos. Elway closed the deal over drinks at the Cherry Creek Country Club by not trying to close the deal. He knew that the worst thing he could do to Manning was to jam him, by virtue of the life and job they had shared. They were the only two quarterbacks to ever be the top-ranked recruit out of high school, the first overall draft pick, and a first-ballot Hall of Famer. Elway thought about Manning. The Colts had cut him. If the Broncos had cut Elway, after all he'd done, he would have been pissed and in shock over it not ending on his terms—and in no mood for a hard sell.

"Quarterback to quarterback," Manning later put it. By then, the hyphens were long gone.

Manning signed, and together, they won four straight division titles and reached two Super Bowls. Manning rewrote the offensive record books and staked his claim on the greatest ever. Elway watched it all from the executive suite in awe—and recognized some of Manning's urges to throw touchdown passes when a run would have gotten into the end zone as well, juicing statistics the way Marino once did. He loved Manning's work ethic and alternated between amusement and annoyance at his controlling personality. They lost Super Bowl XLVIII in a blowout to Seattle. The following offseason was one of the worst of his life, hearkening back to the miserable offseasons in the eighties when he got humiliated. Elway and Manning staged a brutal contract negotiation in 2015, when Manning was starting to slow and Elway knew that to surround him with a team that could win a Super Bowl he'd need to get a quarterback who had taken immense pride in helping quarterbacks get paid their worth to do the opposite: to take a pay cut. The standoff lasted months. Elway knew Manning's future better than he did. He knew the wiring that helped him achieve heights in football would conspire against him in retirement. Midway through the 2015 season, Peyton knew it was over. The ball wasn't coming out of his hand like it once did; passes that used to land where he wanted now floated wide. He didn't want to say it, because he didn't want storylines to be about him. Derek Jeter had told Manning that he regretted announcing his final year ahead of time. Too much attention. The Broncos won the Super Bowl that year, with a stellar defense and a sage Manning. When Manning did retire, a few months later, he hit golf balls and called Elway to tell the team to prepare a press conference. He called ESPN's Chris Mortensen to give him the scoop—and then asked him to hold it until the next morning. Manning told him that he wanted to go to dinner—and have "one last night as an NFL quarterback." Archie had always told Peyton, "You're the quarterback of that town." Peyton liked that feeling. And knew when it ended, it would be over forever.

In the hours following the Super Bowl win over the Panthers in February, Elway sat in his suite in the Santa Clara Marriott, where thirty-three years earlier he had nervously stood with his dad as they faced the cameras and refused to back down from the trade demand. This time, he was celebrating with a small group of friends. Around 4 a.m., the children of Broncos president Joe Ellis egged on Elway to wake up their dad, who had fallen asleep in a nearby suite. Elway pounced into bed and shook Ellis. He was smiling like a boy, but there was something sad and beautiful about where his mind went next.

"We can get better!" Elway shouted at Ellis. "I'm telling you—we can get better next year!"

What's more elusive: a Super Bowl, or inner peace?

The end of Bob and Jane's marriage in 1968 played out in the press. She accused him of "extreme cruelty"; he accused her of "excessive drinking habits." The *National Enquirer* was more blunt: "SHE WAS A DRUNK." When their divorce was quietly finalized, Bob kept the Sherman Oaks house, and Buck mostly lived with him, the house quieter and emptier, bereft of a certain dazzle. Waterfield stayed busy scouting for the Rams, taking care of his ranch, and visiting his little local bar. He sometimes saddled up first thing in the morning. He had a stable inner circle of old friends, and they would stop by, sharing a few drinks and a few laughs. Nobody asked about Jane; she was off-limits.

Years later, when he was asked to pinpoint the happiest time in his life, his answer was swift and simple.

"The days when I played football."

One afternoon I sit with Moon and ask him something I ask all the minted quarterbacks: What's the hardest part of retirement? I thought he would testify to the classic stuff, loss of identity without the game. But no. He had played pro football since the seventies. When he walked away, it was time. "I'll always be a quarterback," he says. He loved the first few years away from the game. His arm worked well. He threw the ball with his kids or with strangers and felt like he still had it. He remarried and raised another son. He kept in shape. He broadcast Seahawks games. He mentored Cam Newton, who was the first overall draft pick out of Auburn in 2011. Newton had a stellar rookie season, then struggled in his second year. It was typical for most quarterbacks—defensive coaches have an entire offseason to study them—but Newton made it worse by pouting after games. That gave critics all the opening they needed. They started comparing him unfavorably to Michael Vick and Vince Young. It was the same old stereotyping—Black quarterbacks being compared only to Black quarterbacks. Lots of quarterbacks whined and moaned after games, including Tom Brady, who threw tablets and sometimes left the field without shaking hands with opponents, and Jay Cutler of the Broncos and Bears, who turned his petulance into a brand. Moon knew what was happening to Newton, and he knew why, and he voiced his opinion, using a platform he was once ambivalent about to back up Newton and impact the conversation.

Moon is a member of many quarterback tribes. The LA quarterbacks, where he's one of the legends. The Black quarterbacks, where he reveres and is revered—where he spoke out in support of Colin Kaepernick, who lost his NFL career after inspiring a movement of players to kneel during the national anthem to protest racism and police brutality; where he introduced Vick into the National Quarterback Club Hall of Fame. Moon is in the club of the greatest quarterbacks ever, where he sits near the center of the table. One of his lots in life, accepted in his fifties and into his sixties, until . . .

"This girl tried to accuse me of sexual harassment," he says.

She didn't try, she did. In December 2017, the *Washington Post* published an exclusive story that a former employee was suing him. She said that he had forced her to share a bed with him on the road and to wear skimpy clothing, forced her to leave the bathroom door open when she showered, and that he had groped her genitals as she slept. When she protested his alleged advances, he allegedly replied, "This is the way it is." This was not an anonymous complaint. Wendy Haskell put her name on it. For two weeks after the lawsuit, Moon was silent. A narrative took hold. Then he spoke to a few media outlets. He said that he was a victim of blackmail, that on his birthday—"So I know this was personal," he said then—Haskell's lawyer had sent him a demand for $3 million. When they settled for an undisclosed sum in 2019, Haskell's attorney said that "justice is served."

In the years after the lawsuit, Moon wasn't out as much, wasn't sitting for as many talks, wasn't himself. He retreated. It was easier to stay home.

That's where he was in 2022 when Hamilton High called, with word that a mural was in progress.

In the years after his parents' divorce, Buck noticed something odd, especially when Dad would go on scouting trips: The gossip columns would report that Bob had been spotted with Jane. She had remarried shortly after the divorce was finalized, but that husband, actor Roger Barrett, died of a heart attack after they returned from a honeymoon in England. Dad started to talk about Mom more often to Buck. One day, Bob told Buck, "I think your mom and I are going to remarry."

Bob expected Buck to be overjoyed. He was not. Buck was only a teenager, but he knew his parents well—maybe better than they knew themselves. "Will you guys stop drinking?" Buck asked.

"No."

"Then don't get married."

Bob and Jane fizzled out again, as always. Waterfield eventually remarried, not to Jane, but to a woman named Jan Greene. He went on long hunting trips, where nobody could reach him. By the early 1980s, Waterfield's health started to slip. He was hospitalized. Doctors told him that if he kept up his current bar hours, he wouldn't last much longer. He changed, buying a few years. But in March of 1983, his breathing was labored. On March 25, he died at age sixty-two. The family threw one last party at the Sherman Oaks house, filled with icons and commoners from football and Hollywood. Legendary *Los Angeles Times* columnist Jim Murray went into full mythmaking mode: "Man and boy, Bob Waterfield was the best football player you or I ever saw. He had gifts that were not given to the rest of us. He came along in the gaudiest era that was Hollywood. The heroes of the time were strong silent types, laconic men of action, not words. He was part Gary Cooper, part John Wayne. As big as any of them. Gable-esque in his public image . . . Waterfield was not only a man's man. First, he was a man, period."

On Easter Sunday, Buck took his father's ashes to Caliente Mountain, where Bob loved to hunt alone, and spread them under pine trees. He cried, and he remembered some of his dad's final words:

"Tell your mother I love her."

———

Jane lived in Arizona in the years after Waterfield's death, married for a third time. One day she was talking to Etta, her assistant who ended up marrying Buck, but really talking to herself out loud. "God, why couldn't we have just stuck it out?" Jane said. Jane didn't need to say who she was referring to. Etta knew. Jane had mentioned Robert's "little escapades" for years. But time and perspective had changed her mind on what Robert did—and on Robert himself. Maybe if he hadn't been a quarterback, life would have been different. But of course, if he hadn't been a quarterback . . .

"Sometimes it was just part of the job," Jane said. "You spend so much time apart. Sometimes you just get weak."

She saw Robert not in the firmament, but as her guy. She missed him.

———

Moon is here today, staring at a mural of himself at Hamilton, before an audience that sees him in totality. He stands alongside politicians, teachers, coaches, kids, ready to give the tarp a pull. "Warren's gotta give it a good tug," an official says.

"Ready?" Moon asks.

"Ready."

He grabs a fistful of curtain and yanks. Moon holds his hands out, smiles, steps back, studying it and himself, what he was and is. Once, sitting in Moon's living room, I asked him about that young man on the wall, who took the bus to school, who dealt with death threats, who became a certain way in the hope of becoming a certain thing, expecting a kind of melancholic longing. "I don't miss that kid," he said. "I really don't." He was too serious, too locked-up, too driven, too distrusting, too hardened, too existentially exhausted. But most of all, Moon doesn't miss the pressure on himself. That's different from missing the crushing headaches. One is from what we imposed on him, the other is from what he gave of himself for us.

"I'm really impressed by this," Moon says, looking at the painting. "I really am." He turns back to the audience. I think about the footballs he threw, arrows into the sky. "If there are quarterback coaches out there," he laughs, "they'd probably tell me to have two hands on the ball at all times."

———

Elway walked away as general manager of the Broncos a few years after the Super Bowl. Pat Bowlen had died, and after years of family litigation the team was sold. When Elway met with the new owner, Greg Penner, chairman of Walmart, he told him he didn't want money, didn't want obligations, didn't want to feel like he owed anything to the franchise, or himself. Penner understood, but he wanted Elway to keep an office at the Broncos facility; he wanted him to know he was always welcome, always belonged.

At the bar in Denver, he is talking about a house he's building from the ground up in Palm Springs. "So many decisions," he says. Elway is starting over, yet again. He and Paige quietly divorce in 2024. A year later, his older sister, Lee Ann McCarthy, dies from pancreatic cancer—the same disease that took his mother, Jan, in 2020. John is the only one left. The familiar urges pull at him. He needs to be out. He needs to win. He needs something to work toward. He loves Palm Springs for the golf courses. "That is what fulfills me," he says. There's the BMW Championship in Denver, the senior opens, the American Century Championship in Tahoe. . . .

"I'll never lose that," he says. "You never lose being a competitor."

It gets worse, doesn't it?

"It does. It gets worse as you get older. It hasn't waned at all."

━━━━━━

In April 2025, at a private course outside Palm Springs, Elway was driving a golf cart carrying some friends, including his longtime buddy and business partner Jeff Sperbeck. They were leaving a party. Sperbeck fell off the cart and hit his head on asphalt. Elway called 911. Sperbeck was transported to a hospital and died four days later. According to the police, there was no indication that Elway was driving negligently. But people close to him started to worry. They knew the dark places his mind might go, missing his friend, replaying the incident, wondering what he could have done differently. When he gets depressed, it runs deep. He has a lot of friends, but not a lot that he truly trusts. Sperbeck was one of the few.

For the second time, Elway's life in retirement was defined by divorce and death and the core feeling that each of us is vulnerable and, in the end, alone. Maybe he felt it from the moment he got out of the Impala all those years ago.

Elway has imagined death—wondered about it. Will his spirit go on? Will it feel compelled to win in some afterlife? He once told me that he's envisioned the end. Cracking that familiar grin and whispering maybe the most Elway thing I've ever heard, he said: "I've always thought I was going to die with a shovel; in case I woke up, I could dig my way out." His eyes widened. "It's never *over* over until it's over."

His back is to the restaurant. He looks toward a TV above the bar. Years and reflection and therapy and time with family have provided some clarity, but finding a measure of peace and contentment, reconciling with what it's meant to have his life, *that* life, remains a work in progress.

"I've compressed those feelings because it hurt so bad," he says. "I wonder, there are times I go, is that still stuck? And I haven't let it go?

"Is that because of what I've gone through in my life?"

People in the bar sneak photos and quietly point in his direction.

"Emotionally, you get a little . . ."

He searches for the word.

"Warped."

The room seems to quiet, as if waiting for him to finish his thought.

"The highs are great. But it's the *lows*. . . ."

Arch Manning starts Senior Night with the freshmen. Dinner at 4 p.m., chicken and pasta, hours before the 7 p.m. kickoff. Most kids sit with friends or phones. Not Arch. He sits with the kids, but he isn't there long. Dinner is fast. Warm-ups are next. As Arch gently throws on the field, a school staffer walks by.

"Hey, Sixteen," he says. "This is my third game this year. Impress me."

A few weeks earlier, the Seattle Seahawks had been in town to play the Saints. They held their walk-through practice at Newman. Stewart met Pete Carroll, then Seattle's coach, and star wide receiver DK Metcalf—who had one question: "Where's Arch?" Stewart went to fetch him, and when the Seahawks broke for the day, they cheered, "We want Arch!" Stewart knew that Arch's senior season was about preparation for Texas as much as it was about winning games for Newman. He often spoke with the Texas staff and used some of their concepts in his offense—especially a play called Hooker. It matters to the Mannings that Newman runs a sophisticated offense, one that matches Arch's drive and ability and challenges him and satisfies its audience of one: Peyton. Arch is also a backup safety, and seems as excited when he gets a few snaps in the secondary as he is when he throws a touchdown pass, fully aware that no matter how long his football career lasts, after a year at Texas or fifteen in the pros, he'll never play defense again. Earlier in the season, when Newman was in a prevent defense, Stewart inserted Arch at safety. An opponent cut him at the knees. Stewart looked across the field. Archie was in the stands, "staring a hole through me," he says.

Stewart walks the field before the game, standing behind Arch, watching the ball come out of his hand, and listening—a fervor is palpable, as the crowd ushers him in and within himself. He knows what it's doing, yet he can't help it. None of us can. "You can hear the ball hiss," he says.

Stewart cruises around, then slips upstairs for a few quiet moments in his office. He pulls a ball off a table and grabs a Sharpie. He wheels out into the hallway and stops, cradling the ball in his left hand, like a baby, as he writes on the white stripes. It's a present for Arch. Stewart knows that Arch will likely break Uncle Eli's Newman record for touchdowns tonight. He texts Peyton and Eli before the game, letting them know that Arch is only two touchdowns away. Both are still protective over their records. Eli jokingly offers to pay Stewart if he'll run the veer—a running play—all game.

TD AT*, Stewart writes. Touchdowns, all-time.

Stewart says a few words to the team, then dips downstairs, where there's a reception for the opening of the Manning Fieldhouse. Pictures are scattered about; stuff is on the floor. Peyton was supposed to be here. Coaches were relieved when he canceled last minute. Four portraits hang on the wall: Archie, Cooper, Peyton, and Eli. Soon there will be a fifth. In the gym, alums drink wine and beer and mingle. Archie is here, leaning on a cane but fit for his mid-seventies. His balance is poor. He's got a numbness in his feet. It's not painful, but it's dangerous. "You can't fall," he says. He stays home a bit more than he'd like.

"I just tell people I'm old," he says later. "I'm giving up the high hurdles. I'm just gonna stick to the springs now."

A few minutes later, Arch jogs his slow jog to meet his parents for Senior Night. Then he runs to his teammates, gathering them at midfield.

"Let's fucking ball! Fucking ball!"

Ten days after his Pro Day, Caleb Williams flew to Chicago. Four Bears players took him to dinner at Sophia Steak in Lake Forest, not far from Halas Hall, the team's facility. The next morning, he visited the offices. Williams wondered how he'd vibe with everyone. Did the team want to win? It "seemed" like they did, Williams later said, but *seemed* wasn't good enough for Carl.

"I can do it for this team," Caleb told his dad. "I'm going to go to the Bears."

"I don't think you should," Carl replied.

"I'm going to do it."

As the draft neared, Caleb still wondered if he should blow it up. By then, there were no obvious routes. Sports lawyers would get random calls from people in Williams's orbit, wondering if there was any option aside from what the Elways had done, what the Mannings had done in a much more careful way, aside from the only one that seemed real: the nuclear one, of torching the Bears and Chicago so badly that there was no choice but to ship him elsewhere. Carl had spent years preparing. Did Caleb have it in him? Did he want to be known for that? If he forced a trade, was he ready for what would happen if, like Elway and Eli, he initially struggled? What if the nuclear option failed, and the Bears stood firm and drafted him anyway? Then what?

"I don't care," Caleb said. "If I need to do it, I will."

Caleb knew where Carl stood. It was Caleb's call. But in the end, Caleb got in line. "I wasn't ready to nuke the city," he later told me. He liked Chicago. If he won there, he knew he would be minted. "I can do it here," he told Carl. "They have good players.

"I guess I'm going to the Bears."

On April 25, 2024, Williams sits in a green room, behind a stage in Detroit, which is hosting the draft. Cameras are on him. A few minutes after Roger Goodell announces that the draft has begun and that the Bears are on the clock, his phone rings, on cue.

"Hello?" Williams says.

"Who's this?" Ryan Poles says with a laugh.

"Who's this?"

"This is the Chicago Bears, man. How you doing?"

"I'm good, I'm good."

They speak for a few minutes, forced and performative. Poles passes the phone, first to Matt Eberflus. The entire thing feels anticlimactic, if not scripted. Williams hangs up, stands up, and breathes deep. He's done it. *They've* done it. He hugs his mom. Hugs his dad. Everyone smiles. The plan hasn't worked perfectly, but it did work. Jayden Daniels goes second overall to Washington. Drake Maye goes third overall to New England, yet another in a series of young men trying to replace Tom Brady. The Patriots are very aware that when asked for the roots of his greatness, Brady—like Maye—begins with being the youngest in a loving but competitive family, fighting for attention. As Williams walks down a long hallway, from green room to stage, past the logos of NFL teams lit on the walls, all of the fights real and imagined he and his family had staged against this weird American institution, one thing is obvious: He is a special kind of happy, one that touches on relief and anticipation and the culmination of one thing and the launch of another. Someone hands him a Bears hat. He curves the brim, and rounds a corner onto the stage. Tens of thousands who have assembled in downtown Detroit for the draft cheer him. He breathes deep, shoulders raised, closes his eyes, and lets out a scream.

Tomorrow, a building of grown-ups would look to Williams for hope. Not all of them would be in his corner. When football season arrived, the Bears started 4–2. Williams was still unsure of the Bears operation. He liked the coaches as people, but struggled to connect with them as football minds. At times, he would watch film alone, with no instruction or guidance from the coaches. "No one tells me what to watch," Caleb told his dad. "I just turn it on." The Bears' success felt fragile, like it always does in the NFL, and soon, it ended. In the final minutes of the seventh game, against Daniels and the Commanders, Williams led the Bears 62 yards down the field and Chicago scored a go-ahead touchdown with thirty-one seconds left. Ballgame, it appeared. But Daniels got the ball, moved Washington to midfield, and as time expired, launched a Hail Mary down the center of the field. It was tipped and caught for a touchdown. Washington won. Daniels essentially clinched the Offensive Rookie of the Year award with that throw. When Daniels was officially given the trophy three months later, it seemed like a formality.

The Bears, meanwhile, self-destructed. After three consecutive losses, Shane Waldron was fired. A little more than two weeks later, after six straight losses—including a Thanksgiving Day clock-management debacle against the Vikings and Kevin O'Connell—Matt Eberflus was fired. The Bears lost four more games in a row after that, ten straight in all, before beating the Green Bay Packers in the final week of the season, on a Williams-led game-winning drive in the closing seconds. Williams generally played well as a rookie. He threw 20 touchdowns, only six interceptions. But the year went close to what Carl had predicted and feared. Caleb was sacked 68 times, third-most by any quarterback ever. He often held the ball too long, failing to see open receivers. In mid-January, the Bears hired Detroit Lions offensive coordinator

Ben Johnson as head coach, and Carl kept trying to remind himself of what he told his son countless times during the joy of his rise: You have to find a way to manufacture belief.

————————

During the exact time Williams is wondering who will be his third head coach and fourth offensive coordinator in seven months, Jayden Daniels and Bo Nix are preparing for their first playoff games. Daniels wins his, pulling off an overtime win against Tampa Bay; he'll lead Washington to the NFC Championship Game against the Eagles. Nix's Broncos are in Buffalo against the Bills. Sean Payton was right about Nix. He started all seventeen games, threw 29 touchdown passes and ran for four more, and helped lead Denver to the playoffs for the first time since winning Super Bowl 50 in 2016. Functionally and practically, he is no longer a rookie. A franchise is depending on him. The day of the Bills game, Payton sits in a cramped corner of the locker room at Highmark Stadium, an office for the visiting coach. The desk has one lamp; he asks an aide to fetch him another. Payton holds two documents. One, on cardboard, is his play-calling sheet for the game. The other, a five-page packet, contains Nix's favorite plays in the game plan, highlighted in blue.

Nix highlighted many pass plays. Too many.

"Can't have too many favorites," Payton says. "It defeats the purpose."

Music thumps in the background from the locker room as players prepare for the game. It's ninety minutes until kickoff. Payton looks at his play sheet, a road map or a prison for a quarterback. Maybe both. After a few hours, and discussions with assistant coaches, the play sheet is done. The game begins. The Broncos score on their first drive on a play called Boston College, a 43-yard bomb from Nix to receiver Troy Franklin. It's Denver's only score of the day, a contrast between a rookie quarterback and an MVP-caliber one. Josh Allen of the Bills is confident and relaxed, leading long drives; Nix is tentative and struggling to find rhythm. After the 31–7 loss, Payton is back in the office, face red from three hours in the cold and wind, eyes tired, experiencing the crash landing of a season ending. Nix is at his locker, taking off his pads. Two disappointed men who know that the season is an undeniable success. Payton has something almost more valuable than a playoff win. He believes he's found his guy for the rest of his career.

"How many Tiger Woods are there?" Steve Young says. "One. How many people want to be Tiger Woods? Ten million."

We're chatting about young quarterbacks. The Woods metaphor, of spectacular achievement coupled with spectacular disaster, is not lost on him. But Young is not stodgy about the current world of quarterbacks. He thinks it's cool that there's an infrastructure and an ecosystem. It's cool that there's a path. It's cool to work with quarterback gurus. "I wish I could have done that," he says, but also adds, "Do I think that it actually helps you, in the end, to lower the odds to where you're the guy? That you're one of *them*? I think it's both. It can help accentuate and burn you out. It's too much."

"Is it healthy?" I ask.

"Depends," he says, his mind spinning in a way that tells me I've asked the wrong question. "None of this is actually a sign that you can do it. So, what are the things that really matter? These qualities of grit, these qualities of spatial awareness, these natural abilities to be humble yet a bastard, you know what I mean?"

He feels for these kids. Worries that it's too much. In what other top jobs do we ask teenagers to assume such a prominent role? Whoever writes on a YouTube video that a teenager is the next Tom Brady knows nothing about what made Tom Brady. "It's all too early," Young says. "And we don't know, and he doesn't know.

"And so we're celebrating the *hope*. . . ."

You know the moment. It happens every game. When the quarterback takes over. When he creates and alters momentum, when he separates himself, when we know, everyone knows, why this job is different. Arch Manning's seminal moment is in the third quarter of a close game on Senior Night, closer than expected. The Greenies face third-and-29. There are no plays for that situation. Arch gets the ball. He stands in the pocket as it breaks from behind, and skips forward, eyes downfield, until nobody obstructs his view, and he sees a chance, a deep post route. He sets. He's at his own 26-yard line. The ball launches into air, above the stadium lights and into the darkness, then down again, nose over nose—how did he throw it that far?—until it drops at the opponent's 15-yard line, into the arms of his receiver for a first down, 60 yards traveled in all. The local television broadcaster says *wow* four times, yet that seems insufficient. After Newman wins, players gather in the end zone. Nelson Stewart addresses them. Arch is on a knee, toward the back. Stewart paces, calling out high and low points. Then he stops. He holds a ball.

"I'm about to embarrass him," he says.

Arch looks down.

"I'd argue tonight was his toughest game," Stewart says. "He got hit a bunch. He got up every time. He didn't yell at the line once. He kept his poise. That's what being a leader is. Now Arch has 129 career touchdowns. He's our career leader."

The team applauds.

Arch brings the team together and gives them a rally cry for the night. The kids disperse, toward the fence separating the stands from the field. Parents and friends gather. Seniors pose for selfies. Arch wanders over, his path stopped for a photo or autograph, half dozen in all. A life is just beginning, and Arch has yet to face the crossroads that his famous family members did. In two months, he would clean out his locker. It was a mess. Cooper shook his head. Arch sifted through stuff, tossing things away as he went, when both men noticed something buried in the back and at the bottom. It was a trophy. It had a football player kneeling. It was what he'd been awarded when he won the Bobby Dodd National High School Player of the Year from the Touchdown Club of Atlanta. Archie had won Touchdown Club's version of the award in 1969. Peyton had won it in 1993. Eli had won a different award from the same club in 2003. Cooper told Arch that it should be in his room or in a trophy case. Arch gave it to his dad to figure out. In three months, he'd be a freshman at Texas, and property of the public in an even greater way than he is now.

In 2024, after he got his first career start and helped the Longhorns defeat Louisiana-Monroe, the life he knew would change; something he had prepared for and thought about caught him by surprise. Kids wanted his photo as he walked through campus. Dinners out took on a new meaning. He could not hide in Austin, and in fact he was easier to spot than ever. You think you know when you're starting to lose control of your life, but you don't until it happens. He texted Eli: *Can we chat for little bit?* Eli figured it was to talk ball. It was to talk fame. *How do you handle this stuff?* Eli had a few rules. It's okay to say no. It's okay to tell people to wait until after dinner. Tell the team: No photos with anyone drinking alcohol. If you blink at the wrong time holding a beer, it'll live on the internet forever, coming up after the inevitable bad game. They were tips, but not answers. Eli didn't offer solutions. There are none.

One morning after Arch is gone, Stewart is at his office when he gets word that Peyton is going to stop by Isidore Newman the next day. He won't be alone. He'll be with his young teenage son, Marshall.

They need a place to throw.

———

It isn't supposed to be this way. Charlie is supposed to be talking to Colin about football, about school, the future starter at LSU, future draft pick, his dream, their dream . . .

"This is a good day," Charlie says. "He swallowed ice."

Charlie hovers over Colin, chatting with him, as nurses remind him that his son needs rest, hoping for . . . it's hard to tell what. For this to be over, for Colin to somehow resume his life from before he got behind the wheel that night. Charlie is still a cop at heart, and so he wonders what everyone else does: Why was Colin driving at almost 3 a.m.? Was it a feeling of invincibility? Was it that he had earned freedom, after all he had sacrificed, all he had given others, from his dad all the way down to coaches and fans and teammates and people like me? Was it just a dumb mistake by a kid? How will Colin and Charlie come to think about the past few years, after Colin has either furthered his career as a quarterback or hasn't: a reminder of the early days—or a deep memory, on the shelf alongside his high school awards, a prior life, a *before*, an account of the years when Colin Hurley went from can't miss to a miss?

On the day that Colin moved into the dorm, a year before his accident, Charlie and I grabbed lunch at a legendary LSU bar and grill called Pastime. We ordered beers and burgers. Charlie told the bartender that his kid was coming to play for the school. The bartender barely glanced up.

"He's a quarterback," Charlie said.

That got the bartender's attention. He pointed to the restaurant's walls, covered with photos and murals of local legends. Quarterbacks seemingly live forever on fading walls of restaurants and bars across America. Charlie and I imagined Colin Hurley up there, framed alongside the icons. I scanned the wall and was stunned to realize one was missing: the greatest ever to come out of LSU, the only one who's in the Pro Football Hall of Fame.

I asked a manager, "Do you have any photos of Y. A. Tittle?"

"Nah," he said. "We don't go back that far."

Y. A. Tittle visited LSU a final time. Saturday afternoon kickoff, September 2014, against Mississippi State. Dianne was with him. Several times in those years she thought she was about to say goodbye to him. He and Dianne waited in the tunnel of Tiger Stadium, ready to be reintroduced. Some quarterbacks wonder how they'll live without the intoxicating roar of the crowd. There's something irreplaceable about stepping out in front of a packed stadium and hearing your name for doing something that's ingrained in you. Once. Twice. For a season. For a lifetime. It's a privilege and a pleasure, earned and fragile, easy to take for granted, that never leaves you. Tittle wondered how he'd live without it. Now he'd hear it for the last time. He wore the symbols of his stature: his Hall of Fame blazer and a blue tie and a purple LSU hat. The cart took him and Dianne to the 10-yard line. Cameras surrounded him. The broadcast aired it live. The announcer yelled his name. A staffer held up his number 25 jersey. Tittle waved. The crowd of 102,321 provided a standing ovation. The ground shook. Y.A. sat down in the golf cart, filled with something indescribable, and turned to his daughter.

"What's all the fuss?"

───────

Three years later, on October 8, 2017, Y.A. was admitted to the ICU. It wasn't a sad day. Dianne danced in the hospital room and belted out Johnny Cash and Willie Nelson songs. Y.A. lay in bed, his head nodding along, tapping his fingers on his chest. Dianne had wondered for decades what a championship would have brought to her dad's life, her life, not only as points on a scoreboard but as a reckoning after all the years that she had watched, with wonder, as her father went down and got up again and again and again and kept trying, regardless of pride or pain. She assumed that championship moment worked some kind of human magic. By now, she knew better. She was experiencing something else in the hospital room, rarer, with an endless stream of stories and love. An unlucky quarterback was a lucky man.

Late afternoon, his heart-sustaining medications were removed. He slipped into sleep. At around 9 p.m., he was ready to go. I attended the funeral a few weeks later in Palo Alto. People told stories, less of a quarterback than of a dad, husband, brother, and son, way back when, who happened to find his calling in a celebrated space. We walked outside to lower the casket. Dianne had prepared herself for this moment, but something about it gutted her. Maybe myths never had happy endings, but her father's life did. Dianne neared her father's headstone, with words that she wanted the world to know about her dad, her parents, her life, *that* life:

Tittle: Beloved Dream-Makers

In March 2024, Steve Young was at BYU for an alumni event, walking around campus, when someone stopped him and said, "You know there is the alumni game tonight."

At first, Young thought, *Don't do it. This could be bad.* But something ignited within him that he hadn't felt for a while. A chance to throw. On a football field, that sacred space. To moving targets. Before fans, under lights on a Friday. An opportunity to unearth a dormant gift. To feel that thing. He was sixty-two years old. What was once high stakes was now reduced, but still pure. What the heck? He decided to see what he could do.

It was warm that evening, in the sixties and partly cloudy. In a hoodie, Young took the field against men half his age, some less. He threw an interception on his second play. Other BYU quarterbacks took some snaps. Later in the game, he drove his team down the field with a few short passes. He was near the end zone. He had coached girls' flag football the previous fall for Menlo Park High. His daughters, Laila and Summer, played. Venus Williams came to one of their games. So did two elderly women, just to watch girls live out a dream that was unavailable not long ago. One of Young's favorite plays for Menlo was called "Shake! Shake! Shake!," named after a Taylor Swift lyric. It called for two receivers to cross and shake each other free. Young told the guys what to do. He got the ball and bounced on his feet. He looked right, then saw a twenty-six-year-old receiver named Aleva Hifo crossing the field left. Young just *reacted*, fluid and quick. The ball was out of his hands, toward the corner of the end zone, where Hifo caught it with inches to spare. People cheered. The guys surrounded Young, then lifted him on their shoulders. He leaned back, raised his arms, and yelled, not unlike when he was handed the Lombardi Trophy.

That night, Young was staring at his phone in bed, when he received a video of the play. The angle was from behind, a perfect look to study himself. His footwork was elegant, his release high and fast, the ball a spiral, with the right mix of touch and power. "A reminder of what's *in* me," Young says. He watched it again. And again. And again. And again. And again. And again. And again. And again. And again. And . . .

Three and a half days after Colin Hurley hit the tree, he opens his eyes for more than a flicker. He's on heavy sedatives and pain-killers, but aware that he's in the hospital and that he's injured.

"What hurts?" a nurse asks him.

"My hip and my elbow."

"What's your name?" she asks.

"Colin Hurley."

"Where do you go to school?"

"LSU."

"Do you play sports?"

"Football."

"What do you do?"

"I'm a quarterback."

―――――

Doctors discharge Colin from the hospital, and he goes to a rehab facility in Jacksonville. He spends a few weeks there, rebuilding strength. As February becomes March, doctors predict he has a good chance to be a fully functioning adult again. Quarterback is another question entirely.

I visit the Hurleys one day in the rehab center. Colin rests in bed, staring at his phone. He moves slow. He says little, compared to himself before January. It's quiet, except for the beeps and clangs of a medical center, the rolling walkers down the hallways. Colin has a lot of time to think. I want to ask Colin if he understands the situation. His situation. How. And why. But I don't. The mere presence of someone besides his dad in the room—seeing him like *this*, when everyone is used to him like *that*—seems humbling enough. I can feel him replaying decisions and regrets.

Over lunch, Charlie picks at his food and allows himself to go there, to what now might be beyond reach.

"I still can't believe this is real," he says. "We were so close."

―――――

Colin puts in the work, as always, this time teaching his body to do what once came easily. He's released from the rehab center and goes back to his old house, outside of Jacksonville. He sleeps in his old bed. He trains with his old tutors, Tom Gormely and Will Hewlett. How he was raised. What he knows best. At the CORTX gym one morning, he sees Caleb Williams, who greets him and says, "Don't do dumb shit again." Colin nods, then turns back to a barbell with large plates on each side. It's leg day.

By April, Colin receives news that he's medically cleared to play football. He's starting over, back at the bottom of the mountain, but not nowhere. When he returns to college, he'll now bring another asset with him. Call it luck, call it gratitude, call it the fear and knowledge that quarterbacking, at a minimum, can vanish in a blink. But something else will be at work, too. Lots of college students get in dumb and potentially fatal car wrecks. How many of them have the focus and fight to make it back? If being a quarterback almost killed Colin—chasing the feeling of invincibility and speed—can being a quarterback also save him?

Before long, the Hurleys are back on the old field outside of town, under the morning sun. It's quiet, except for the soft sounds of practice: the pat on the ball, the shuffle of cleats on turf, the tight exhales, the spiral's subtle whistle in flight. Colin sets and resets his feet, eluding imaginary pressure, and throws deep left. Charlie films it all from behind. Two men, father and son, still out there, with a goal.

I remember my first meeting with the Hurleys more than two years earlier, on a field a few miles away. Colin was throwing, of course. Charlie was behind him, of course. Before them was the future. As Colin fired passes, Charlie turned around. Something caught his eye. He saw a man and a boy in the other end zone, probably a father and son. They had a football. The child's drop-backs were all over the place. The ball was too heavy for him. He didn't throw it far, and it flopped in the air. But the touchdown celebrations were funky and cute, and you could hear their laughter on our side of the field. Nowhere to be, nowhere to go, no one to impress or slay.

Charlie nodded to his son.

"Remember, Colin?"

Colin turned his head.

"That was us."

⸻

I leave Colin, thinking about him at the ICU. On the ride to my hotel, I think about John Elway in his father's Impala and Warren Moon's migraines. Buildings pass outside the window. I remember Steve Young's solace in room 9043 at the Marriott, Johnny Unitas's walk home with a burlap bag full of coal, Joe Namath in rehab, Tom Brady starting over in his late forties, and Peyton Manning onstage with Larry David. What did they expect, and what did they find? I've been looking for a grand universal theory on quarterbacks, proof of existentialism or grit or cosmoses or goddamn magic. But the thing that once seemed so mysterious and unattainable—the perfect pass, delivered in the crucial moment—is maybe the simple part. They don't have to think about that. The living with what it takes, what it brings, and what it costs, is the mystery.

⸻

One night, I'm at a bar in downtown Indianapolis. It's Combine week. Quarterbacks with something to gain and lose walk the streets in nondescript gray sweats. I'm having a drink with an old friend: Aaron Collins, the center on our high school team, the one who sat next to me and put his hand on my helmet after I threw the interception in the October rain. We catch up, then our conversation takes an inevitable turn. I think about my junior-year self, being seventeen, that boy who haunts me.

"Why do you think I didn't make it as a quarterback?" I ask.

Aaron's answer is swift and declarative, as if he'd thought about it.

"You had no chance. We couldn't block."

I've blamed myself for so long, felt like that one practice revealed to me, and others, a fatal weakness that would one day derail me again. But Aaron keeps talking about what kind of quarterback I was. He says that my belief in my ability and in my team was palpable, infectious. That I was always optimistic. He says that I could throw, in the pocket or on the run . . . stuff I had either forgotten or blocked out or couldn't trust. Stuff that made me sound like what I was: his quarterback.

A few hundred of us wait for Joe Willie Namath at a Long Island country club on a fall day in 2024. Former NFL players mingle. Other quarterbacks, too. Even Hall of Famers. But there's only one of *him*, only one whose memorabilia makes up most of the auction items, and when he enters, over on the far side, starting gates are lifted. The room tilts his way. He stands near a bar but doesn't drink. Someone asks Namath what he is up to nowadays.

"Stayin' healthy," he says.

He looks it, at age eighty-one, despite the damage done and dues paid. He moves better than you might think. He's also a little guy now; the inches have come out of his neck and famously rounded shoulders.

He still throws. Just the other day, with his granddaughter. He says she's got a good arm—not from him, from her mom, he insists with a smile.

By now, I've been to a few of these receptions with Namath, when his duty is to turn it on, provide a glimpse, provide a feeling. On a spring night in 2023 at the University of Alabama, a group of cheerleaders waved Namath over. He positioned himself in the center, still an earthquake of a man. They turned to a photographer and smiled, but that wasn't enough—wasn't *Broadway* enough—so they kicked their legs, to the left and right, like Rockettes, and he was grinning like it was two in the morning in 1969 and he was leaving the back room at P.J. Clarke's, past the Sinatra Table, through the narrow bar, with a pit stop at the men's room and the iconic saloon doors, out onto Third Avenue at dark and all its wonder, knowing he can keep the party going a little longer and still sleep for seven hours before practice. Namath doesn't get away with everything, but damn, he always pulls it off.

Earlier today, Namath sat with friends signing auction memorabilia. Jerseys, footballs, helmets—and then someone slid him a few baseballs to sign. That brought back memories. The Cubs wanted him out of Beaver Falls, you know. He was an outfielder who could drive the ball, and it was the sixties, when baseball was the biggest game in America. What if he'd reached the bigs, a friend asked him? What if he was good in the majors, or even great? Namath might have become a superstar, but he wouldn't have become Joe Willie.

And so at the reception in Long Island, I ask Namath: Knowing what you know now, what this job took and what it provided, would you want to be anything but a quarterback?

He looks away for a beat, out into a swirling cocktail hour, revealing that profile: nose and chin as advertised, the face of a young man who won and an old man who survived. He turns to me.

"I'd have to give that some thought," he says. "But thank God I'm still here."

———

One summer evening, I'm in the Idaho mountains with John Elway. He's nursing a beer after a round of golf with Wayne Gretzky, Sean Payton, and a few other friends. I had bumped into him on the putting green that morning as he was loosening up. "My body . . ." he groaned with a smile. We're at Gozzer Ranch, a hidden club for the stars near Lake Coeur d'Alene. Chris Pratt and Justin Bieber are members. Various Kardashians, too. Elway and his friends call themselves the Breakfast Club. Eggs and screwdrivers as the sun rises. Links all day. Breathtaking amounts of money wagered hole by hole. A few drinks at golden hour. Their everyday, until who knows when.

A pile of what must be thousands of dollars in cash is at the center of the table. Elway holds the score cards, doing the math. Gretzky orders food. He rooted for Elway, he tells me, long before they were buddies. The Broncos were his team, Elway his guy.

Talk turns to the old days. To championships and eras and the passing of time. Gretzky mentions the way names are replaced on the Stanley Cup. Dating back to 1907, the roster of the championship team is engraved on it each year. Gretzky's name is on it five times. But the Cup is running out of room. To create space for a new team, an old team must fall off. Gretzky's last Cup was in 1988. He knows his grandkids will probably see his name, but that's it.

"I've got another twenty years," he says. "Then I'm gone."

I turn to Elway and expect him to join in, with his own story of fading away. He nods and sips his beer, but it's hard to tell if he's paying attention. He tallies their scores, and collects the pile of bills, and leans back satisfied.

"I'm not sure I believe in reincarnation," he says in the last of the afternoon light. "I know there's no way, if I come back, it's going to be as good as the life that I had, right?"

A little while later, the Breakfast Club calls it a night. Elway shakes my hand goodbye, and I walk to my car and drive back down the mountain, watching them fade away in the rearview, losing elevation with each quarter mile, winding toward the valley floor.

ACKNOWLEDGMENTS

A running joke among my friends is that writing a book is no way to live—and is a great way to live. For this project to approach my vision for it, I needed help.

Thank you:

To the quarterbacks, their families, coaches, and support systems, who were generous with their time and insight. Steve Young sat down with me four times. John Elway and Warren Moon, three times each. The Mannings—Archie, Cooper, Peyton, and Eli—were open about their lives, and Arch Manning and Nelson Stewart allowed me to be a fly on the wall for the days leading up to Senior Night. Caleb and Carl Williams were honest about a wonderful and strange year. I met Colin and Charlie Hurley in five different states and witnessed some of the most glorious and horrific moments in their lives. Dianne and Steve de Laet discussed Y. A. Tittle, in California and in Greece. The Unitas family—Sandy, Joe, Chad, and Paige, and Kevin Warntz—provided a loving and honest look at what it meant to live with a legend. Buck and Etta Waterfield spent two days taking me through a lost America. Also, thanks to Jake Browning; Mack Brown; Joe Burrow; Kirk Cousins; Tom Gormely;

James Harris; Will Hewlett; Marion Hurley; Jim Kelly; Vanita Krouch; Will, Mike, and Beth Levis; Jake Locker; Andrew Luck; Drake, Mark, and Aimee Maye; Josh McDaniels; Kevin O'Connell; J. T. O'Sullivan; Sean Payton; Dak Prescott; Lincoln Riley; Mike Shanahan; Joe Sloan; Alex Smith; Randy Trivers; and Kurt Warner, among others. I'm also grateful to Matthew Stafford, Sean McVay, Patrick Mahomes, Tom Brady, and Tom and Galynn Brady for their past help.

To Kari Anderson and Katie Carter King, for the expert research assistance.

To Tricia Huerta, for the transcriptions.

To David Black, for advice and belief.

To the Hyperion Avenue team, especially executive editor Adam Wilson, who dealt with early morning and late evening calls, who deftly helped cut, rework, and polish many of the words—and who gave me an audience to share memories of being a Broncos fan in the eighties and nineties. Guy Cunningham provided a jarringly thorough read and saved me from myself many times. Intrepid art director Amy C. King has the gift of formulating a vision into a cover design. Kelly Forsythe left me in awe of her preparation and creativity in public relations. Also: Tonya Agurto, Jennifer Levesque, Monique Diman, Daneen Goodwin, Olivia Zavitson, and Sara Liebling.

To these dear friends, within my business and beyond, a constant source of inspiration, encouragement, perspective and laughs: Greg Bishop, Albert Breer, Taffy Brodesser-Akner, Jason Cole, Ryan D'Agostino, Bruce Feldman, Peter King, Phil Levis, Chad Millman, Ian O'Connor, Tony Rehagen, Michael Silver, Kevin Stange, Rick Telander, and Steve Walentik.

To my ESPN bosses and colleagues who care about the work to the bottom of their souls: Stephania Bell, Scott Burton, Jeff Darlington, Joe Disney, Chris Duzan, Andy Hall, Jena Janovy, Kalyn Kahler, Tim Keown, Elizabeth Merrill, Mina Kimes, Burke Magnus, Gueorgui Milkov, Tony Moss, Jimmy Pitaro, Stacey Pressman, Jason Reid, Scott Siebers, Pete Thamel, Pablo Torre, and Dave Wilson. Specifically: to Khalid Salaam, for clearing the runway and for constantly looking out for me, to Mike Drago and Don Van Natta Jr. for the challenge, joy, and continuation of partnership and friendship that our series of Dan Snyder stories provided, and to Chris Buckle, who wanted this to be the best book possible and provided the time and resources for me to try.

To Matt Moscardi, Courtney Rowe, Jonathan Small, and Mike Hren for happy hours and comic relief.

To Kevin Van Valkenburg, who constantly reminded me that quarterbacking is about an earned magic, and to Tom Junod, who constantly reminded me that it is about an earned artistry.

To Justin Heckert, for sending funny quarterback social media posts—and worthy epigraphs.

To Wright Thompson and Eric Neel, for the blessing beyond belief of putting the success of others as high if not higher than their own.

To my parents, Kirk and Beth Wickersham, and my sister, Lauren Rice, for catching passes in the early nineties, often in the ice and snow, because they knew what I wanted more than anything.

To my family, for navigating my travel schedule—sixty-three work trips in all—long hours, deadlines, creative bursts with patience, love, and support. Alison, Maddie, and Grant: I love you.

NOTES ON SOURCES

The vast majority of the material in these pages is derived from more than a hundred interviews during the past three years specifically for this book, and hundreds more during my two-decade career as a writer at ESPN. Among them, in alphabetical order: Tom Brady, Bill Belichick, Joe Burrow, David Carr, Derek Carr, Kirk Cousins, Trent Dilfer, John Elway, James Harris, Colin Hurley, Jim Kelly, Vanita Krouch, Jake Locker, Andrew Luck, Patrick Mahomes, Archie Manning, Cooper Manning, Eli Manning, Peyton Manning, Drake Maye, Sean McVay, Warren Moon, Kevin O'Connell, Sean Payton, Lincoln Riley, Mike Shanahan, Alex Smith, Matthew Stafford, the late Y. A. Tittle, Kurt Warner, the late Bill Walsh, Caleb Williams, and Steve Young, among others.

Most of the interviews were on the record. Some, especially when it came to sensitive information, were on background, meaning that I agreed to not identify the subjects by name but would use a general title—a coach or player or executive or friend, or on deep background, meaning that I agreed to not identify them at all. Where dialogue is within quotation marks, it comes from the speaker, a firsthand witness, or notes or recordings from that moment. Where dialogue is paraphrased, it reflects only a lack of certainty about precise wording. Where specific thoughts or feelings are noted, they come from the person identified—either directly to me or from the bevy of press conferences, books, newspaper and magazine articles, and films the person has participated in over the years—or someone to whom they have expressed those thoughts or feelings directly.

I relied on many books, including: *A Matter of Style* by Joe Namath and Bob Oates Jr., *All the Way* by Joe Namath, *Armed and Dangerous* by Jim Kelly and Vic Carucci, *Dan Marino: My Life in Football* by Dan Marino, *Elway* by Jason Cole, *Football Done Right* by Michael Lombardi, *Great Football Writing* by *Sports Illustrated*, *Gunslinger* by Jeff Pearlman, *I Can't Wait Until Tomorrow 'Cause I Get Better-Looking Every Day* by Joe Namath and Dick Schaap, *I Pass!* by Y. A. Tittle and Don Smith, *I'm Still Scrambling* by Randall Cunningham, *Joe Namath and the Other Guys* by Rick Telander, *Luckman at Quarterback* by Sid Luckman, *Monday Morning Quarterback* by Peter King, *Namath* by Mark Kriegel, *Out of the Darkness* by Ian O'Connor, *Payton and Brees* by Jeff Duncan, *Super Bowl Blueprints* by Bill Polian and Vic Carucci, *Quarterback* by John Feinstein, *Quarterbacks Have All the Fun* by Dick Schaap, *QB: My Life Behind the Spiral* by Steve Young with Jeff Benedict, *Taking Flak* by Dan Pastorini with John P. Lopez, *The Art of Smart Football* by Chris B. Brown, *The GM* by Tom Callahan, *The Pro Quarterback* by Murray Olderman, *The QB* by Bruce Feldman, *The Why Is Everything* by Michael Silver, and *The $400,000 Quarterback* by Bob Curran.

I relied on hundreds of newspaper articles, magazine pieces, films, and online stories from the past twenty years. I'm especially grateful to those who have covered quarterbacks so well on various

ESPN platforms, especially but not limited to ESPN.com, *ESPN The Magazine,* espnW, Andscape, *Grantland, SportsCenter, E60,* 30 for 30, *NFL Live, NFL Sunday Countdown,* and *SportsCentury.*

Thank you in particular to Jon Kendle and Hailey Kasney at the Pro Football Hall of Fame for allowing me to post up in the archives for a few days. To media relations folks Patrick Smyth of the Broncos, Michael Bonnette of Louisiana State, Robbie Bohren, then of the Titans, Jon Ekstrom of the Vikings, Katie Ryan of Southern California, Tad Carper of the Cowboys, Jeremy Sharpe of North Carolina, and John Bianco and Thomas Stepp at Texas, among others. To Chris B. Brown for filling in some blanks on the Air Raid offense. To Juston Lewis at the *Florida Times-Union* for his work on Colin Hurley.

Below are additional section-by-section notes.

PART I: ORIGINS

The information in this chapter comes primarily from events that I witnessed firsthand and interviews with John Elway, Nelson Stewart, Archie Manning, Cooper Manning, Peyton Manning, Eli Manning, Arch Manning, Warren Moon, Leigh Steinberg, James Harris, Caleb Williams, Tom Gormely, Will Hewlett, Carl Williams, Russell Thomas, Mark McCain, Michael Lombardi, Scot McCloughan, Bill Walsh (2002), Bill Belichick (2009), Sean Salisbury, Steve Young, Mike Shanahan, Colin Hurley, Charlie Hurley, and Marion Hurley. It also came from a visit in 2024 to the Pro Football Hall of Fame. Also:

Alex Kirshner, "Behind the Scenes at Heisman Weekend with
     Caleb Williams, the Face of the New College Football,"
     GQ.com, December 12, 2022.

Bill Polian and Vic Carucci, *Super Bowl Blueprints*, Triumph Books, 2021.

Jason Cole, *Elway: A Relentless Life*, Hachette, 2020.

Jason Reid, *Rise of the Black Quarterback: What It Means for America*, Andscape Books, 2022.

Jeff Pearlman, *Football for a Buck: The Crazy Rise and Crazier Demise of the USFL*, Mariner Books, 2018.

"Just a 92-Yard Walk in the Park," ProFootballHOF.com, December 31, 2001.

Leigh Montville, "Father Moon," *Sports Illustrated*, September 27, 1993.

Louis Moore, *The Great Black Hope*, Hachette, 2024.

Michael Lombardi, *Gridiron Genius: A Master Class in Winning Championships and Building Dynasties in the NFL*, Crown Archetype, 2018.

Michael Lombardi, "Seven Habits for Drafting a Highly Effective QB," TheRinger.com, April 5, 2017.

Michael Silver, "Last Hurrah?" *Sports Illustrated*, December 13, 1999.

Peter King, "How Peyton Manning Changed the Game," SI.com, March 7, 2016.

Peter King, "Inside Deion Sanders' Football Realm at the University of Colorado-Boulder," NBCSports.com, October 2, 2023.

P. J. Green, "Mahomes Pays Homage to HBCU Legends During Legacy Bowl," Fox 4 Kansas City, February 20, 2022.

Richard H. Price, William C. Moss, and Timothy J. Gay, "The Paradox of the Tight Spiral Pass in American Football: A Simple Resolution," *American Journal of Physics*, September 1, 2020.

Rick Gosselin, "Does the NFL Know What a QB Looks Like?" RickGosselin.com, April 24, 2024.

Seth Wickersham, *It's Better to Be Feared: The New England Patriots Dynasty and the Pursuit of Greatness*, W. W. Norton, 2021.

Seth Wickersham, "Only the Name Is the Same," *ESPN The Magazine*, October 8, 2008.

Seth Wickersham, "The Book of Coach," *ESPN The Magazine*, January 24, 2013.

Ric Serritella, "Bill Walsh: The QB Blueprint," All Access Football, April 22, 2024.

Steve Young with Jeff Benedict, *QB: My Life Behind the Spiral*, Houghton Mifflin Harcourt, 2016.

"The John Elway Story: From High School Prodigy to the Hall of Fame," *In Their Own Words* produced by NFL Films, aired on June 28, 2017 by NFL Films, YouTube.

Tom Brady with Patrick Bet-David, 2023 Vault conference.

"Warren Moon Settles Sexual Harassment Lawsuit," ESPN.com, August 3, 2019.

William C. Rhoden, *Third and a Mile*, ESPN Books, 2007.

Wright Thompson, "Joe Montana Was Here," ESPN.com, February 8, 2023.

PART II: QUARTER-BACK TO QUARTERBACK

The information in this section comes primarily from events that I witnessed firsthand and interviews with Buck and Etta Waterfield; Y. A. Tittle (2014); Dianne and Steve de Laet; Sandy Unitas, Joe Unitas, Chad Unitas, Paige Unitas; Maxx McNall at Wesleyan University; Timothy Bennett at Yale University; and Rich Marazzi and Sue Riehl at Carroll University. Also:

Rob Fernas, "Complete Package," *Los Angeles Times*, December 25, 1999.

Bob Oates, "Right Time, Right Place : Pete Rozelle's Career in Pro Football Started 40 Years Ago, Quite by Accident," *Los Angeles Times*, August 15, 1986.

Christina Rice, *Mean . . . Moody . . . Magnificent!: Jane Russell and the Marketing of a Hollywood Legend*, University Press of Kentucky, 2021.

Cleveland News, "Courage in the Clutch—That's Rams' Waterfield," November 23, 1945.

Cleveland Plain Dealer, "At Home With the Waterfields," November 16, 1945.

Dave Anderson, "Namath Is Retiring From Pro Football," *New York Times*, January 25, 1978.

Dianne Tittle de Laet, *Giants & Heroes: A Daughter's Memories of Y. A. Tittle*, Steerforth, 1995.

Edith Gwynn, "Inside Hollywood," December 8, 1942.

Franz Lidz, "Y. A. Tittle, Somewhat of a Folk Hero as a Quarterback, Finds Folk Art," *Sports Illustrated*, December 12, 1983.

Jane Russell, *My Path and My Detours: An Autobiography*, Franklin Watts, 1985.

Jerry Crowe, "It Turned Out to be the Biggest Snap of His Career," *Los Angeles Times*, January 28, 2008.

Jim Murray, "Waterfield Couldn't Keep Drive Going," *Los Angeles Times*, March 31, 1983.

John Y. Brown, *Legend of the Praying Colonels*, J. Marvin Gray & Associates, 1970.

"Josh McDaniels Breaks Down Tom Brady's Best Comebacks," Patriots.com, June 12, 2024.

Joshua Neuman, "Why Isn't Kenny Washington an American Icon?" Slate.com, December 19, 2021.

Los Angeles Evening Herald and Express, "Cravath Sleepless as He Worries Over Waterfield's Passing," December 11, 1942; "Waterfield's Not Only Spark, He's the Main Voltage," December 12, 1942.

Los Angeles Examiner, "Commission and a Kiss!" September 24, 1943.

Los Angeles Times, "Jane Russell Wed to U.C.L.A. Football Star," April 27, 1943.

Mark Kriegel, *Namath: A Biography*, Viking, 2004.

Marsh Clark, "Joe Namath and the Jet-Propelled Offense," *TIME*, October 16, 1972.

Miami Herald, "YA Tittle Keeps Some of NY, Namath Bids for Share" by Jimmy Cannon, January 28, 1965.

Michael MacCambridge, *America's Game: The Epic Story of How Pro Football Captured a Nation*, Random House, 2004.

Michael MacCambridge, *The Franchise: A History of* Sports Illustrated *Magazine*, Hyperion, 1997.

Michael Oriard, *Reading Football, How the Popular Press Created an American Spectacle*, University of North Carolina Press, 1993.

Murray Greenberg, *Passing Game: Benny Friedman and the Transformation of Football*, Public Affairs, 2008.

Murray Olderman, *The Pro Quarterback*, Prentice-Hall, 1967.

Otto Friedrich, *City of Nets: A Portrait of Hollywood in the 1940s*, Harper Perennial, 1986.

Oxford English Dictionary, "quarterback (n.), sense 2.c," July 2023.

Pasadena Star News, "One Hope of West," January 1, 1943.

Richard Hoffer, "A Great Year for Sports . . . And a New Sports Magazine," *Sports Illustrated*, July 14, 2003.

Robert H. Boyle, "Show-Biz Sonny and His Quest for Stars," *Sports Illustrated*, July 19, 1965.

Robert W. Robertson Jr., *The Wonder Team: The Story of the Centre College Praying Colonels and Their Rise to the Top of the Football World, 1917–1924*, Butler Books, 2008.

S. C. Gwynne, *The Perfect Pass: American Genius and the Reinvention of Football*, Scribner Press, 2016.

Sally Jenkins, *The Real All Americans: The Team That Changed a Game, a People, a Nation*, Doubleday Press, 2007.

St. Louis Post-Dispatch, "New Football of Surpassing Interest," Charles Chadwick, October 4, 1906.

St. Louis University yearbook, Fleur de Lis, 1906–1907.

Tex Maule, "Y. A. Tittle Is the Best Policy," *Sports Illustrated*, November 18, 1963.

The Record, January 23, 1965.

The Waterfield Family Archives, which contained articles from: *California Daily Bruin, Los Angeles Evening Herald and Express, Los Angeles Examiner, Los Angeles Daily News, Pasadena Star News*, and *Los Angeles Times*.

Tim Brulia, "A Chronology of Pro Football on Television: Part 1," *The Coffin Corner*: Vol. 26, No. 3, 2004.

TIME, December 7, 1931.

Tom Callahan, *Johnny U: The Life and Times of John Unitas*, Crown, 2006.

Washington Post, "This Morning, with Shirley Povich," December 17, 1945.

Y. A. Tittle, "A Good Quarterback Has to be His Own Man," *Sports Illustrated*, August 16, 1965.

Y. A. Tittle with Kristine Setting Clark, *Nothing Comes Easy: My Life in Football*, Triumph Books, 2009.

PART III: LEVERAGE

The information in this section comes primarily from events I witnessed firsthand and interviews with John Elway, Cooper Manning, Peyton Manning, Eli Manning, Arch Manning, Nelson Stewart, Caleb Williams, Carl Williams, Colin Hurley, Charlie Hurley, Will Hewlett, Tom Gormely, Warren Moon, Russell Thomas, Mark McCain, Randy Trivers, Lincoln Riley, Patrick Mahomes, Adam Cook, Pat Mahomes Sr., Andrew Luck, Nicole Pechanec, Anthony Castonzo, Alex Smith, David Carr, Kurt Warner, Trent Dilfer (2007), Mike Nolan (2007), and Jeff Ulbrich (2007). Also:

A Football Life, "Warren Moon," produced by NFL Films, aired on NFL Network, October 2, 2014.

Aric DiLalla, " 'The shock waves may never subside': An oral history of the Broncos' franchise-altering trade for John Elway," DenverBroncos.com, May 02, 2023.

Bill Simmons, "Curious Guy: Malcolm Gladwell," ESPN.com, March 2, 2006.

Bruce Feldman, *The QB: The Making of Modern Quarterbacks*, Crown, 2014.

Bussin' with the Boys (podcast), September 3, 2024.

Chris Tomasson, "Chris Hinton looks back 40 years after being 'the guy traded for John Elway' by Broncos in 1983," *Denver Gazette*, April 19, 2023.

"College Football 150 Conducting Tennessee Band a Special
      Memory for Manning," ESPN, November 19, 2019, https://
      www.espn.com/watch/player/_/id/28146160/redirected/tr

Dana Hunsinger Benbow, "Archie Manning: 'Peyton would like to
      be back in football,'" *IndyStar*, September 24, 2019.

David Johnson, "Lane Kiffin Appears to Make Stop at Arch
      Manning's High School," 247Sports.com, January 31, 2020,
      https://247sports.com/college/ole-miss/article/arch
      -manning-quarterback-lane-kiffin-appears-to-make-stop
      -high-school-peyton-manning-nfl-143161961/

David Remnick, "Elway Mania," *Washington Post*, August 5, 1983.

Douglas S. Looney, "In Denver, Delirium Is Spelled E-L-W-A-Y,"
      Sports Illustrated, August 15, 1983.

Dwight Clark Legacy Series. "A conversation with Steve Young,
      Alex Smith, Jeff Garcia, and Brock Purdy," May 16, 2024.

Elizabeth Merrill, "Why don't more NFL prospects try to dictate
      landing spots?" ESPN.com, April 15, 2024.

Elway to Marino, ESPN 30 for 30, April 23, 2013.

Jim Saccomano, "Sacco Sez: John Elway and the Start of the
      Broncos Media Frenzy," DenverBroncos.com, May 2, 2020.

John Ed Bradley, "Like Father, Like Son," *Sports Illustrated*,
      November 15, 1993.

John Elway interview with ESPN, October 18, 2001.

Lindsay Jones and Mike Sando, "The Comeback, No. 19: John
      Elway Engineers The Drive," *The Athletic*, August 21, 2020.

Marc Delucchi, "New Evidence Shows How Badly NFL Teams
      Discriminate Against Black QBs in the Draft," SF Gate,
      September 11, 2023.

"NFL 100 All-Time Team," NFL Network, 2019–2020.

"Rich Gannon: NFL quarterbacks aren't being taught well
enough," *Los Angeles Times*, January 28, 2012.

Rick Reilly, "Making His Marks," *Sports Illustrated Presents
Champs Again! 1998 Denver Broncos.*

Seth Wickersham, *It's Better to Be Feared: The New England
Patriots Dynasty and the Pursuit of Greatness*, W. W.
Norton, 2021.

Stephania Bell, "How Caleb Williams, Brock Purdy and Others
Are Resetting the Way Quarterbacks Prepare," ESPN.com,
November 2, 2024.

Steve Kelley, "Elway: Brilliant, Enduring," Knight Ridder News
Service, January 25, 1998.

The QB Plug Instagram, September 23, 2023, https://www
.instagram.com/reel/CxjEc1pOTg_/?utm_source=ig_web
_copy_link&igsh=MzRlODBiNWFlZA==

Yogi Roth and Joey Roberts, *5-STAR QB: It's Not About the Stars,
It's About the Journey*, 2022.

PART IV: CRISES

The information in this section comes primarily from events
I witnessed firsthand and interviews with Steve Young, Frank
Vuono, Warren Moon, John Elway, Arch Manning, Colin Hurley,
Charlie Hurley, Marion Hurley, Caleb Williams, Carl Williams, Kirk
Cousins, Tom Brady (2013), Mike Shanahan, Drake Maye, Aimee
Maye, Mark Maye, Mack Brown, Jake Locker, Matthew Stafford,
Cooper Kupp, Sean McVay, Sean Payton, Dak Prescott, Will Levis,
and Mike Levis. Also:

A Football Life, "Houston '93," produced by NFL Films, aired on
NFL Network, December 10, 2013.

A Football Life, "Steve Young," produced by NFL Films, aired on NFL Network, October 7, 2016.

Andrew Carter, "For Drake Maye, the Youngest in UNC's Unofficial First Family, the Time Is Now," *The News & Observer*, September 1, 2023.

Colin Hurley's social media, September 9, 2023, https://x.com/JStCyrTV/status/1700376298021913051

Elway interview with Mark Seal, Pro Football Hall of Fame archives.

ESPN SportsCentury: John Elway, January 26, 2001.

Greg Bishop, "Vince Young's Journey North to Rewrite the Ending of His Football Career," *Sports Illustrated*, June 27, 2017.

Jason Cole, *Elway: A Relentless Life*, Hachette, 2020.

Jill Lieber, "Too Cool in Defeat?," *Sports Illustrated*, February 8, 1988.

John Elway with Tom Friend, "It's My Call," *ESPN The Magazine*, February 22, 1999.

Josh Clark, "Former Quarterbacks Disagree Over Key Dak Prescott Play," Audacy, January 23, 2023.

Mark Kiszla, *Denver Post*, 1998, Pro Football Hall of Fame archives.

New York Times Staff, "Moon's Wife, on Stand, Blames Her Temper," *New York Times*, February 17, 1996.

NFL 100 All-Time Team, produced by NFL Network, 2019–2020.

Patrick Mahomes press conference, Super Bowl LVII, February 2023.

Pete Thamel and Caleb Williams conversation, *ESPN College GameDay*, September 30, 2023.

Rick Reilly, "I'm About to Suffocate," *Sports Illustrated*, November 6, 1989.

Rick Reilly, "Ultimate Losses, Ultimate Victory," *Sports Illustrated*, February 2, 1998.

Sam Schube, "The New King of College Football," *GQ*, September 6, 2023.

Steve Young with Jeff Benedict, *QB: My Life Behind the Spiral*, Houghton Mifflin Harcourt, 2016.

Sue Anne Pressley, "From Football Star's Wife, a Reluctant, Painful Story," *Washington Post*, February 21, 1996.

TMZ Sports, March 7, 2021, https://www.tmz.com/2021/03/07/jeff-george-jr-nfl-dad-football-combine-draft/

W. Timothy Gallwey, *The Inner Game of Tennis*, Random House, 1974.

PART V: ECHOES

The information in this section comes primarily from events I witnessed firsthand and interviews with John Elway, the Unitas family, Buck and Etta Waterfield, the Manning family, Nelson Stewart, Matthew Stafford, Tom Brady (2013), J. T. O'Sullivan, Kevin Barry, Kurt Warner, Tom Gormely, Will Hewlett, Kevin O'Connell, Caleb Williams, Carl Williams, Josh McDaniels, Dianne and Steve de Laet, Warren Moon, Leigh Steinberg, Sean Payton, Vanita Krouch, and Joe Namath, at a reception for his foundation. Also:

Bill Belichick, Maxx Crosby, and Peter King (hosts), "Tom Brady," *Let's Go* (podcast), January 10, 2023.

Chantal Fernandez, "Gisele Rides Again," *ELLE*, September 13, 2022.

Chris Mortensen, "Johnny Manziel Cuts Camp Short," ESPN.com, July 14, 2013.

Courtney Cronin, "Caleb Williams Not Thinking Beyond No. 1 Pick in NFL Draft," ESPN.com, March 1, 2024.

Craig Whitlock, "Retired NFL Star Warren Moon Is Sued for Sexual Harassment," *Washington Post*, December 6, 2017.

Dave Sheinin and Emily Giambalvo, "The Changing Face of America's Favorite Sport," *Washington Post*, December 18, 2023.

Dan Pastorini with John P. Lopez, *Taking Flak: My Life in the Fast Lane*, AuthorHouse, 2011.

Dan Pompei, "Bills Legend Jim Kelly Used to Be Mad About All He'd Lost. Now He Focuses on What He's Found," *The Athletic*, November 8, 2023.

Fred Katz, "Manning, Plunkett, Kern and Theismann Sound Off," *Sport*, October 1970.

Greg Stoda, "Class of '83 Touches Marino's Heart," *Palm Beach Post*, August 24, 2000.

Ian Mohr, "Dan Marino Hid Love Child from Bosses at CBS Sports," *New York Post*, February 1, 2013.

Jane Russell, *My Path and My Detours: An Autobiography*, Franklin Watts, 1985.

Jenn Baluch, "After leaving ASU, Jack Elway Quits Football, Forges Own Path," Cronkite News, May 3, 2017.

Jenny Vrentas, "How the Texans and a Spa Enabled Deshaun Watson's Troubling Behavior," *New York Times*, June 7, 2022.

Jesse Will, "Terry Bradshaw's Secret to Career Longevity," *Men's Journal*, September 6, 2022.

Jessica D, "Facing Mental Illness: My Hero, Terry Bradshaw," Bleacher Report, 2009.

Kelli Young, "Flashback to 1965: Enshrinees' Gold Jacket Dinner,"
    Canton Repositor, July 22, 2016.

Larry Mayer, "Inside Look at Bears' Vetting Process of Caleb
    Williams," ChicagoBears.com, May 2, 2024.

Late Show with David Letterman, November 19, 2004.

Leigh Steinberg and Michael Arkush, *The Agent: My 40-Year
    Career Making Deals and Changing the Game*, Thomas
    Dunne, 2014.

Lisa Ryckman, "First and Foremost Janet Elway Remains a Mom,"
    Associated Press, April 17, 2006.

Mark Kriegel, *Namath: A Biography*, Viking, 2004.

"Matt Ryan's Early Thoughts on Super Bowl LIX," CBSSports.com,
    January 28, 2025.

Michael Lewis, "Coach Leach Goes Deep, Very Deep," *New York
    Times Magazine*, December 4, 2005.

Nathan Hague, "Marshall Native, Hall of Fame QB Tittle Dies at
    90," *Marshall News-Messenger*, October 9, 2017.

Peter King, "FMIA: How KC landed Patrick Mahomes in 2017,"
    NBCSports.com, February 19, 2024.

Peter King, "Letting Go," *Sports Illustrated*, March 20, 2000.

Peter Keating, "Out of Thin Air," *ESPN The Magazine*, July
    14, 2015.

Peyton's Places, ESPN+, 2020.

"Prayers and Praise at Funeral for Unitas," Associated Press,
    September 18, 2002.

"QB Caleb Williams Gets the Draft Call from the Bears,"
    ChicagoBears.com, April 25, 2024.

Raw Room, February 26, 2025.

Rhythm Masters, produced by ESPN Films, aired on August
    14, 2024.

Rich Cimini, "A Day in the Life of Jets Legend Broadway Joe Namath, Octogenarian," ESPN.com, May 31, 2023.

Rich Cimini, "Benched QB Zach Wilson Apologizes to Jets for Postgame Comments," ESPN, November 23, 2022.

Robert Klemko, "Where Patrick Mahomes Gets His Cool," SI.com, October 5, 2018.

Saturday Night Live, NBC, March 24, 2007.

Seth Wickersham, "Black Coffee, F-Bombs, Cell Phones & Super Bowls," *ESPN The Magazine*, August 26, 2008.

Seth Wickersham, "How One Super Bowl Loss Helped Define Matt Ryan's Legacy," ESPN.com, April 22, 2024.

Terry Bradshaw: Going Deep, HBO, 2022.

"This Is Football," Kevin Clark, ESPN2, September 4, 2024.

Tom Brady speech at 10x Growth Conference, February 2023.

Tom Brady, "Inside Tom Brady's Private Football Collection (and how to win one)," YouTube, October 10, 2024, https://www.youtube.com/watch?v=Js_xU1F4Wwc

Warren Moon's enshrinement speech transcript, ProFootballHOF.com.

"Wife Charges John Unitas with Adultery," Associated Press, January 23, 1971.

Wright Thompson, "Joe Montana Was Here," ESPN.com, February 8, 2023.

Wright Thompson, "The Inheritance of Archie Manning," ESPN.com, December 11, 2020.

Zak Keefer, "What Did NFL Learn About S2 Test After C. J. Stroud?," *The Athletic*, February 26, 2024.

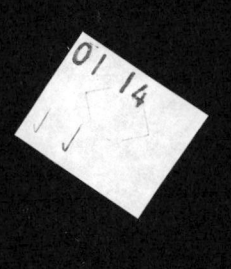